D0354789

Lucking Out

Also by James Wolcott

ATTACK POODLES AND OTHER MEDIA MUTANTS:
THE LOOTING OF THE NEWS IN A TIME OF TERROR

THE CATSITTERS: A NOVEL

Still from *Blank Generation* © 1975 Ivan Kral/Blank Generation LLC

Lucking Out

MY LIFE GETTING DOWN AND
SEMI-DIRTY IN SEVENTIES
NEW YORK

James Wolcott

DOUBLEDAY
New York   London   Toronto
Sydney   Auckland

Copyright © 2011 by James Wolcott

All rights reserved. Published in the United States by Doubleday, a division of Random House, Inc., New York, and in Canada by Random House of Canada Limited, Toronto.

DOUBLEDAY and the portrayal of an anchor with a dolphin are registered trademarks of Random House, Inc.

Portions of this book previously appeared in *Vanity Fair* in somewhat different form.

Page 260 constitutes an extension of the copyright page.

Book design by Michael Collica
Jacket design by Emily Mahon
Jacket photograph © Serge Clément/Agence VU'

ISBN 978-1-62090-061-1

MANUFACTURED IN THE UNITED STATES OF AMERICA

To my parents and, as always, Laura

"We come into this world with our little egos equipped with individual horns. If we don't blow them, who else will?"

—Addison DeWitt (George Sanders), *All About Eve*

"I love this dirty town."

—J. J. Hunsecker (Burt Lancaster), *Sweet Smell of Success*

CONTENTS

PART I:

Lucking Out

So much is gone, stricken from the scene, but it's still there, a landmark site in nobody's mind but my own—the Latham Hotel, in lower-midtown Manhattan. On those rare occasions when I go by, I half expect to see my younger self exiting the lobby, eyebrows steadied for battle. Shelved at Twenty-eighth Street just off a motley stretch of Fifth Avenue, the Latham belongs to one of those square, unfabled pockets of Manhattan that never quite got around to developing a personality. I had discovered the Latham Hotel in a used paperback guidebook bearing the now-aching title of *New York on $10 a Day*. Catering to the frugal-minded, the Latham held the faint whiff of former glory that attaches to places that lodge permanent transients. It was there that I checked in after arriving from Maryland, my single-bed room offering an air-shaft view with the flapping and chirring of pigeons on unseen ledges. Street noises sounded distant and abstract, as on a Hitchcock soundtrack. Seedy hotel rooms were quieter then, more media-sparse, enabling guests to hear the ticktock beneath their own thoughts. Downstairs was no frantic beehive either, the hotel partly a way station for old people on pensions and Social Security, for some of them the last stop before the last exit. The women in particular suggested minor characters in Dawn Powell novels who had slipped down several rungs in life and were left with nothing but late-inning rituals and brief flurries of bother. I overheard one elderly lady remark to another about the gentleman lolling between them on a bench or sofa, his eyes shut, his head slumped sideways, and the flap of his tongue showing, "He was so *lively* this morning." I shared the shower on my floor with a bent-double woman whose hunchback rose like a rock formation out of her thin robe. She startled me once, coming out of the bathroom as I was going in, but she was unaware of my double take, her head crooked floorward. The radio in her room was always on.

Next door to the Latham hunkers another low-profile holdover, the Prince George, which, before the gold medallions and furry testicles of disco descended, was a popular layover for flight crews whose trim blue uniforms and clippy stride made everybody else on the sidewalk look like clumps. During a passing fancy in the seventies the George's banquet hall was rumored to have been converted into a swing room. "For swing dancing?" an editorial assistant once asked me with the bluebird chirp of youth, picturing jive couples in ballroom competitions, like she had seen on TV. Not that kind of swinging, I said, implying unspoken volumes of decadence to which she would never be privy. I wasn't privy to them either, relying on picturesque hearsay of spiderlike couplings on the mats and the tentative, evolving etiquette of threesomes (permission to come aboard was requested with a shoulder tap). "The Seventies in New York smelled like sex," I recently read one veteran of the decade rhapsodize (sex and urine, he amended), but it wouldn't be until I moved into the West Village that the musk of debauchery would strew the air, and there and then too I would be a bystander. Being raised Catholic in a pressure-cooker household besieged by alcohol and bill collectors enforced and heightened a sense of sentry duty in me, the oldest of five children and the one most responsible for keeping everything from capsizing. Wild indulgence was for other people, the non-worriers.

Eastward on Twenty-eighth Street blazed the Belmore Cafeteria, where cabdrivers and other late-shifters—whose pithy grumblings of indigestion helped furnish the columns of Pete Hamill, Jimmy Breslin, and the sportswriter Dick Young with working-stiff lore—hunched over cups of coffee and heavy carbs while flipping through the night owl editions of the *New York Post* and *Daily News,* whose front-page headlines carried the latest earthquake reports from the Watergate investigation. A few years later the Belmore would achieve cinematic landmark status in Martin Scorsese's *Taxi Driver,* where Peter Boyle tried to impart a little wisdom Robert De Niro's way as the Belmore's cursive red neon sign bathed them in a tainted glow. I was no great fan of *Taxi Driver,* I found it a thesis statement shot from a spatter gun, but I was able to look up at the screen and feel as if I owned part of the experience, a souvenir piece of the squalor. I had been on that same lousy corner, and now the Belmore and its venereal neon are gone, consigned to fond history.

How lucky I was, arriving in New York just as everything was about to go to hell. I had no idea how fortunate I was at the time, eaten up as I was in my own present-tense concerns and taking for granted the lively decay, the intense dissonance that seemed like normality. Only F. Scott Fitzgerald characters (those charmed particles) feel the warm gold of nostalgia even while something's unfolding before their enraptured doll eyes. For the rest of us, it's only later, when the haze burns off, that you can look back and see what you were handed, the opportunities hidden like Easter eggs that are no longer there for anybody, completely trampled. To start out as a writer then was to set out under a higher, wider, filthier, more window-lit sky. A writer could still dream of climbing to the top, or at least getting close enough to the top to see who was up there enjoying themselves.

What had brought me to New York in the autumn of 1972 was a letter of recommendation written by Norman Mailer, the author of *The Naked and the Dead* and American literature's leading heavyweight contender, to Dan Wolf, the Delphic editor of the *Village Voice.* It was the reason I had left college after my sophomore year, spoiling my parents' dream of my becoming a teacher, collecting a regular salary, wearing a grown-up tie to work, and getting those great summers off. How I got to Mailer was the equivalent of firing a paper airplane out the window and having it land at JFK. I had been a hero-worshipper of Mailer's since being zapped by his writing, the closest my brain has come to hosting a meteor shower. I was in high school, Edgewood High School to be exact, just down the highway from Cal Ripken's hometown of Havre de Grace (known to the local

Restoration wits as "Haver Disgrace"). I was lounging around the local library and flipping through the latest magazines, which may lend the impression that the library was simply an after-school hangout for a teenage layabout, a sanitarium to hole up in before heading home to listen to everybody holler. Not so, or at least not entirely. It was also the portal into that strange, unfamiliar near-distant realm where the smart people were, the adults I longed to join. From its shelves I discovered Gore Vidal, William F. Buckley, George Plimpton, and similar Bengal lancers. Mailer I was aware of only because I had once cracked open *The Naked and the Dead* and shut it soon after, the few pages I waded through striking me as thick, ropy, and swampy, making me feel as if I were in the jungle too. I didn't want to be stuck in the steaming jungle fighting fungus, not at that stage of my literary upbringing, when I was more at home with *The Catcher in the Rye,* identifying with Holden Caulfield to a distressingly conventional degree. But on this particular afternoon I fished up the latest issue of *Harper's,* which was devoted entirely to Mailer's report on the antiwar march on the Pentagon, just to browse. The warp drive in my brain accelerated, and I remember looking up from the magazine ten or fifteen minutes later and staring through the library window to the sun-bright parking lot of the supermarket across the way, as if checking to make sure everything was still where it was the last time I looked. I was imprinting into memory the time and place of the point of impact when Mailer's writing first hit, the wow moment. The solo blitzkrieg that became *The Armies of the Night* has subsided into its proper rest spot in journalistic-literary history, many of its passages now reading lathered-up and rhetorically Wagnerian, and never again would Mailer gleam at his own egotistical foibles and others' through a monocle of mocking irony (as with the drawing-room comedy of Mailer and Robert Lowell trading lofty compliments like exquisite slices of bologna). But at the time, which is the only time that matters when it comes to the transfiguring moment that divides before and after, it was like having the power grid switched on, inaugurating a cerebral hum that I still hear when I read Mailer at his best. Writing about yourself in the third person as an actor in a newsreel drama struck me as a genius device on Mailer's part. Other writers may have done it before, but they did it as recording angels or passive lenses (camera eyes with fancy lashes), whereas here was Mailer writing about himself from the panoramic outside while documenting himself in the thick of it, a militant subjectivity that swept all before it. I had no idea who most of the names were that Mailer was banging into—I hadn't read Lowell's poetry, had only the haziest notion of who Dwight Macdonald was, and the jibe at Paul Goodman ("the literary experience of encountering Goodman's style . . . was not unrelated to the journeys one undertook in the company of a laundry bag") I found completely mystifying, and still do (*what* journeys one undertakes in the company of a laundry bag?)—but turning them into real-life fictional characters nullified the need for knowing their backstories. For someone as cautious, culturally limited, and socially corner-pocketed as I was (I could later relate to the character in Barry Levinson's *Diner* who muses, "You ever get the feeling there's something going on we don't know about?"), Mailer dynamited a way open, revealed a combat mode any writer could emulate if he could pry himself free from all those inhibitions handed down from loving parents and kind teachers to help keep you in line.

I proceeded to read everything of Mailer's I could lay grip on, swan diving into *Advertisements for Myself* and *The Presidential Papers,* attempting and giving up in defeat on the novels *Barbary Shore* and *The Deer Park* (whose characters I found to be finger puppets filled with gassy monologues), diving back into *Cannibals and Christians,* and molding myself into Edgewood High School's premier Norman Mailer imitator. I acquired a sparring verbal rhythm and a belligerent waddle that supplanted the place of a useful hobby. Since few of my classmates had read Mailer and even fewer had seen him on TV, they didn't know who or what I was imitating, though my frequent use of words like "existential" and "nugatory" must have tipped them off that I was dipping into somebody else's vocabulary bag (much like those young conservatives who rolled out the full regalia of William F. Buckley Jr.'s rococo tics—the tongue flicks, eyebrow lifts, purring vowels, pencil-eraser nibblings, and Oxbridge stammerings that often preceded a tart retort—as if they were conducting Latin mass on Mars). My high-school papers, my college application essays, read like Norman Mailer packed in a crunchy peanut butter sandwich.

My Mailerisms became even more pronounced in college at Frostburg State in western Maryland, whose bleak winter spells reminded me of Pennsylvania coal country after the coal mines had closed (I had relatives in Hazleton from my mother's side of the family). It was a college utterly without pretenses in a town that felt remote from the rest of Maryland, an obscure poor cousin exiled to the end of a long, winding bus ride. It was really Frostburg or nothing. Not only couldn't I afford the University of Maryland or (dream on) Johns Hopkins, but my grades had plummeted my junior year of high school, when I worked nights as an assistant dishwasher at the country club where my father was bartender and where my youngest brother later served as general manager. It was then and there that I acquired the insomnia, caffeine addiction, hangdog eye pouches, and teenage-caveman habits that became integral elements of my identity kit and prepped me nicely for my freshman year at Frostburg, where I holed up in a study room as if in solitary self-confinement and felt homesick, but not for home. For what then? For some scribbled-over patch of the past before I climbed into the isolation booth and locked it from the inside. For all my autodidactic appetite (I read like a fiend, devouring Dostoyevsky until I developed Siberian wolf breath), I didn't entertain high expectations for myself. High expectations weren't nurtured in my neck of nowhere back then; children weren't fawned over from an early age as "gifted" and groomed for a prizewinning future; self-esteem was considered something you had to pluck from the garden yourself. Attending Frostburg certainly wasn't touted as the slingshot to a soaring tomorrow. I remember the then head of Frostburg's English department—in whose office hung a framed letter from T. S. Eliot, the closest thing to a saint's relic—drawing on a cigarette in class and pronouncing, "Some of you will make something of yourselves in life [here he took a juicy pause worthy of Charles Laughton as Captain Bligh], and some of you will end up wiping the lunch counter at Woolworth's." I rather doubt my generational counterparts at Princeton and Yale had their chains yanked so. Then again, he prided himself on his crusty curmudgeonliness, and another one of my English-lit professors, who later went on to become a prison chaplain, loaned me money when I decided to leave for New York, an act of generosity that I wouldn't want to go unrecorded. Anyway, adversity isn't the worst thing to have on your side. Frostburg's inferiority complex helped stoke an underdog attitude that made you want to prove everybody wrong. And by "you" I mean "me," since I don't know if any of my classmates felt the same way, or if they were even listening. They may have had a whole different narrative playing through their internal sound systems.

During my sophomore year at Frostburg, my Mailer radar system flashed red alert with news of an episode of *The Dick Cavett Show* set to broadcast featuring Mailer, Gore Vidal, and *The New Yorker*'s Paris correspondent, Janet Flanner. Today every self-respecting dorm suite is equipped with communications technology of which Stanley Kubrick could only stroke his beard and dream, but in those frontier days on the lower slopes of academe students didn't have entertainment devices tuned to the matrix; we had to get our TV intake from the big ugly raised-up, bolted-down set in the basement rec room. My avid anticipation of the *Cavett* broadcast was unshared by my fellow primates. (My freshman year had been spent in an all-male dorm, providing an immersive experience in de-evolutionary living for which even growing up with three brothers hadn't prepared me—it was like boot camp at the chimp house.) Those used to slumping with one leg slung over the chair at that late hour in front of the TV were less than captivated by the prospect of watching a ninety-minute program starring two novelists and some elderly bird embroiled in bladed repartee. But somehow I and a couple of confederates were able to commandeer the set from the jock contingent and ward off sporadic guerrilla attempts to change the channel, attempts that were preceded with comments along the lines of, "Shit, there must be something else on." Finally, resistance melted, and we were able to watch the show in relative peace.

Who knew the show would go down in broadcast history? At the time TV programs were mostly preserved on kinescopes, and taped shows were routinely taped over, so that invaluable archives of the old Johnny Carson, Steve Allen, and Jack Paar shows were rinsed down the void. But this ninety-minute show from December 2, 1971, has not only survived but evolved into a time capsule that, opened, still emits a white-blast radioactive force, like the atomic suitcase in *Kiss Me Deadly*. It was shown in 2007 as part of the Paley Center for Media's film and video retrospective *The Mistress and the Muse: The Films of Norman Mailer*, triggering a slew of commentaries and remembrances, including a memory-lane recap by Cavett himself, who had no idea that what was intended as a literary evening with three accomplished practitioners would soon require the services of a lion tamer. What transpired was like a tension-headache grenade going off on Cavett's tiny set (Cavett himself being quite the clever teacup) with the audience rooting and booing as if at an old-fashioned melodrama, Mailer eating up his role as villain.

> [*Mailer turns his chair away from us and to the audience.*]
> Mailer: Are you all really, truly idiots or is it me?
> [*A chorus replies, "You!" Then, applause.*]
> Cavett: Oh, that was the easy answer.

(Forgotten today is that one of the *Cavett* show's most frisson-y highlights belonged to Flanner, who, after describing how the dancer Isadora Duncan died when her scarf got tangled in the wheels of a car, noted, "She was nearly decapitated"—producing an audible intake of breath from the audience.)

Riveted by the most lacerating exchanges of rancor since the Gore Vidal–William F. Buckley skate-off at the convulsive 1968 Democratic convention in Chicago (where, as one of the ABC News commentators, Buckley, making a fist, snarled, "Now listen, you queer, stop calling me a crypto-Nazi or I'll sock you in the goddamn face and you'll stay plastered," and Vidal didn't even *flinch*), I decided to write about the show for Frostburg's student paper, the *State-to-Date*. I analyzed the verbal punches and bristling subtext much as Mailer would cover a prizefight or a gunslingers' duel, as if he were wired into the opponents' nervous systems, their jabs the extensions of his own perceptions. Decoding comments that in the original context sounded cryptic and were (as when Mailer disapprovingly alluded to Vidal's revealing in his nonfiction novel *Two Sisters*—excerpted in the *Partisan Review*—that he had sex with the Beat novelist and lumberjack bodhisattva Jack Kerouac), I reconstructed the evening as if it were a clash of two storm fronts within whose black clouds the motives were buried. The piece was called "O.K. Corral Revisited," and why the *State-to-Date* thought a meditation on an episode of *The Dick Cavett Show* by a sophomore was worth publishing across an entire page wasn't entirely apparent then, but there it was, my first appearance in college print, and I thought, Why not send a copy to Mailer? He had gotten such a drubbing for his boorishness that I thought he might appreciate someone who was tuned in to his broadcast frequency covering the verbal fisticuffs. I looked up an address for Mailer in the college library's edition of *Who's Who* and sent off a copy of *State-to-Date,* not sure if the issue would even reach him and expecting nothing in return.

Here is what I received.

"I think you have a career," Mailer's letter began, and external noise washed away, as if my brain needed to be rid of sound to take in what it was reading. It was so clear-cut, what he was saying, that I couldn't from that moment imagine my future heading any other way. Mailer went on to compliment me for peeling back the tense skin of Cavett's show and perceiving the blood currents and nerve wiring underlying the animosity between him and Vidal; and for noting the significance of his allusion to Vidal's outing of Jack Kerouac in an excerpt from *Two Sisters* that had been published in *Partisan Review,* and his shooting down of Vidal's echoing of Degas's rebuke of Whistler—"I'm going to give you a line that Degas said to Whistler—two celebrated painters—and Whistler was a great performer like Norman, and Degas said, 'You know, Whistler, you act as if you had no talent'"—by snapping, "Come on, I read that quote the same place you did, in Edmund Wilson's answer to Nabokov in this Sunday's *Times Book Review*." So don't try pulling any of those fancy erudite moves on me, buster! Mailer went on to talk about his experience in reporting and writing *The Armies of the Night,* the importance of getting the dramatic feel of the action right rather than burying your nose in the notepad and missing the marrow of the moment. He was talking shop to me, someone who had no shop to talk! Guaranteeing no certain result, he offered to write a letter of recommendation for me to Dan Wolf, the editor of the *Village Voice,* whenever I graduated from college, and I decided then and there to drop out of college at the end of my sophomore year and leave for Manhattan. Well, I didn't decide "then and there," holding the letter in my hand, but I decided to decide, and knew that in a deeper sense the decision had been made for me. I felt that if I didn't take the gamble soon, in two years I might be afraid to take a shot and that Mailer might have forgotten by then his earlier promise, and who knows what could happen between now and then? So I wrote back to Mailer, immediately taking him up on his offer, and he was as good as his word, writing to Wolf:

Dear Dan:
    I have taken the liberty of telling a young college kid, 19, to go and look you up for a job. His name is James Wolcott and he sent me a piece of reporting he did about the Cavett show I did with Vidal which I must say impressed me. Not only because it was kind to your aging ex-partner, but for the sharp recall of the quotes and the feeling Wolcott had for what the participants were up to and how they were feeling inside as the show went on. This is a long way of saying that I think this fellow has talent which I don't feel too often about young writers, and in fact it wouldn't surprise me if he

was the best I sent your way since Lucian Truscott. (Let me hope I sent Lucian your way—all I know is that I corresponded with him for a couple of years and this name popped up in the *Voice,* so I may take credit for a connection I don't deserve.)

At any rate, Dan, I wrote to James Wolcott, told him how much I liked the piece and asked him if he would be interested in getting an interview with you for working on the *Voice.* He answered all the way in the affirmative and I think he would be willing to live on hot dogs for a while, which can't be said of all of our sterling reporters these days, can it? I guess, therefore, you will hear from him before too long and I would appreciate it if you would let him have a little of your time and give a try out on a story or two.

Cheers,
Norman

Hear from me Wolf did, and in return he sent a note a bit less up-tempo.

"Dear Mr. Wolcott," he began and, after some preliminaries, cautioned:

There are very few staff writers on the *Voice* and those we put on are drawn from the ranks of our contributors. However, we have a number of fairly regular contributors.

If you decide to come to New York I would certainly be glad to talk things over with you and try to evaluate the situation. But I must stress the fact that everyone is represented by what he does rather than what he says. You wrote a piece on N.M. I would like to see it if you have a copy.

Sincerely,
Daniel Wolf

Obviously, this wasn't an urgent summons to pack up my dreams and hop the next hay wagon north, but I decided to read this yellow signal as go-ahead green, and after a summer spent dosing and weighing rats in a biomedical lab at Edgewood Arsenal (where one of the technicians and I discussed Proust to everyone else's amused indifference), I arrived in New York in the fall, fording my way through the Port Authority Bus Terminal, where a well-entrenched troupe of winos, pimps, panhandlers, and assorted other characters amenable to fucking you up sideways on the airiest pretext introduced themselves to newcomers. Using the Empire State Building as my guidepost, I turned south and strolled dozens of blocks downtown (not knowing how to use the subway and afraid of ending up in the Bronx with my bloodied head on a stick) and showed up at the *Voice* reception desk, ready for induction. They weren't ready for me, so I spent the first night, then a second, at the Y.

I met with Wolf in his office on the fifth floor of the *Voice,* then at 80 University Place and Eleventh Street. I had been briefed by Mailer in a letter that Wolf was largely deaf "and you have to make certain that he has heard what you just said," advice reiterated by the receptionist that I shouldn't mumble, "but don't shout either." Now that I am deaf in one ear, I understand better the cock of Wolf's head as he seemed to lean both into and away from a visitor. Wolf, like *The New Yorker*'s William Shawn, was a master of indirection, implication, and the silent nudge, operating on a Zen druid frequency that offered maximum maneuverability with a minimum of words; they practiced an art of listening that bordered on the telepathic unless they tuned you out altogether, which they were too polite to do, though in Wolf's case you could sense his meter ticking. He was patient with me, amused at the huge rolled-up copy of that day's *Washington Post* poking out of my coat pocket, which whanged around whenever I shifted in the chair to favor a particular butt cheek. In Wolf's office hung a framed photograph of Mailer leaning forward with his hands braced on his thighs, his mouth open as if in mid–lion roar or bawling orders at a junior officer.

Mailer was an initial investor in the *Voice* and one of its original columnists and provocateurs, famously getting into a roiling snit when the paper (whose lax copyediting left Mailer's text acned with minor, grating errors) printed "the nuisances of growth" in lieu of "the nuances of growth," arousing the finicky wrath of a writer whose style tended more toward steel wool. What provoked him was perhaps not so much the errors themselves—which could be corrected in the next week's column—as the suspicion that they were deliberate sabotage from gremlins hoping to make him look the fool. Each handful of mistakes was like having thumbtacks thrown under his wheels. Those who had to accommodate his Zeus bolts in the late hour had a different perspective. One of the *Voice*'s original pilgrims, John Wilcock, whose column The Village Square was one of the paper's most popular features, along with Jules Feiffer's cartoon strip abounding with bohemian dancers in black leotards and neurotic mama's boys as tense as rolled-up umbrellas, recalls in his *Manhattan Memories* trying to put the issue to bed only to have Mailer roll in, fully armored. "We'd all be beavering away at this grotty printing plant when our new columnist Norman Mailer would arrive bearing his lengthy column, insisting it appear word for word in the already made-up tabloid. This would involve cutting a story here and another one there, jig-sawing in the Great Novelist's priceless prose an inch or two at a time. Here was this young guy who'd written a best seller while barely out of his teens, who'd thus acquired all the arrogance of a star without any of the graciousness. The worst thing, as I saw it, was that unlike my newspaper friends he'd never been edited—and was never likely to be. There's something about being paid several dollars per word for one's writing that doesn't encourage brevity and so, good writer though he was, he could have been infinitely better. Like most of us he would have benefited from a good editor, one not intimidated by his instant fame."

The ongoing combat over Mailer's late copy being inserted unmolested wasn't the determining factor in his split from the *Voice*. As Mailer acknowledged in *Advertisements for Myself*, his dispute went deeper, to a philosophical schism between his desire that the paper be radical Hip (a word he capitalized as if it were a religion, which it was at the time for him) and the paper's more conventionally bohemian and "politely rebellious" stance of opposition. Mailer's discernment of the conservative temperament guiding the paper's pirate course hit on something that's often overlooked. It is one of journalism's more interesting parallels that the *Village Voice* and William F. Buckley's *National Review* were founded in the same year, 1955. Though the *Voice* was to become an embattled clubhouse for the scruffy urban left and *National Review* the flagship for the preppy urbane right, their birth canals were not as antithetical as it might seem. Both were founded in opposition to a liberal consensus that had gone blah and paternal with platitude and complacency. In the foreward (the misspelling is intentional) to *The Village Voice Reader,* Dan Wolf wrote, "Those of us who started the *Voice* had long since been left cold by the dull pieties of official liberalism with its dreary, if unspoken, drive to put every family in a housing development and give each child his own social worker." That was a sentiment to which *National Review*'s founding editor, William F. Buckley Jr., could assent with a splash of holy water. The difference was that Buckley wanted to convert ideas and ideology into electoral, legislative, and executive power. Wolf didn't. He and the *Voice*'s publisher and co-founder, Ed Fancher, a psychoanalyst whose defusing calmness was a credit to the Freudian playbook, weren't fixed upon some future sun-risen horizon, conjuring a hero on horseback (a Goldwater, a Reagan). Wolf didn't harbor national ambitions that might someday be inscribed in capital marble.

At the *Voice* the answer to the pukewarm pieties of official liberalism and the remedy for boredom were the unofficial individuality of locals sounding off in print as if the paper were their personal mike. Anticipating the blogosphere, the *Voice* thinned the distinction between professional keyboard peckers and stir-crazy amateurs in fifth-floor walk-ups, presenting a Beat-flavored alternative to the vaunted notion of the author as member of a sacred novitiate whose brow was sprinkled with the beneficent ashes of Lionel Trilling's cigarette. Dainty aesthetes and goateed pedants could apply elsewhere. For me, discovering the paper at a historic newsstand in Baltimore called Sherman's that stocked underground weeklies and rad-hip incendiaries such as *Ramparts* and *Evergreen Review,* the *Voice* threw off a black soot that no other rag could match (I must have been the only person to hook school in order to hit the Enoch Pratt Free Library and spend the afternoon marching through its bound volumes of *Partisan Review,* then scoot over to Sherman's to stock up on the latest bombardments in the *Berkeley Barb* and the *East Village Other,* then drop in to the Marxist bookstore whose basement was piled with mildewy back issues of the *Nation, Saturday Review,* the *New Republic,* before catching the Greyhound home). You couldn't even read the paper without getting your hands smudged with what looked like powder burns. In a time of strife it was the real fisticuffed goods. While so many underground papers went paisley wild with psychedelic art and five-alarm headlines fresh from the police-state blotter, the *Voice*—from the photography of Fred McDarrah to the barricade reporting by byliners whose press credentials were slung around their necks like militant dog tags (as witness the photo of the valiant *Voice* reporter Don McNeill on the paperback cover of *Moving Through Here,* blood trickling down his Dylanesque face)—practiced front-page cinema verité. It doled out a rough cut of history steeped in the radical hubbub and bohemianism of the Village but with a lot more riding on the outcome, a sense that each week might be pivotal as the war in Vietnam raged and American cities rioted and burned. Reading the *Voice,* you could practically hear the clomping hooves of police horses as a protest threatened to get disorderly, tear gas canisters about to hit the cobblestones. Since New York didn't actually have that many cobblestoned streets, my aural imagination must have been using its embellishing brush.

By contrast, the phantasmal histrionics of Hunter S. Thompson in *Rolling Stone* never commandeered my cadet allegiance because I always found them something of a masquerade, a grown man with a cigarette holder playing outlaw dandy for his fan club. The jeweled brocade of Tom Wolfe's New Journalism bedazzled, popcorn kernels of laughter exploding alongside the typographical fireworks, but his tours de force were such feats of mind reading and magicianship that they and he didn't seem quite human. I wasn't into baroque caricature then, when the brick-hard reality of the sixties seemed berserk enough, and Wolfe's dandyism wasn't something I could relate to—in his author's photos he looked like a painted flat posed in front of another painted flat. But each issue of the *Voice* was a barrage of articulate gabble, crackling with radio static and overlapping quarrels (like the gangster families in *The Godfather*, the *Voice* convulsed into feuds every few years to purge the bad blood and begin a fresh cycle of animosities), hitting you from an ambush trap of different angles while sticking to the actuality of what was happening, offering the cinema-screen field of view. *Voice* writers could be as egotistical as anybody else who packed words into snowballs for a precarious living, but it wasn't a high-buffed, cachet-seeking, English-majory-brunette,every-comma-hung-like-candy-canes-on-a-Christmas-tree exercise in fine craft and delectation. *Voice* writers tended to be more direct, shooting their sentences from shoulder level. You were always aware of the hard surfaces and clashing forces off of which everything caromed—the noun-verb combination punches that had traveled from Hemingway to Jimmy Cannon to Pete Hamill—and you could almost hear the mousy scribble of quotes scratched into their reporters' notebooks that would yield the killer payoff, the fatal clincher. So to be accepted into the *Voice* was to be initiated into a fight club where you either fit in or were flushed out. Or so I fancied, never doubting I'd make the cut if given a chance. Such confidence I had, a healthy by-product of not knowing any better.

To return to the office where Mailer's photograph silently roared: The questions Wolf asked were basic and general, mild probes befitting an informal interview with a noncandidate for a nonexistent job. I wonder if he thought I was a rough diamond or a raw carrot. From my end, I thought—truthfully, I'm not sure what I thought, or if I was even thinking from inside the swirl of expectations I had spun out of the daydreams of glory that owed less to literature than to Hollywood films such as *Youngblood Hawke,* where the barefoot, bare-chested author straight from the provinces landed

Suzanne Pleshette as his editor ("Shall I call you Youngy or Bloody?" is the line Gore Vidal cherishes), and TV's *The Waltons,* where John-Boy and typewriter longed to sprout the heavenly wings of *Look Homeward, Angel.* But if I had envisioned that Wolf would be so impressed that I had quit college and left home to apply to the *Voice* that I would be accepted at once and sent out with an assignment to prove myself worthy of Mailer's sword tap (and I had), the helium soon left that balloon. This wasn't Hollywood, and a handshake wasn't going to welcome me into the fraternity of fire jumpers. The meeting ended with an invitation to submit something and they'd be happy to take a look at it, the editorial equivalent of "Drop by if you're ever in the neighborhood (but call first)." It was up to me to prove myself, not up to them to nurture the tender bough and outstretched leaves of some greasy kid popping in from nowhere. I didn't need a blackboard diagram to understand that they hadn't been waiting all their lives for me to emerge from the woods like a natural wonder, jangling my pocketful of epiphanies. Wolf didn't try to discourage me, direct me back to college for more seasoning, so there was at least that.

What I didn't understand until later was that by the autumn of 1972, Wolf had wearied of the *Voice* and its perennial teething problems and gnawing neuroses, tired of being father-confessor/mentor-guru/chief rabbi to a restive band of underpaid, psychological dependents. They, in turn, resented their dependency, confronting Wolf in December 1971 (the same month as the Mailer-Vidal fracas) to demand more money from management (was this what Mailer was slyly alluding to in his letter to Dan about "sterling reporters" unwilling to live on hot dogs?), their demands undercut by their expressions of devotion. After the death of Don McNeill in August 1968, a drowning accident that devastated Wolf, he wasn't looking for new candidates to fill the role of rising son. (One historian of the paper wrote, "There was no young writer [McNeill was only twenty-three] who had ever shown more promise, or to whom Dan Wolf had ever gotten closer, and . . . in all his years as editor of the *Village Voice,* no event ever hurt Dan Wolf more than when Don McNeill left it.") It was exhausting enough trying to keep everybody happily unhappy within the fine *Voice* tradition of constant uproar without the stress and disappointment of tending another litter of possible protégés. He was beginning to tune out the conflicting *Voice*s to a pinched whine, dialing out the indoor traffic. Which, had I known, would have been okay because I wasn't searching for a father figure, not even in Norman Mailer, believing (or so I believed that I believed) that discipleship was best practiced from the on-deck circle, where you were less likely to get on the font of wisdom's nerves.

Every few days I would visit the *Voice,* asking if anything had "opened up," varying the timings of my visits to lend them an air of happenstance, as if I were just popping in on my way elsewhere, some trifling errand perhaps, toeing that delicate line between harmless nuisance and complete pest. In the meantime, I had gone through the little money I had brought, living on Cokes and powdered donuts, a regimen that would yield so many negative dividends in future years. I also went in search of other work, one job agency declining to send me out on interviews because I didn't have a proper coat—"I can't send you into a personnel office with you dressed like that," one young man said with a note of kindness that I appreciated. A less choosy outfit sent me to apply for a dishwasher's job at a restaurant where there was so much steam, slop, and cursing it was like a submarine taking on water. I responded to a newspaper ad for holiday-season helpers at a department store—was it Altman's?—where everyone there already looked as if their feet hurt and we were sent home as soon as the available slots were filled. I had perfected a modest pantomime of entering and departing the Latham Hotel in a slow, eyes-averted, nonchalant hurry to avoid detection, which didn't stop the billing notices from sneaking under my room door, making a little whisking sound that I learned to dread. Perhaps if I had had other contacts in the city, I could have used them to score temporary work, but I didn't know anyone yet and hadn't made any new friends, a gift for friendship not being a prominent item in my golf bag. I had only one ladder propped against the wall, and that ladder led to the *Village Voice,* but the ladder only went so high— I couldn't get over that wall.

Once the money dwindled until there was just enough for a bus ticket back to Baltimore, I packed to leave, having just barely arrived. My suitcase was spread open on the hotel bed, thinly packed, my having brought just enough clothes to throw on in case of fire. I had made it through the previous winter at college in the whistling-cold mountains of western Maryland in a single pair of sneakers and, when not feeling sorry for myself, fancied myself quite the Spartan pioneer. I told myself I was beating a tactical retreat and would return once I had saved more money and mapped things out better, but an alternative reel in my head had me returning to Frostburg to get my B.A. and maybe move on to graduate studies in English lit, where I would scoff at John Barth to show what a rebel I was. I put through a last phone call to the *Voice* and asked for Dan Wolf, who, surprisingly, took the call. (When I had asked for him before at the front desk, he was either out or in meetings.) I explained my situation without laying on too much melodrama and told him I wanted to leave a forwarding address in Maryland where I could be reached if anything opened up in the future. I wasn't bluffing or making a pity ploy; my mind was made up to go. But instead of taking down my address, Wolf sighed and said: *"Ohhhhh,* all *right,* why don't you come down, we'll see if we can find something."

And, really, everything that's happened to me since swung from the hinge of that moment, the gate that opened because one editor shrugged and said, *Ah, what the hell.*

The *Voice* did find me something, not in editorial, but in the circulation department at the rear of the first floor, where I processed subscription orders and fielded telephone complaints about late delivery or copies lost or chewed beyond recognition in the mail, the latter task requiring patience, a caring tone, and similar affiliated "people skills" that made every phone call an adventure. Were I to man a crisis hotline at some volunteer center today, I could muster the soothing tones of a late-night jazz DJ and defuse most minor crises, but back then I met friction with friction, which was the house style at the *Voice,* but no treat for the nervous system, mine or anyone else's. It was my first extended contact with that hardy, nasal species of persistence known as the New York Complainer, capable of raising the smallest dispute into *Judgment at Nuremberg,* and it made the head hurt. Although it's the writing that's remembered, one of the major drivers in the *Voice's* downtown bible status back then was the classified-ads section for apartment rentals and job listings that no prospector could do without. An urban legend had taken hold that there was a special secret drop-off point on Tuesday nights where early birds could get the jump on everybody else to prospect the classifieds before deliveries were made in the rest of Manhattan. It wasn't true. If memory serves, the first bundles were always dropped at Sheridan Square early Wednesday morning, but the rumor mill kept churning about a treasure-map rendezvous point on Tuesday nights whose location was known only to a cunning few. I fended call after call from job seekers and apartment hunters wanting, pleading, *demanding* to know where the first bale of *Voices* landed so that they could get the paper before anyone else and circle the real-estate ads in ink. Nothing I said could disabuse them. It got to the point a few times when I would say, in a whispery, scared voice, "I'm sorry, I'd like to tell you, but I can't, I can't—" then hang up as if a black glove had landed on my receiver, cutting off the transmission to Allied forces. Some would then ring back and ask to speak to my supervisor, for whom I was already an albatross, a cross to bear, and a daily penance. For justifiable reasons, I was nearly fired on a number of occasions—I called in sick one Friday to catch the opening of Sam Peckinpah's melancholy canter through auburn-drenched mortality, *Pat Garrett and Billy the Kid,* returning on Monday to find my desk had been completely cleared off by my boss, as if a crime scene had been eliminated—but was given more stays of execution than I deserved.

On the inside looking out, I managed to become a minor fixture in the aquarium, part of the sandy grit at the bottom of the *Voice*'s ecosystem. I dated a co-worker, though dating isn't exactly what we did. I'm not sure what it was we did, recalling only the prison heat of her five-floor walk-up on Eighth Street—a street as unpicturesque today as it was then—where she once chucked her shoes at me as I exited following a minor spat in which it had been determined I was in the wrong. This being the seventies, it wasn't standard-issue footwear she was hurling but chunky platform shoes worthy of Carmen Miranda or a member of the New York Dolls, real clompers that, her aim slightly awry, landed against the door with a murderous thud. I'm not even sure her firetrap of a studio had a bed, since I recall the two of us spending a lot of time on the floor listening to the jazz station on the radio. She was a luscious string bean, the woman I'll call Leanna, an Italian-American tempest with a raucous, dirty laugh and chocolate eyes who enjoyed a smattering of rough sex, the bruisier the better. In this area, as in so many other areas where she and her mattress were concerned, I was frustratingly half-measured, reluctant to close the gap between a light open-hand slap and a closed hard fist. Once she accused me of trying to choke her after we came out of a Robert Altman movie called *California Split* over whose merits we differed, she finding it completely sucky and me being somewhat more judiciously appreciative. Our disagreement escalated until my hands floated into a choke position around her throat without actually touching. "But the other night you *wanted* me to choke you," I said after she had let out a yelp on the street, to which she replied: "Yeah, and of course you wouldn't— you never want to do things when I want to, only when you want to." It was soon clear that I wasn't the considerate brute she was craving. Months after our brief office non-affair ended without having established enough traction for a genuine breakup, Leanna, playing show-and-tell after work, lifted her loose blouse here and there to display purple-blue nebula-like bruises bestowed by her latest beau, a member of the NYPD. It was as if—no "as if" about it—she were taunting me about finding someone macho enough to give her what she wanted, a *real* man who didn't putter around and hide behind some nice-guy bullshit. Leanna later moved to Los Angeles, where she lived with a well-known character actor who, during one cocaine fugue, chased her around the lawn with hedge clippers, threatening to cut off her nipples. "You have a *lawn?*" I said, and she laughed. Despite my allegiance to Norman Mailer and Peckinpah movies, I had too much altar boy in me to seize the bitch goddess of success by her ponytail and bugger the Zeitgeist with my throbbing baguette. That just wasn't me. I was so unmacho I couldn't even pronounce the word properly, giving it a hard *c* until someone in the circulation department corrected me so that I wouldn't embarrass myself further.

When one of the receptionists ducked out for lunch or to run an errand, I would pinch-hit at the front desk, seated in the cockpit, as it were, and afforded a wide-angle view of University Place. Once or twice Anaïs Nin majestically floated by, her face powdered like a geisha's, a blue cape trailing behind her in the Kodak sunlight. Anaïs Nin—her name carried a music-box lilt then, seldom heard now, her cult fame a peacock feather that literary fashion has left behind. In the seventies, however, she was a prefeminist upright odalisque idol and a milky apparition of Paris past, her diaries with their familiar covers clutched and carried everywhere by young women whose devotion to passion and literature had an idealistic ardency ripe for disillusionment. But in 1973 the backlash against Nin's queenly deportment—the narcissism slathered like moisturizing lotion across thousands of pages—had yet to commence, and she swanned through the Village like the last dollop of dyed splendor in a Sidney Lumet world of screeching tires and clogged sinuses. Donald Barthelme once dropped by at the front desk, a confabulator whose stories in *The New Yorker* were whirring devices constructed from exquisite diagrams with sadness peeking from the corners, leaving residue. Jill Johnston, the dance writer turned Joycean stream-of-consciousness riding-the-rapids diarist, would wait for someone to open the back stairs (she was phobic about elevators), occasionally plucking a seashell from her denim vest to leave on the counter as a souvenir. I always liked Jill's entrances because she seemed to bring a playful breeze with her, a sense of salutation that was like a greeting from a grasshopper, owing no allegiance to the daily grind. *Voice* writers talked a good game of being uninhibited, but for them it was more of a policy statement, a plank in the countercultural platform. She was more performative. It was Jill who would roll on the floor with a lesbian pal at the Town Hall debate on feminism starring Norman Mailer and Germaine Greer, an antic that provoked Mailer to snap, "Jill, act like a lady!"

Strangers would pop in with unsolicited manuscripts in manila envelopes to leave at the front desk for the editors. When the stack had reached a suitable height, I was given permission to open the envelopes and sort them into piles according to the appropriate department. Semi-idealistic as I was then, I accepted as gospel the democratic notion that there was all this rough undiscovered talent Out There crying out for discovery, rescue, tender care, bunny food, and a shot at publication—a phantom legion of mute, inglorious Miltons waiting for their big Broadway break. Within one of these manila envelopes ticked the explosive arrival of some railroad-flat genius or untenured academic drudge whose individuality would leap off the page like a police bulletin and knock them off their bar stools at the Lion's Head, where men were men and their livers were shot. Boy, was I ever misaligned with reality. Based on my slush-pile diving, it was dishwater all the way down. Given the *Voice*'s status as a mouthy paper that didn't aspire to starchy respectability, I was amazed at how so many of the manuscripts droned on with the dental-drill lecturing of letters to the editor at the *New York Times* or moused along with sensitive whiskers aquiver, emulating the crinkly-leafed, diffused-light impressionism of a *New Yorker* sketch—the kind of Talk of the Town piece *The New Yorker* hadn't published since the fifties, not that I had read *The New Yorker* in the fifties. But as soon as I saw a manuscript with each comma perfectly tucked like a lock of hair behind a shy ear, the end of each paragraph landing with a muffled, dying fall, I pictured the author picturing himself as Updike or E. B. White, lit by an attic window.

The stabs at relevance were worse—ham-fisted and all over the canvas. The Watergate bombshell of the eighteen-minute gap in the Nixon tape produced an inundation of speculative humor pieces about what was missing on the tape, Russell Baker–Art Buchwald exercises that occasionally escalated into Paul Krassner necro-buggery fantasy without being funny. (Krassner was the creator of the champion sick-humor hoax in his satirical magazine, *The Realist,* where an exposé titled "The Parts Left Out of [William Manchester's] Kennedy Book" claimed that the former First Lady Jacqueline Kennedy had caught LBJ sticking his penis into the mortal hole in JFK's throat on the flight back from Dallas. I never found that put-on funny either, but the controversy hung jester bells on Krassner that he's been jangling ever since.) The fact that so many sharp brains—I recognized some of the names as belonging to occasional *Voice* contributors—were mining the same Nixon-fucking-the-Constitution-and/or-Rose Mary Woods fantasies showed that the imaginative lodes of collective fantasy were much thinner and chalkier than I had thought, that there was much more mental conformity below the surface than one would have guessed from all the flying elbows being thrown from these gag writers. Everybody seemed to be staring at the same targets through the same pair of binoculars.

I do recall seeing an account of jury-duty service submitted by Alfred Kazin that stood out from the rest of the laundry—wow, an actual writer, I thought, one whose authority was evident from the first footstep he took on the page. (It had originally been commissioned for *Playboy* in one of its wild, impetuous moments.) Years later I would be invited to appear on Dick Cavett's PBS show with Kazin and a pair of fellow reviewers, taking part in a literary panel discussion in which Kazin did his blinky best to pretend the rest of us were lawn ornaments while he held forth like a highbrow hound dog bemoaning the intellectual erosion at the *New York Times Book Review,* a topic always dear to people's hearts. He found it perturbing that the *Book Review* had given front-page treatment to Gay Talese's snorkel submersion into the hot tub of the American libido, *Thy Neighbor's Wife,* an editorial decision he felt deserving of reprimand and reproach. That the rest of us weren't perturbed allowed him to have the heath all to himself. Somewhere along the line the monologue in his head and the monologue out of his mouth wedded into an uninterrupted melody that you longed to interrupt, to give that murmurous, sonorous eloquence a rest. It wasn't his conceit that rankled (hard-earned conceit being acceptable as long as it's not ringed with barbed wire and rude to waiters); no, it was the pained moral conscience that accompanied it, the sigh of weary resignation worthy of a Moses with no followers, as if he were the last literary soul in the five boroughs who cared.

Sifting through the slush pile served the useful purpose of pointing me in the direction of what not to do as I tried to break into print from inside the building. Avoid parody, which slides too easily into facetiousness. Avoid political satire, which has the shelf life of a sneeze. Avoid preamble—flip the on switch in the first sentence. Find a focal point for your nervous energy, assume a forward offensive stance, and drive to the finish line, even if it's only a five-hundred-word slot: no matter how short a piece there has to be a sense of momentum and travel, rather than just allotted space being texted in. A number of *Voice* regulars with their own weekly beats had lapsed into a chummy informality with beer suds at the top and not much below, an anecdotal approach that struck me as a drought waiting to happen, and not just because I had so few anecdotes to call my own. Writing that was too talky lacked the third rail below the surface that suggested untapped power reserves, an extra store of ammo. Mailer's writing could be verbose, but he never relaxed his knuckles; it never devolved into chat. Loosely fortified with these scraped-together guidelines, bent like a concert pianist over a borrowed typewriter and barely able to think further than one or two sentences ahead, I applied myself to whatever chanced by in order to break into the *Voice* with my own byline, enhanced with the versatility of a novice willing to essay a variety of subjects because I was equally unversed in all of them. American history, European history, New York politics (Carmine De Sapio, who he?), the performing arts, the drug scene, the dominant schools of psychotherapy, the factional feuds between the rugby squads of sixties radical movements, these were but a smattering of the blank regions on my intellectual road map to points unknown. My lack of education and expertise didn't hold me back; if anything, it made me feel free, unbuckled. I didn't know what I was capable of doing as a writer, because I didn't know what I was *incapable* of doing, because I hadn't done anything yet. Everything was so new to me that nothing seemed ruled out. Niche journalism hadn't yet whittled too many writers into specialty artists, dildos for rent.

In those lax days that were soon to end sooner than anyone anticipated, the *Voice* had an idiosyncratic system for stocking the shelves of its review departments. Freelance reviews were left in a vertical folder for the arts editor, Diane Fisher. Because these reviews were unassigned, there might be three unsolicited reviews of the same rock concert or some new album trying to squeeze through the same tunnel, reviews of events and items that might have already been assigned to a regular. It was like playing darts in the dark, hoping to hit the board. It may not have been the most efficient system, but it was ego sparing. When something turned in on spec didn't make the cut, I didn't know if it had flunked because it wasn't good enough, if it was a victim of column-space shrinkage, if one of the regulars had already called dibs, and so on. The pieces were never actually *rejected,* handed back with a skull and crossbones slashed in ink across the top, they just weren't accepted, which enabled you to avoid discouragement but also left you dangling, until the next elimination dance. So I kept trying, trying to figure out the combination to the lock, find the elusive sweet spot.

Having intercepted a publicist's phone call one day at the front desk, I zipped uptown to interview Groucho Marx, who was in town to promote a Marx Brothers festival. It was the last interview of a long day, and he was flagging but cordial (if a little puzzled), a cheery tam-o'-shanter perched on his head as he humored this obvious novice, his sharpest retort coming when I asked what he remembered most about working with Marilyn Monroe on *Love Happy,* and he said: "She had square tits." His minder was Erin Fleming, who had played the NYU graduate with pretentious airs ("For me, Norman Mailer has exactly that same sort of relevance—that affirmative, negative duality that only Proust or Flaubert could achieve") whose portal Woody Allen's anxious sperm prepared to ford in *Everything You Always Wanted to Know About Sex*. Fleming was later sued and removed as Groucho's legal guardian by his family, who accused her of pushing him into public appearances past the limits of elderly fatigue, resulting in numerous minor strokes. Falling by the wayside, Fleming eventually died of a self-inflicted gunshot, but nothing was foreshadowed on that late afternoon; she was charming and help-ful, papering over awkward pauses with diplomatic interjections and bringing the interview in for a gentle fade so that Groucho could have a nap before the carousel restarted in the evening. The Groucho article didn't run, but brief reviews I did of rock albums, downtown plays, and TV programs began to be published. Upon appearing in print, I realized that I possessed an asset that I had never reckoned on, something given to me at birth.

My name.

My byline, James Wolcott, it sounded so *mature,* so English, so litty-critty and stamped with authority. It was a byline that sounded as if it knew what it was talking about and had an extensive library for backup. That the impression my byline gave bore little resem-blance to its owner didn't matter, because no one could see me eating lunch at my desk. It would be years before people realized I was nowhere near as lineaged, assured, and stately as my byline suggested, one well-known editor from Knopf exclaiming upon meeting me, "And here I always thought you were a member of the fucking *gentry.*"

These small incursions not only bolstered my confidence but gave me something to clip from the paper as proof to my parents and other interested parties that I wasn't just gazing out the window in the circulation department wishing the phone wouldn't ring.

Then the everyday drift of events picked up speed and went over the falls into the thundering foam. In 1974, the founding fathers of

the *Voice* were dethroned in a coup that sent Dan Wolf and the publisher, Ed Fancher, packing into exile, or as far as "exile" could take
you while still maintaining an abode in Greenwich Village. In a
buccaneer move that none of us underlings saw coming (and caught
nearly all the overlings off guard), the paper was sold by its principal
owner, the patrician pretty boy and former New York City council-
man Carter Burden, to Clay Felker, who had made *New York* magazine the flagship station of the New Journalism, the only weekly
worthy of the racing silks and the dusty roar of career jockeys working the far turn. The sale was a culture clash fused with a shotgun
wedding. Where the *Voice* was a downtown scrappy collage, a bulletin board that shot back, *New York* was a midtown, Madison Avenue, starfucky, glossy display window where the contributors shone
with the reflected glow of their glamorous subjects, achieving their
own celebrity shellac—Tom Wolfe, Gloria Steinem, Jimmy Breslin,
John Simon, Albert Goldman, Gail Sheehy, Nick Pileggi, Nik Cohn,
Judith Crist. If the *Voice* still fancied itself as something of a rogue
enterprise, punching above its weight with wicked uppercuts, *New
York* aspired to the cocktail party in the penthouse suite where every
name was boldfaced and the tinkling of ice was musical delight. In
this, my first experience with an editorial coup, I had the psychic
cushion of being a bit player not worth waging a custody battle over.
I had little stake pro or con in an editorial changeover because I was
still down in the circulation department, hiding incriminating mistakes in my desk and fielding phone calls from the highly frustrated.
It was far more emotionally whipsawing for most of those around
me, whose histories with the paper went back a decade or more
and had become integrated into their cellular structure. For those
of such braided loyalty, the *Voice* was the only journalistic home
they had ever known, the only hut on the island willing to accept
the idiosyncratic and unclassifiable and provide refuge. Dan and Ed,
Ed and Dan (their names went up and down together like a teeter-
totter), were soft-spoken patriarchs whose presences were taken for
granted as enduring. The sense of dismay and betrayal at the paper

being sold cut deep and cross-angled, serrated with the knowledge of how much Dan and Ed had profited from the original sale to Carter Burden while writers were subsisting on financial scraps. As would later happen at *The New Yorker* when William Shawn was deposed, some would never recover from Wolf's departure, banking their bitterness for long-term capital losses and never quite finding themselves again.

What Felker perceived with pirate zeal was that the *Voice* was a brand and the brand was being left to fend for itself, unexploited, unemblazoned. He compared the current operation of the *Voice* to a college paper, a country store. Following the model of *Rolling Stone,* he intended to platform the paper into a national weekly less immersed in the parochial joustings below Fourteenth Street and packing more throw weight as a political and cultural resonator. To accomplish this, the national edition had to pipe up and pump out trend pieces that translated into every urban zip code. Such trend spotting and trumpeting were antithetical to the *Voice* ethos, where eyewitness testimony was prized over billboard statements plastered over every passing craze. And the wider spectrum Felker sought involved a different, alien set of metrics; he commissioned a profile piece of the impressionist Rich Little—whose personality was considered bland even by Canadian standards and whose takeoffs had none of the fanged bite of David Frye's (his tongue-darting, eye-popping William F. Buckley suggested an iguana on mescaline)— based mostly on Little's high Q ratings, which were considered a gauge of likability. Likability! This from a paper dedicated to chafing and championing the difficult underdog. He brought in designers and illustrators and introduced a blue band to the *Voice*'s front-page logo, a minor twirl-up that was considered a trashy violation of the paper's monochromatic aesthetic. It didn't take long for the verdict to be rendered on Felker's tenure at the *Village Voice:* guilty—guilty of journalistic manslaughter and reckless malpractice. In the histories and memoirs of the *Voice* that soon followed, Felker was cast as both usurper and undertaker. The front cover of Ellen Frankfort's unauthorized account *The Voice: Life at the "Village Voice,"* published in 1976, featured a mock front page of the *Voice* pasted over a tombstone. "Here Lies Independent Journalism" was the graveyard message. Kevin Michael McAuliffe's less emotionally shredded, wider-lensed view of the ongoing psychodrama, *The Great American Newspaper: The Rise and Fall of the "Village Voice,"* published in 1978, offered a more detailed damage assessment that also consigned the *Voice* to the junk pile of broken dreams. To McAuliffe, and in this he was far from alone, Clay Felker's conquistadorial reign had ushered in a dry-hump orgy of debauchery, profligacy, and groupie adulation of power and celebrity:

> Clay Felker had taken over a paper in 1974 that was unique, populated by a community of writers who constantly agreed to disagree and who were edited, if that is the word, by a man who simply loved good writing for its own sake. By the end of 1976, Felker, whatever his own politics might be, had discovered that New Left rhetoric was a commodity that could be bought and peddled just like any other, and that was what he had done. For the first time in its history, it was possible to predict, in advance, what position the *Village Voice* might take on anything. The paper that had never had an editorial line now had one, a smug, institutionalized hippie leftism. The paper that had always been open to every point of view was now cravenly jingoistic. Clay Felker had taken the most ambitious, the most experimental, the most exciting American newspaper of its generation, and he had built a monument to vulgarity with it.

All that may be true, but I have to admit it worked out swell for me. Up blew the whale spout and on a spume of foam I flew. Those may sound like the words of an ingrate, but denying is lying, and I can't deny that the Felker takeover turned out to be the best thing that could have happened to me at the *Voice,* and not just me. That rude injection of vulgarity invigorated a vein of new blood that revitalized the paper and cocked it forward, despite the masthead carnage and the premature burials of the *Voice*'s relevance. Due to Felker's meddling and despite Felker's meddling, the paper was poised for a lightning streak that would make the *Voice* the definitive seventies paper, a bucking bronco reborn. Punk, disco, the emergence of gay culture, the morphing of political feminism into personal memoir (as exemplified by Karen Durbin's ardent, reflective, influential essay "On Being a Woman Alone"), the triumphant swell of the Hollywood blockbuster, the celebrity portraiture that would displace street photojournalism—the *Voice* was primed for these phenomena by the new observation deck Felker installed in nearly everyone's thinking. New editors boarded the vessel, and the old system of unassigned reviews filling the in-box each week like church flyers was junked in favor of a bullpen rotation. One day I was slicing open envelopes like a Victorian clerk when the new music editor, Robert Christgau, boistered in, holding loose manuscript pages in his hands and flapping them with authority. In future years it would be hard to picture Bob empty-handed, so familiar was he for reading copy on the flat-footed fly, doing his own version of bumper cars years later when a new device known as the Sony Walkman came on the market, enabling him to avoid seeing *and* hearing where he was going. (Empowered by the music pumping into his head, he assumed he had the right-of-way.) Bobbing was what Bob did, the top half of his body—clad in record-company T-shirts that had shrunk considerably in the wash while retaining their impudent panache—rocking back and forth as he thought, expostulated, paced like a prosecutor in front of the jury, laid down the editorial law, or let loose with a laugh that seemed to explode with a timing device, two or three beats after something struck him as funny and he had rolled it around in his head awhile.

The introductions over in a flash, Bob got down to business, letting me know with a minimum of gift wrapping that of the two most recent rock reviews I did for the *Voice,* one was smart and funny (a review of a solo effort by the Doors keyboardist, Ray Manzarek) and the other (here memory draws a blank) pitifully inadequate.

(He would later describe most of the music reviews published by the previous regime as "a waste . . . slack, corny, and anonymous.") In miniature preview, this was Bob's method in boosting and sub-duing contributors: the praise-up and the slap-down, the latter an ego check up against the hockey glass to let you know who was boss, king, keeper of the keys, samurai master of the red edit pen. Although Greil Marcus would come to command more intellectual throw weight with *Mystery Train* and similar expeditions into the mythic depths and marshy fringes of the American Gothic, Les-ter Bangs would survive in legend as the Neal Cassady of Romilar and epic rhapsodies at the typewriter, and Jon Landau and Dave Marsh would eventually earn joint custody of Bruce Springsteen, it was Bob who was the self-proclaimed, scepter-wielding Dean of American Rock Critics, an honorific that sounds as esoteric today as some ecclesiastical title. With the decline of the album as message statement and the rise of the iPod, rock critics no longer exist as a recognizable category of cultural journalist with its own career ladder, schlubby mystique, battle stripes of cultural rebellion, and backstage lore. Like jazz, pop analysis has become academicized, with Christgau himself practicing his deanhood at the Clive Davis Department of Recorded Music at New York University and cart-ing his buckshot-packed capsule Consumer Guide review column from one set of temporary digs to another, retiring and restarting it in 2010. But back then Christgau commanded the pulse center, enveloping himself in an energy cone of charisma that made writers want to be admitted into the big chief's teepee while worrying that, once in, they might find themselves cast out again through the flap door for some flub or faux pas against the canons of rock-crit ortho-doxy. Under his editorship, the pop music pages of the *Voice* exerted a force field that made the review section of *Rolling Stone* look like minor-league box scores.

As an editor, Christgau practiced the opposite of Zen. Indirection wasn't in his playbook; pro or con, he gave it to you straight, with extra mustard. The upside was that Christgau made you want to please him, impress him, fuse two circuits together for an electric insight no one had made before, use the performance anxiety all writers have as the impetus to dig deeper and be on the receiving end of one of his triumphant war whoops. He would share his enthusiasms with the other editors, the congratulations multiplying until your swelled head barely fit into the elevator. The flip side fell when you failed to execute your mission, letting down Bob, the fellow Bobsters, and your membership in the fertility cult. Once, hazily hovering over the opening paragraph of a review I did of the Hollies performing at the Bottom Line, Bob said, as if reprimanding himself for overruling his better judgment, "I knew I should have assigned this to ———," since I had made such a hash of it, revealing myself as Hollies-inadequate. Another time, looking over a revise I had done, he said, "Well, I'm glad you incorporated my suggestions, but I didn't think you'd do it so *faithfully,*" making me feel like a retriever bearing the master's slippers in its mouth. Bob didn't always edit at the office, burning eyeholes in your copy and sounding the sentences in his head as if doing ballistics tests. Sometimes he edited at home, which was a trip, in both senses of the word. Once I made explorer tracks over to the apartment that Bob and his future wife, Carola Dibbell, shared in the alphabet side of the East Village, where a mound of garbage burned in the middle of the street like an anarchist's bonfire as taxis slowed to navigate around it. Inside Bob and Carola's apartment it was a Dickensian cove, as if their decorator had been a chimney sweep with a load of cinders to spread around. The focal point in this Stygian picture of domesticity was the spectacle of Bob, wearing nothing but red sheer bikini underwear, attending to something at the kitchen stove and pensively scratching his ass. Bob wasn't one to stand upon formalities, adopting a more Tarzan stance. After he and Carola moved to a sunnier place on Twelfth Street (a street I too later shared, where the crunch of crack vials met the hoarse cries of hookers having an intimate conversation at the top of their charred lungs from ten or twelve feet apart), Lester Bangs told me that Bob once edited him in the nude, lying on the carpet with his butt-crack smiling northward as in a baby picture. The buzzer rang and it was Bob's apartment neighbor, Vince Aletti, announcing himself. Bob got up and went into the other room to slip on a pair of underwear. Lester wondered, he told me, why Vince's presence necessitated underwear from Bob while his didn't, and then he remembered that Vince was gay—"And, you know, Bob probably didn't *want to tempt him,*" Lester said, laughing.

In his return to the *Voice,* Bob brought with him an air of embattlement that had a soap-opera backstory. He and fellow rock critic/ politico-cultural journalist Ellen Willis had been the reigning rock critic couple on the counterculture scene, the John and Yoko of the downtown set, the future Norman Podhoretz and Midge Decter of the Ministry of Pop Sensibility. If as a couple they functioned as a dual-processor dynamo, their intellectual status was separate but unequal. While Christgau had enjoyed a trapeze platform as a columnist at *Esquire,* which was a "hot book" in the magazine world under the ringmaster editorship of Harold Hayes, Willis haunted even higher, holier rafters as the rock critic of *The New Yorker* and a contributor to the *New York Review of Books* and Theodore Solotaroff's *New American Review* (where her somber epitaph on the riots at the 1968 Democratic convention, "Lessons of Chicago," appeared). Given his intellectual carriage and male pride, this uneven ranking must have been a cactus prick to Christgau, who was denied entrée into the more exclusive cloisters of prestige. Bob told me of the phone ringing when he and Ellen lived together and hearing the quavery, eggshell-walking voice of William Shawn at the other end and his handing the phone to Ellen with a mock-annoyed "It's for you." Their breakup—discreetly memoirized by Willis in a journal for the short-lived paperback magazine *US,* edited by Richard Goldstein, a wunderkind who would also rejoin the *Voice* in its radical Felkerization and not win any popularity contests—had been unamicable in the extreme. The betrayal of Ellen's briefly taking up with some hippie dude ("The last time I got my hair cut, Ellen dumped me for somebody else," was how I remember Bob explaining his subsequent aversion to barbershop scissors) incurred a wrath almost Sicilian from Bob, who refused to share the same public confines with his former comrade-lover. It was a logistical headache for record-company and concert publicists, who had to ensure that the rock critic of *Newsday* and *Esquire* didn't find himself under the same roof enjoying freebies (there were freebies then—buffets even) as the rock critic of *The New Yorker.* Urban legend had it that Bob once spotted Ellen at a record-label event and was so incensed that he threw a pie at her, an incident that became as inscribed in rock-crit myth as R. Meltzer (*The Aesthetics of Rock*)'s peeing into the punch bowl at some press event, a stunt I was cautioned not to emulate, lest I develop the wrong kind of reputation—an invaluable piece of advice for any promising youngster. Bob assumed everyone knew the saga of his breakup with Ellen, as if it ranked with Grendel on the Richter scale, and its unfinished business dragged through the office like an anchor.

Bob's wounded pride and obstinacy prevented Ellen from being given a full editorial role at the *Voice,* Bob deploying a her-or-me ultimatum that was eventually lifted after mutual friends and colleagues, tired of being tugged in the middle, impressed upon Bob that his gruff resolve made it appear that he still hadn't gotten over the breakup despite the intervening years, which wasn't very flattering to Carola, who was by then his wife. I had no great opinion to drop one way or the other on the scale of justice because I never quite "got" the Ellen Willis cult of genius, the whole Rosa Luxemburg mystique aureoled around her curly Ed Koren cartoonish head and goggled squint. Written as if her words represented the patter of rain, Willis's pop music reports for *The New Yorker* had none of the toreador flash and headlong plunge of the best rock writing being done in the sixties and seventies; they lacked the authority she stamped into her political essays, as if she were doing a series of liner notes, keeping the grown-ups informed about what the kids were up to. Not that I liked her political writing any better. I liked it less. It ground forward like an earthmover along with the worst liabilities of left-wing pamphleteering, her Marxist-feminist-Reichian calls for erotic freedom and social liberation laid down with the iron clang of railroad spikes hammered to the heavy metronome of jargon. It was evident from the worship and emulation Willis inspired that she possessed a personal charisma that transcended the page, but that charisma and I never cloud-mingled, so all I had to go by were pieces that seemed weighed down by their pedagogical intent, bottom-heavy correctives to liberal orthodoxy, and radical cant that made the pages you were holding in your hands turn to lead. But I was in the minority when it came to Willis's acuity and importance and would remain so, not that it mattered then or now. What was important then was this sense, this supposition, that sixties scenes-bursters such as Christgau, Willis, and Goldstein were destined to inherit or hijack in slow motion the intellectual-journalistic establishment of *The New Yorker,* the *New York Review of Books, Commentary, Partisan Review,* and *Dissent* and become the presiding grown-ups of this generational power bloc. They had the brains, the ambition, the range and grasp, and the lengthening track record of a countercultural commissariat set to inherit the big desks in the editorial offices and give culture its marching orders. Yet it didn't happen, they never assumed command; their schemas never got off the drawing board. Ice formed on the ceiling, the elevators got stuck between floors, they were no match for Harvard—choose your own metaphor, but the upward push that seemed inevitable was somehow arrested and the books never completed that might have planted their flags on the surveying heights. That's one of the advantages of sticking around in life long enough: you get to see how other people's stories turn out, though it doesn't do your own story any good, the future having laid its own special snow-covered wolf traps just for you.

Having done just about as much damage as I could do to the circulation department short of embezzlement, I was promoted to a writer-receptionist's job on the fourth floor, a hybrid role almost as lottery-winning as landing a rent-controlled apartment. It provided the ideal setup for a pinball-machine brain embedded in a body content to be indoors, off the streets—wherever the action wasn't. Three days a week I was assigned to man the reception desk for the fourth floor, where staff writers had their offices, some of them outfitted with cots for those all-night word-bashing deadline-looming marathons and, presumably, the occasional tryst or hangover nap. My job entailed sorting mail, answering the phones, clipping articles, doing some light filing, nothing requiring heavy mental lifting or seamless multitasking. The two days I wasn't desk jockeying I could retreat to my own private Yaddo and attend to my own articles. Today writers would *murder* to have their own offices and the opportunity to interrupt one another's work (one reason there will never again be *Here at the "New Yorker"*–like memoirs is that there is no more office lore to mine—writers are now relegated to their own bobbing life rafts, requiring guest IDs to enter the editorial mother ship), and here I was in my early twenties with a sunlit parlor of my own. I didn't have a cot or napping sofa. More than once I stayed up all night to meet a deadline and slept curled up on the floor, stiff as a carp. But there was something romantic and borderline roughing it about staying up all night writing and crashing on the floor—this was one of the reasons one came to New York to become a writer, to impress yourself with your own determination. The writer with whom I shared receptionist duties had an even sweeter deal, or so it seemed to me. He only had to cover the desk the two days a week that I had off. Not being given an office of his own, he wasn't obligated to occupy the premises for the other three days; he had liberty leave to do whatever he wanted—go to the movies, visit museums, do library research, sit on a bench and study humanity, or just stay home and make with the jeweled prose there. But I didn't reckon with the passionate hold of the nesting instinct for those looking to consolidate their position from within, hoping to secure their niche inside the editorial command module. I didn't understand that in New York, real estate trumps everything, that the territorial imperative didn't care how small an amount of square feet was involved.

The co-receptionist's name was David Tipmore. I wonder what

became of him. His was an individual talent, even for a boxing academy like the *Voice,* where the rumble of rough promise kept the thunder going. Tall, blond, thin (after he close-cropped his hair, he was teased for looking like an Oscar statue), T. had a lavish way of expressing himself, especially when ladling out superlatives. "I *love* Blair," he would verbally skywrite about Blair Sabol, the *Village Voice* fashion writer whose father was the head of NFL Films; he would say it in anticipation of her arrival on the fourth floor and repeat it again once the elevator had deposited her back on the ground floor for her reentry into society. I began to look forward to her visits; it was like having Princess Margaret drop by. David could make me laugh by the catholic enthusiasms he displayed and then would laugh at my laughter, as when he exclaimed, after reading one of Al Goldstein's foulmouthed, turd-brained tirades in *Screw* magazine (where all the porn-star fornicators looked like topiaries with their hippie hair), "I *love Screw* magazine!" Sometimes he forgot to fasten the safety lock on his mouth, and his impromptu expressions of delight would go badly astray. Once Christgau punctured our airspace with his presence, looking uncommonly fluffy. "Bob," David exclaimed in congratulatory surprise, "you washed your hair!" It was his transparent lack of malice that made this most backhanded of compliments hard to resent, and Bob accepted the comment with near-gracious chagrin, mentioning something about a new shampoo. The exclamation marks that punctuated Tipmore's talk were astringently absent from his writing, which had some of the tactically efficient lack of affect, eyewitness testimony, and finely manicured irony that George W. S. Trow was making a house specialty at *The New Yorker,* to which Bret Easton Ellis would later add a chic coat of anomie. Tipmore's best sentences had a white birch quality, lean, upright, singular. He did a review of Peggy Lee in performance at the Empire Room of the Waldorf that remains a gleaming artifact of sly dissection: "With a burst of white light Miss Lee appeared stage right in Stavropoulos chiffon, acknowledged the audience reception, and segued directly into 'I Don't Know Why (I

Love You Like I Do).' She was difficult to see because intense lighting gels obscured her face in an opaque sheen. She was difficult to
hear because the orchestra, which Miss Lee conducted periodically
during the show, played with Sousa-march volume. Scanning the
orchestra, I saw three violins, French horn, clarinet, saxophone, syn-
thesizer, electric guitar, an intimidating percussion section, and, in
the far corner, a black back-up trio, whose names Miss Lee did not
seem to remember."

He and I were the supporting players on the floor, the star roster
consisting of staff writers such as Clark Whelton, whose cover story
about staying overnight in Central Park, an assignment that in those
crime-ridden days was worthy of combat pay, was ridiculed by an
up-and-comer named Jamaica Kincaid; Lucian K. Truscott IV, the
combative grandson of a decorated general who had served under
Patton ("Lucian was probably one of the few urban sailors who could
spot a corpse floating in the river . . . and then write about it for the
Village Voice" [McAuliffe]); and Ron Rosenbaum, whose orange-red
beard burned with biblical fervor and Blakean prophecy. "Ron's the
real genius of the *Voice*," a writer named Robin Reisig whispered just
loud enough for posterity to hear. (Reisig was given to gnawing on a
pencil in a state of spellbound distraction, emerging from inner tran-
sit to ask, "Did somebody just say something?") Rosenbaum's genius
aura, unlike Ellen Willis's, did have a dynamic element, a roaming
shadow existence. Investigating far-out terrain and the machinations
of secret societies closed off to all but the chosen, he seemed to haunt
the night like an Edgar Allan Poe story, alternating between his
apartment and his office at the *Voice*, a restless nocturnal commuter.
The columnist Nat Hentoff, whose beard was as wise and Talmudic
as Rosenbaum's was insurrectionist, tore articles out of the *Times*
as he walked the Village and tucked them into his pockets; by the
time he arrived at the office, he had so many columns of newspaper clippings spilling out of his pockets that he seemed to be
going into leaf. His wife, Margot, a contributor to the *New York
Review of Books,* had a sharpshooter mouth that could knock a tin

can off your head from across the room. Other contributors were more raconteurish, their bottoms finding a home on many a bar stool, their sentences leaving footprints across the sawdust floor. As, for instance, Joe Flaherty, who wrote a ruefully funny memoir called *Managing Mailer* about his misadventures as Mailer's campaign manager for his mayoralty run in New York City (Mailer's running mate was Jimmy Breslin); their campaign went afoul when the candidate laced into his loyal supporters at a rally for being "spoiled pigs." And Joel Oppenheimer, who personified the poet as billy goat and whose lowercase columns were devoted to the Mets, losing his teeth, and the valuable protein in semen. But a weekly paper like the *Voice* was more than the clashing palette of its high-profile personalities. It was ribbed with writers who went about their work with self-effacing dedication to their beat, such as the theater reviewers Michael Smith, Julius Novick, and Michael Feingold. The dance critic Deborah Jowitt had the fine-boned fortitude of a frontier settler with eyes forever fixed on future horizons; her merciful consideration of even the most flailing effort and her descriptive set pieces suitable for framing set her apart from the tomahawk throwers. The classical music critic Leighton Kerner, with his stooped posture and ever-present briefcase, resembled a sad pachyderm covering Willy Loman's old rounds. Andrew Sarris, the chief movie critic and godfather of the auteurist school of film criticism, had the dark circles under his eyes of an honorary member of the mole people, the wag of his head and his staccato laughter the marks of a man who was pacing inside his head.

Upstairs, on the fifth floor, there was enough snapping-turtle turmoil to keep *The Caine Mutiny* afloat. Office renovation removed private sanctuaries for a more open cubicle layout that allowed greater visibility for frank exchanges of differing opinions that could be overheard the length of the floor, depending on wind conditions. Monarch of his midtown principality, Felker never conned himself that he would be welcomed and embraced as an emancipator below Fourteenth Street, but he couldn't have anticipated how much resistance he would draw as the *Voice*'s new stepfather. *"Why am I being thwarted?"* he would bellow. Accustomed to barking orders, he didn't expect to hear so much barking back, often from the very editors he had hired to execute his game plan. Sometimes the back talk was accompanied by rude slapstick, as when Richard Goldstein poked Clay in the panda stomach. Felker would also find himself at the receiving end of Ron Rosenbaum's dramatic farewell when Rosenbaum crumpled up his paycheck and flung it with bite-me gusto at Felker, who reportedly asked in bafflement after Rosenbaum steamed off, "Who was that?" Felker ran into headwinds trying to install punctuation, proper capitalization, and paragraph breaks into Jill Johnston's cataract of free association, and his top lieutenant, Judith Daniels, would face the wrath of a writer scorned when Truscott, just back from the Middle East on a reporting mission, gave a command performance of outrage and invective comparable to Jack Nicholson's monologue in *Carnal Knowledge.* Standing over Daniels's desk, Truscott railed, "While I was risking my fucking life over in the Middle East, you had the fucking nerve to not run the fucking pieces that I was fucking over there to do"—or words to that fucking effect. (In McAuliffe's book, he has an exchange where Daniels, over drinks, explained to Lucian that his pieces had just sort of "evaporated," to which Truscott exploded: *"Evaporated? . . .* What do you think my typewriter prints—little teacups full of water?") Unlike for others who left the *Voice* during the transitional trauma, it panned out for Truscott. He went on to write a best-selling novel about West Point called *Dress Gray,* adapted into a made-for-TV miniseries scripted by Gore Vidal. Years later, ringing me up for reasons obscure, Lucian asked me if I knew how long fame lasted for a best-selling author. Unfamiliar with the experience, I said no. Four years, he said. The first year, you're in the exalted thick of it. The second year, you're still bobbing in the success, carried with the current. Third year, the gold plating has chipped away, and people are asking you if you're working on anything new. Fourth year, they're no longer asking, and you might as well drape yourself over a coat hanger in the closet and get accustomed to the dark. Truscott sounded almost resentful, despite having hit the jackpot that so many writers daydreamed about in those days when a fiction best seller didn't require the bestowing tap of Oprah's sparkly wand. A lesson it would take me a while to learn was that *nothing* makes writers happy for very long, there are always ravens pecking on the roof.

The Dan Wolf cone of silence over his run-silent-run-deep decision making gave way to a more democratic airing of what was in the works at the regular editorial meetings on the fifth floor. The more rambunctious ones sometimes yielded the raw disclosures of an encounter session. At one meeting a senior editor casually shared that although his penis might be on the snubby side, what he lacked in size he more than made up for with dedicated effort. ("It takes a liberal to brag about how small his dick is," one of the staffers wisecracked, he being more old-school in such matters.) The point-blank pillow talk of popular feminist fiction in the seventies—best sellers such as Lois Gould's *Such Good Friends,* with its forest of desultory blow jobs, Alix Kates Shulman's *Memoirs of an Ex–Prom Queen,* and, most famously, Erica Jong's *Fear of Flying,* which introduced the "zipless fuck" into the lexicon and established the runway for Carrie Bradshaw to parade her stilettos in *Sex and the City*—empowered frisky mouths. My then editor, my latest piece lying before her ready to undergo the blue pencil marks of what Terry Southern immortally called "tightening and brightening," once apologized for not yet having the opportunity to give my copy a proper going-over. She was just feeling too worn-out that morning, she said. She didn't look worn-out to me; if anything, her Annie Hall cheekbones shone even brighter, a beacon to guide us. Perhaps because she was feeling worn-out in a good way. "I didn't get much rest the last couple days," she explained. "I spent the weekend with—well, let's just say I was in the hands of a master." The picture theater of my imagination immediately opened with multiple screens, all of them showing X-rated material. Whatever insufficient comment I was about to cough up was interrupted by one of the paper's feminists leaning over the cubicle and saying, "So tell me, what happened with the guy you left with?" *"Later,"* my editor promised in a stage whisper of smoky texture while I sat there feeling sexually hangdog from the knowledge that my editor, on whom I had a crush (we all did, those cheekbones being apples of the gods and her hair so glowy), had spent the weekend being royally serviced by some renowned instrumentalist with magic fingers while I was hunched over the stupid typewriter, laboring to get my opening graf to "breathe." It was so unfair, especially since I was being deprived of the choice details that give erotic envy that extra dash of spice.

Wired under the dashboard of the chatty byplay was a serious work ethic, a professional rigor. Writers today are assigned and edited almost exclusively over the phone and computer screen, physically cut off in their own monadic domains. That's why we're all so *lonely.* But at the *Voice,* as at *The New Yorker* and the *Boston Phoenix* and so many other newspapers and magazines then, editing was a face-to-face procedure, a surgical operation where each paragraph was gone over in pencil, each phrase subject to query, word reps circled and remedied, your best passages complimented, your muddier passages met with a concerned moue as the two of you tried to untangle the seaweed, retrieve a sunken thought from the morass. (In those primitive, pre-word-processing times, Richard Goldstein would sometimes take scissors and paste together the paragraphs of a writer's piece, reconfiguring them in a different progression as if cutting a film, only to misplace a graf on his messy desk, necessitating a scavenger hunt.) The weekly sit-downs fostered an apprenticeship attitude that no true writer ever outgrows, if he or she is smart, because there's always more to learn, habits to break, imprecisions to sharpen, excisions that bring out the muscle of a sentence sausaged in flab.

There was another home-brewed brand of criticism practiced at the *Voice*—informal, unsolicited feedback that was delivered like a body check in hockey and intended to put you on notice. It was not uncommon for a fellow writer, in a warrior spirit of collegiality, to let you know that the piece that ran in last week's issue or the new one teed up in galleys carried the risk of making you look like a fool. Not simply mistaken, not merely misguided, but a fool—a dupe who made everybody else look bad. One year at the *Voice* Christmas party, a columnist in ambush mode, having filled his tank to excess capacity with holiday cheer, intercepted me, even though I was standing still, to put me wise that a campaign piece I had done about a presidential candidate that was set to run proved that I didn't know a thing about politics and if it were published I would look like a *fool* and the editors would look like *fools,* a diatribe/dire prediction he delivered so close up his face nearly went out of focus. He was telling me this for my own good, he said, but nobody at the *Voice* ever told you anything for your own good unless they were up to no good. Another *Voice* staffer, whom nobody dared call a fool for fear he'd do a calypso number on their heads with his fists, speculated that the weaponized use of the word was rooted in Old Left discourse, evidenced by how often *Voice* writers would quote August Bebel's pronouncement "Anti-Semitism is the socialism of fools," one of those thundering dicta certainly intended to stop an adversary dead in his rhino tracks. (As Diana Trilling would write of thirties radicalism, "Everyone judged everyone else . . . today's friend was tomorrow's enemy; whoever disagreed with oneself had sold out.") Or perhaps "fool" simply caught on in the office because some alpha force began using it and everyone else added it to their repertoire, just as so many writers picked up on Ellen Willis's use of "cranky" as a positive descriptive, indicating someone out of sorts with the prevailing political norms. Whatever its origin in the lingua franca, "fool" was a strangely shame-laced word, intended to make you feel like an object of ridicule based on the snickers and scowls of some invisible jury. It would later chime in my head with Piper Laurie's crackpot mother taunting Sissy Spacek in *Carrie* before the senior prom: "They're all gonna laugh at you! They're all gonna laugh at you!" I resented being bullyragged for making a fool of myself because making a fool of yourself was one of the hard-earned liberties Norman Mailer had fought for in his boxing trunks. But I have to say, I don't regret my days in gladiator school. Having your ego slapped around a bit helped the blood circulate and would prove a superb conditioning program for a future sub-career in blogging, where a tough hide would come in handy every time the Hellmouth opened. Every time I'm abused online with a battery of scurrilous remarks of a personal nature, I'm able to let them bounce off like rubber erasers, having been called an asshole by *professionals,* experts in the field.

My stay on the fourth floor was an idyll destined to die early. My installation as a regular fixture was resisted by the person whose opinion mattered most—my boss, Mary Perot Nichols. I had been hired against her wishes, as I soon came to understand from her verbal inflections and facial expressions, which were generally lemon flavored. Nichols, for whom I did guard-dog duty at the desk, was the paper's city editor, a veteran of Village activism who had led the fight opposing Robert Moses's plan to drive a road through Washington Square Park and whose fearsome inside-dope column, Runnin' Scared, was to local politics what *I. F. Stone's Weekly* was to the Washington lie machine—a caustic disinfectant. She thrived on feuds and court intrigue, her turf war with the political muckraker Jack Newfield resulting in huge shifts in barometric pressure inside the building when some vital piece of information was up for contention. It wasn't her idea to hire me, and had I been a better butterer-upper, I might have schmoozed things over to the point where I wasn't looked upon as an intrusive specimen, a bug found in an ear of corn. But I was too untutored in the art of deference, oblivious to the danger signs, and lackadaisical in the time-honored mime of looking busy when there was a significant lull in the action. It was about fifteen or twenty minutes before end of regular hours, and returning to the office when she would normally have been leaving, Nichols crossed in front of my desk, which had been cleared so that I could begin the next day with a clean slate (having stuffed everything I needed to do in the drawers), paused, surveyed my near-empty desktop, factored in my bland demeanor, which apparently contained a subcutaneous layer of insubordination, and asked: "Don't you get bored sitting there all day doing nothing?"

A question whose tone and implication I considered a trifle inconsiderate, since I hadn't spent "all day" doing nothing, reserving relative inactivity for that brief interval before it was time to head out. Rather than defend or explain my idle appearance, I replied amiably enough: "I meditate."

Nichols blinked without actually blinking, looking stunned, and not in a delighted way. I'm not sure why I had replied as I had, since it would be another twenty years before I even took up meditation, enrolling in the Transcendental Meditation course in a class that included a Frenchman who later complained to the instructor that he wanted a different mantra from the one he had been assigned ("My mantra is working *against* me"), but whichever imp of the perverse activated my tongue didn't matter: my blithe attempt at airy deflection proved to be more infuriating than any edgy comeback I might have made. I acted as if I were out of her jurisdiction, which no boss can countenance. It may have also confirmed Nichols's (correct) suspicion that the world of hard-boiled politics was no place for a potted fern like myself. It was recorded in McAuliffe's excellent history that upon hearing my insolence, Nichols snapped, "Then go meditate at the unemployment line." Dramatically neat as that plays, the truth was klutzier, as it usually is. She got back into the elevator, hit the button for the fifth floor, and—so I was later informed—told the editor in chief: "I can't do anything with Wolcott. I tell him to do something and he tells me he's meditating." Instead of firing me on the spot, she waited until I returned after a holiday weekend to send me on my merry way. I don't recall the dialogue on that occasion being particularly snappy, only how compressed the air felt as I left her office, packed quiet with the knowledge shared by everyone on the floor that I had been axed. As soon as I walked in that morning I knew that they knew that I was a goner from the funny little fidgets their mouths made as they forked over the usual Monday-morning hellos. I was standing in front of my former desk with the hollow, bomb-struck feeling of the just fired when Tipmore, trying and failing to sound offhand now that the news was official, asked: "So, Jim, given any thought as to what you're going to do with your office?"

"Well," I said, "seeing that I'll no longer be working here, I don't imagine I'll get to *keep* it."

Which he knew full well, just as he knew that the logical next occupant of the office would be himself. With a cool twist of the swizzle stick he was letting me know that he had felt the office was rightfully his all along and now he was going to inherit it and too bad for me, buddy boy. Good-bye, good luck, and get lost. We never spoke again, one of the many noncommunication pacts formed at the *Voice* that furnished the elevator with awkward silences and straight-ahead stares. Though if anything I owed Tipmore and Mary Perot Nichols (who would go on to become the president of WNYC Communications and leave a priceless legacy to public broadcasting and the arts as the founder of the WNYC Foundation) a gift basket of gratitude. Released from duty, I drew unemployment and used my ejection time to write full out, placing pieces not only at the *Voice* but at rock magazines such as *Circus,* where I interviewed Todd Rundgren, then at the height of his musical wizardhood with attitude to match. From that point onward I never worked a regular office job again, solely writing for a living, something that would have been impossible if New York hadn't been a city of low rents and crappy expectations that didn't require a trust fund or a six-figure income for the privilege of watching everything fall apart before your eyes. The availability of affordable, problem-plagued, loosely enforced sublets made zigzag lateral movement throughout the city relatively easy, not like it would become a decade later, when each real-estate decision would pyramid under the worry load of upward mobility. In the early seventies, New York landlords were less choosy about whom they rented to, more laissez-faire as long as you didn't give off a whiff of arson. When one of the *Voice* receptionists decided to get married and vacate the city, she offered me her apartment to sublet on West Ninety-second, between Amsterdam and Columbus. Though I had never been that far north before, above Forty-second Street being total terra incognita, I accepted her offer without a glimmer of thought because one of the advantages of being young in the city is that you can say yes to things without feeling it's an irrevocable decision that scripts your fate. At that age apartments were just places to stay, temporary launchpads or secluded cubbyholes, not outward constructs of your identity that required Hamlet-style agonizing for fear that at the root of your being, you might not be an "uptown person."

My new apartment and I were relatively well suited. An acceptable holding cell for the unchoosy bachelor/bachelorette, it was a studio shoe box slightly below street level, affording a window view of feet going by. Because the former tenant was an attractive young woman living solo, she occasionally drew peepers on balmy days when she raised the blinds and cracked open the window in futile hope of a breeze. (No air-conditioning.) Neighborhood men of varying ages and maturity levels who had watched her lug in groceries would sometimes pretend they were picking up a stray dime or quarter, craning their necks forty-five degrees in hopes of a floor show. Sometimes they wouldn't even bother with the loose-change pantomime, simply bent over double and gawked. So for the first few weeks I had my share of prospective admirers who either hadn't gotten the news that she had vacated the address or were hoping I was just a temporary sitter and were checking to see if she had returned. On the sunniest of days, the studio admitted barely enough light to imply the slim hope of redemption in a prison movie, and no bulbs seemed bright enough to keep the kitchen from looking depressed. The studio was also right next to the stairs, which reverberated like a bowling alley with each arrival and departure of lead boots and echoing laughter.

When the weather was warm enough for raised windows, I could sometimes hear the couple upstairs making love like a train chugging into the station, picking up speed as they reached the final whistle and ground to a halt. The male partner of this duo was the burly playwright John Ford Noonan, who would often be confused with the playwright and director Tom Noonan (whose eggplant head would loom so spookily in Michael Mann's *Manhunter* and *Heat*). The Noonan upstairs had a knack for catchy titles— *Heterosexual Temperature in West Hollywood, Raunchy Dame in the*

Chinese Raincoat—but the play that made his name was the widely produced *A Coupla White Chicks Sitting Around Talking.* Years later it was on one of our first dates that I took my future wife, Laura, to a play written by Noonan and performed with his daughter called *Talking Things Over with Chekhov.* (Before the play we had dinner at the Lion's Head, whose glory years as a writer's bar were now as faded as the book jackets on the walls, a too-neat analogy, but there it is, go bother somebody else.) And years after that I was crossing West Twenty-third Street when I spotted Noonan buffaloing toward me with undiminished life force. Though we hadn't seen or spoken to each other in decades, I recognized him, he recognized me, and without breaking stride, he spread his arms and shouted what we were both thinking, "Hey, we got older!" and kept on barreling.

The IRT stop closest to my Ninety-second Street apartment was a convenient four blocks north, but those four blocks often required nimble footwork and ninja awareness of impending action. So much of New York did. Most of the parks were safer walking around than through. (I was warned about venturing into Riverside Park, where, I got the impression, dead bodies were always being discovered after having rolled downhill the night before.) Entire neighborhoods were considered no-go areas where you never knew what the hell might fall from the fire escapes, and even sections of town that didn't resemble standing rubble had stretches that you avoided, had you been properly briefed. Otherwise, you'd be walking down some leafy block, moderately carefree, turn the wrong corner, and find yourself staring down the barrel of a hostile street, forced to either retrace your steps or run for your freaky life like Cornel Wilde in *The Naked Prey.* It wasn't just the criminality that kept you radar-alert, the muggings and subway-car shakedowns, it was the crazy paroxysms that punctuated the city, the sense that much of the social contract had suffered a psychotic break. That strip of upper Broadway was the open-air stage for acting-out episodes from unstable patients dumped from mental health facilities, as I discovered when I had to dodge a fully loaded garbage can flung in my direction by a middle-aged man who still had a hospital bracelet on one of his throwing arms. Then, as now, the Ninety-sixth Street crosstown nexus was an irredeemable eyesore that served as a magnet for unmanned shopping carts abandoned on their sides or commandeered as a homeless moving van. It was at the newsstand at the southwest corner of Ninety-sixth that I picked up the copy of the *Daily News* with the arresting headline FORD TO CITY: DROP DEAD, and it was the perfect spot to receive notice of impending collapse.

My uptown address had the down-market advantage of being within walking distance of two of the major revival houses in the city, the New Yorker and the Thalia. Shopping-mall multiplexes were unknown when I was growing up in Maryland, the only two theaters being on the Edgewood Arsenal military base and in the nearby town of Bel Air. The programming at the army theater never erred on the side of daunting pretension. Each weekend offered a carousel of the latest Elvis Presley musical, Jerry Lewis comedy, or garish war epic (such as *Merrill's Marauders* or any other World War II film set in the Pacific with malaria and leeches), and to this day I can dazzle myself with piquant, mindless details from *It Happened at the World's Fair* or *Follow That Dream* or *The Delicate Delinquent* that are stuck like gum to the roof of my mind. I knew nothing about directors but was aware when I saw *Ride the High Country* (Peckinpah) and *Hell Is for Heroes* (Don Siegel) that the guys behind the camera were a different breed of cat from the ones who gave us Elvis making with the hips at a back-lot luau. Though I had taken an introductory film course at Frostburg, where screenings of the classics of German Expressionism (*The Last Laugh, The Street*) failed to fire my classmates' synapses, judging by their simulated snores, it was at the New Yorker and the Thalia, especially the former, that I was inducted into the Eleusinian mysteries of art cinema. Nesting in the balcony of the New Yorker, I wondered why strangers sat so close to each other, given the availability of vacant seats, and then, as if answering a cue, migrated to the men's room together, missing much of the movie. I soon divined that these weren't instances of bladders in harmonic sync. The other patrons seemed to be solitaries, like me, perhaps because I tended to avoid the theaters on week-end date nights, my dating life still in the starting blocks. Many a time I sensed that the men in the audience weren't going to the movies as much as getting *away* from something, stealing a few hours in the hideaway cove as a temporary reprieve. The prints of classic foreign and Hollywood films in those pre-DVD days were legendarily scuffed like locker room floors, with washed-out colors, bleached black and white, frames missing, vertical lines slicing the frames, strange blotches appearing like fungus, fuzzy sound, the screen going blank as a reel came unsnapped and the audience groaned, what little audience there was in the dead of afternoon. But the imperfections in the prints made the experience more dreamlike, closer to an unfinished rough draft from the unconscious, the subtitles a ghostly reduction of dialogue that sounded so much more expressive and layered than the plain words at the bottom of the screen. Needing no translation, the serious Hollywood heavyweights—*On the Waterfront, High Noon*—carried their own echo of the hereafter, a sense that you were watching glorious figments reenacting a heroic rite that now belonged to immortality, where self-importance savors its just reward.

And so the uptown revival houses combined art and elegy in a delinquent atmosphere that made Susan Sontag's vaunted cinephilia seem like basic training for cultural sainthood, membership in a monastic order of paleface prunes. It was different downtown at Theatre 80 St. Marks, which specialized in Hollywood musicals and screwball comedies, its seats a chiropractor's delight; after a double feature you might hobble out like Walter Matthau with back trouble, but that was the price of admission to movie-queen heaven, where the name Norma Shearer could prompt militant debate and Ruby Keeler's tap-dancing glee was categorized as a genial species of dementia. At the time the double bills at Theatre 80 St. Marks seemed lighter, fluffier, less canonical than the Euro classics at other houses, but those crackling relics of the Hollywood studio system have retained a vigor, rigor, elegance, ivory spine, and starglow that (for me) have proven to be hardier, more sustaining than the signature originalities of Godard, Truffaut, and Bresson or the surly realism of *Room at the Top, Saturday Night and Sunday Morning, Look Back in Anger,* and similar English indictments of the class system's rotting carcass and the ghastly fucking wallpaper put up to seal in the gloom. Each year the mystery appeal of Eleanor Powell's horsy clumping deepens, the piquancy of Myrna Loy's uptipped nose romantically beguiles, while Godard's *La Chinoise* seems like a set of fancy card tricks and the lyricism of Truffaut's films looks ever more wispy and attenuated. I went to old movies alone, my occasional dates preferring to see something new in venues that didn't seem haunted. Apart from Peckinpah films and the occasional high mass such as Jean Eustache's black-and-white three-and-a-half-hour *The Mother and the Whore* (the first masterpiece of miserabilism whose spellbinding power owes nothing to anything except its own bleak recalcitrance), I was reading reviews of new movies more than I was actually attending them, keeping just pseudo-informed enough to hold up my weak end in any conversation. That was about to change. I was about to receive my draft notice.

One day I was puttering around the apartment, trying to unstick one of the drawers in my captain's bed, washing a fork, who knows, when the phone rang. I picked it up and heard a voice that carried a ripple of laughter even as it said hello.

"Hi, you're a hard person to get ahold of. It's Pauline Kael."

PART II:

Like Civilized People . . .

We hadn't met, though there had been a near encounter.

In 1974, the *Voice* winched me into a coveted screening of *Lenny*, the director Bob Fosse's fancy switchblade farrago on the life, career, and fury of the comedian Lenny Bruce—an existential X-ray shot in high-contrast black and white where the nightclub spotlight blasted Dustin Hoffman like a prison searchlight as he did his sardonic thing. I had arrived at the screening room early, knowing it would be a packed house, and, having snagged an aisle seat, swung my legs to the side as a couple slid into my row. "Excuse me," a young woman apologized in a cool-mint voice, her elbow apparently having grazed my arm as she settled, and I nodded no problem before glancing sideways and recognizing her as the actress Cornelia Sharpe, whose piquant nose, high-end-model cheekbones, and creamy surface rendered questions of acting ability incidental, irrelevant, almost rude. No problem indeed. Sharpe had appeared in *Serpico*, riding on the back of Al Pacino's motorcycle and wrapping her adorning arms around him as his reward for rejecting police graft and embracing a free-spirited lifestyle that won him entrée into the grooviest loft parties. But since the most recent film I had seen her in was a loutish buddy-cop number called *Busting*, where she splayed her legs wide in a dentist's chair as a call girl who made office calls, I decided not to risk saying anything gauche and so said nothing at all, hoping that my courteous follow-up nod conveyed the mark of a young gentleman, despite my cruddy sneakers.

A few minutes before the lights were due to darken, I heard a minor bustle behind me. The last row, which appeared to have been kept unofficially empty, filled. This arrival seemed to slide a tray of quiet import under the ongoing chatter, and the chatter became self-conscious, inorganic, as if everyone's awareness had split and doubled and effort was being made not to crane one's head in reverse. Whoever was in the last row was chatting away merrily, and there was the paper rustle of notebooks being opened. The man escorting Cornelia Sharpe tipped his head her way and whispered, "Pauline," and it was as if the mention of Pauline's name were the cue for the lights to dim, the movie to begin.

It was a loud movie, *Lenny* was, a real yeller, understandable given its sainted antihero's propensity to propound harsh truths like a renegade prophet laying down some heavy jazz on the varsity sweaters and nine-to-five squares and all those queasy liberals hung up on newspaper editorials. But between the rants and the verbal shivs could be heard the unmistakable scratch of a pencil scribbling notes, invading our collective head space like graphite graffiti. It wasn't that the note-taking called attention to itself, it wasn't loud or continuous; it was the collective awareness that of those of all the movie critics, her notes mattered most, and whatever she was scribbling might be added to the bill of indictment or provide the embroidery of a fantastic rave. Each note could be a nail in Fosse's gaudy coffin or a diamond stud for his vest. She had loved *Cabaret,* after all, helped it smash a wall of resistance. But it was coffin nails being driven that night. Melodramatic as that might sound, Kael's review of *Lenny* proved to be such a devastator that Fosse, carrying a grudge until he stooped, immortalized its aftershocks in *All That Jazz,* where his pill-popping stud-choreographer alter ego—Roy Scheider in a Vandyke beard in a portrait of the artist as prodigious genius-phallus, the self-professed bastard that everybody can't help but love—has a heart attack after *his* Lenny Bruce opus is coolly panned by a local-news critic. That part was played by Chris Chase, a former actress and then-current *New York Times* Arts and Leisure contributor who, not incidentally, was a friend of Pauline's. Casting Chase instead of Pia Lindström or Leonard Harris or some other local New York television reviewer was intended to flip the bird at Pauline, blaming her for blowing a hole in his chest with her blast at *Lenny*. Little did I sense as I sat there next to Cornelia Sharpe's shadowed profile the line that was being cast into the future, the ripple effect.

When the lights came up again, I didn't have the assurance to intrude upon the loose scrum of people around Pauline to introduce myself, unable to think of anything to venture that wouldn't sound inane. It wasn't just who she was that was intimidating. Saying anything at all seemed poor form, a violation of church doctrine. It was somehow communicated to me without being articulated that the shuffle from screening room to elevator or stairwell was an interval that called for politesse and murmur, like the orderly procession to sign the guest book in a funeral service, comments being kept to the neutral minimum since it was rude and imprudent to broadcast your opinions, not knowing who might be within earshot. Save the evil cackle of delight for when there's no danger of the director's mother overhearing or the film's editor, who's been in a bat cave for the last three months trying to string this spaghetti together. No such strictures applied to a movie that had "hit" stickered all over it. Nobody cared if you uncorked your carbonation then, I would learn. It wasn't happiness that needed to be reined in, but disdain and disapproval, at least until you got outside. From the almost cowed way the elevator passengers kept their eyes lifted and fixed on the floor numbers as they ticked down to the lobby, it was evident that everyone had formed a temporary collective of silent collusion. My reading was: everyone respected the effort Fosse had put into *Lenny,* but respecting effort is what you do when something hasn't succeeded. So into the night the audience dispersed, as if jury duty had been adjourned. Pauline's group must have taken a later elevator, because when I reached the sidewalk they were nowhere to be seen, and they didn't strike me as a fast-moving amoeba. I didn't hang around to wait for them to show, not wanting to seem like a stage-door Johnny. I didn't want to be a nuisance until absolutely necessary, but now, to bring us back into my apartment, where I'm holding a phone to my ear, I didn't need to contrive a proper moment to introduce myself— she was the one who threw out the first ball.

What had prompted Pauline's call? She had read and enjoyed a piece I had published in the *Voice* about stand-up comics, a reported essay that had me posting myself night after night to the Improv, a comedy showcase located on a stretch of Forty-fourth Street in Times Square where one tended to pick up the pace just in case it became necessary to race for survival. The hostess at the Improv was Elayne Boosler, who also performed and would make a high mid-level name for herself later, a bright presence with a non-demeaning approach to self-deprecation (as opposed to Joan Rivers's militant ugly-duckling persona that converts Jewish masochism into an assault weapon). If anything, she tended to err on the side of "viva-cious," more *Cosmo* Girl than cutting edge. The regular comics— nearly all of them men—were a mixed bag of promising minor leaguers trying to nail together a tight set that might win them a spot on *Dick Cavett, Merv Griffin,* or (the heavenly blue light at the top of the ladder) *Johnny Carson,* along with more experienced pros who had been around long enough to pick up a fine bouquet of ran-cor. It was the lull before the waterfall roar of *Saturday Night Live*'s arrival on NBC, a paradigm shifter that would upend the dues-paying pecking order of stand-up comedy, launching a new battery of clowns—Chevy Chase, John Belushi, Dan Aykroyd, Gilda Rad-ner, later Eddie Murphy and Bill Murray—whose success bypassed the club circuit and the Vegas strip and didn't require even the cool nod of Carson's papal blessing for induction into the golden ring.

(Not long after *SNL* had altered the gravitational field, I inter-viewed a veteran comic named Milt Kamen, well-known at the time for doing absurdly detailed plot summaries of the latest movies on *Merv* and *The Mike Douglas Show.* After a few cordialities, he spat fire through the phone at how fucking unfair it was that these fucking sketch artists who simply read off of fucking cue cards and never knew what it was to play shitholes and learn their fucking *craft* got treated like rock stars while older comics got the bum's rush, a rant that went on so long that he seemed to forget there was somebody listening on the other end of the line, finally braking to say, "But what the hell, to each his own," which made us both laugh. A few weeks later, Kamen died of a heart attack in Beverly Hills.)

For this same *Voice* piece I also interviewed Peter Cook and Dudley Moore, then co-starring on Broadway in *Good Evening* (the show where Moore hopped out as a one-legged actor auditioning for the role of Tarzan). We met in Tuesday Weld's apartment in the Astoria, an interview that I dragged out so long through nerves and inexperience that when I said, "Well, that's all I got," Cook snorted, "That's all *you've* got?" indicating how tapped dry they were after having so much of their time taken hostage. I left the Astoria mortified, vowing to be less of a yammerer in the future, one of those quick-dissolving vows forgotten as soon as the next round of journalistic stage fright hit.

"And I see that you're also not a big fan of Marcel Marceau," Pauline said, his Everyman school of mime being something I had made fun of, like watching Mickey Mouse put on an existential show. She invited me to a screening of a movie whose name has been erased from memory, but I wasn't invited afterward to join her and the others for whatever they were doing, and I returned to the apartment feeling that we hadn't quite clicked and it was my unspecified fault. Perhaps I was dressed poorly, a potato to be thrown back into the pile. (Though Pauline was no snob about clothes or social class—one profile of her from the seventies quoted an unnamed publicist who said that Pauline had once shown up at a New York event wearing a dress with a hole under the arm, "and it was really The Scandal.") But I was invited to another screening and another. I made an unnamed appearance in Pauline's review of *The Goodbye Girl,* as the friend who shared her "stony silence"—yes, that was me, I told people, Mr. Stony—as the paying audience roared at Neil Simon's mixture of gum-snapping dialogue and therapeutic hugging that would come to be known, horribly, as "dramedy."

We continued to talk on the phone at an increasing tempo until I began to know it was her when the phone rang, even amid a volley

of other calls, to the point where even close bystanders could identify the party at the other end before I picked up. Once I got into
trouble with my then girlfriend when she spotted another young
woman, a friend of hers, leaving my apartment as she arrived for our
date. It was an innocent crossing of paths—it was Halloween and T.
had dropped over on her way to a party to show off her costume, a
skintight Peter Pan number complete with feathered cap and plastic
dagger—but my girlfriend was in none too trick or treat a mood,
and no sooner had she taken off her coat than the phone rang. As my
hand reached the receiver, she said, "That better be Pauline."

It was.

"Hi, have I gotten you at a bad time?" Pauline asked.

"Oh, no, not at all," I said with an extra dash of debonair.

My girlfriend lowered herself into the one comfortable chair in
my apartment and picked up a magazine to browse, as if she were in
a waiting room. She knew the next fifteen or twenty minutes were
Pauline time.

It wasn't only movies we went to. One thing that distinguished
Pauline from the critics who have come after, even those she had
encouraged and promoted, was that she had an interest in the arts
that didn't begin and end at the popcorn stand. (Most of the post-
Pauline reviewers, by comparison, were so enthralled by the burning
roads that she and Sarris and others cut that they couldn't imagine being anything *other* than movie magistrates. One of Pauline's
most doted-upon protégés turned down a book-review request by
sputtering, "But, but—that would be writing about writing!" Yes,
the editor explained over the phone, that's what book reviewing
is, writing about writing, been going on for centuries.) The liberal
arts were what she liberally pursued. She was an opera fan, a jazz
enthusiast, and a pop music appreciator (she grasped immediately
what made the Talking Heads compelling, whereas John Simon
walked out fifteen minutes into the screening of *Stop Making Sense,*
Jonathan Demme's concert film of the Heads). And although she
didn't attend dance performances when I knew her, she was up on
everything going on and thought it was a howling oversight for *The*

New Yorker to be ignoring dance in the seventies while devoting so much acreage to classical music concerts. It was her lobbying for dance coverage that paved the archangel arrival of Arlene Croce—she pressed clips of Croce's essays from *Ballet Review* (of which Croce was the founding editor) on William Shawn until the brilliance and necessity of Croce's critical voice became crowningly self-evident and she was hired. Her arrival gave the magazine the strongest and widest contingent of women contributors ever, not only Kael and Croce but Penelope Gilliatt, the theater critic Edith Oliver, the book critic Naomi Bliven, the city hall correspondent Andy Logan, and the Washington political reporter Elizabeth Drew. On any roster of male feminist heroes, William Shawn earns high salutation, even if Drew's longueurs drove many readers, including Pauline, mad.

Pauline, unlike movie critics today, was a theater lover. "I loved Charles Ludlam," she told the interviewer Ray Sawhill, a fellow member of Pauline's fraternity, who worked at *Newsweek* magazine. "I once took Claude Jutra, the French Canadian director, down to the Ridiculous Theatrical Company. And Claude said, 'This is theater.' And he had tears streaming out of his eyes, he laughed so hard. I loved Charles Ludlam's shows, and I thought there was a real craft and polish and crazy elegance in what he was doing." She was also an early flag-waver for the playwright John Guare, whose lyrically bent *Lydie Breeze* and *House of Blue Leaves* she urged on listeners (his big breakthrough was *Six Degrees of Separation,* which also appears to have been his cresting peak), and she was a regular patron of the Williamstown Theatre Festival, where we saw Christopher Reeve in *The Cherry Orchard* together. Pauline didn't posit the theater and movies as irreconcilable, evolutionary rivals, rejecting the notion that movies were the supersonic present and future, theater the dowdy, upholstered past. She thought her former disciple David Denby had loaded the dice when he did a theater dispatch for the *Atlantic* that disposed of Broadway as slow, stodgy, dust-bunnied, and mausoleum-ish compared with the sexy, magnified immediacy of movies; she found Denby's piece a fact-finding mission by a mind already made up. (In the fullness of time, Pauline would decide that music criticism would be Denby's proper sphere, if only he would awaken to the idea and embrace his true calling and stop mucking about. "All that *boring* intelligence," she would say of his movie reviews, as if they were overdone meat loaf.)

Pauline thought the theater invaluable and exciting because it was where you saw actors at their most uninhibited and unhindered, unchopped into edited bits. I once went with her to see Blythe Danner in *The New York Idea,* Danner being one of those actresses Pauline adored. (Especially her husky, inimitable voice—"That voice has levels in it; it's a French 75—you get the champagne through the chipped ice and cognac," she wrote of her plucky performance in *Hearts of the West.*) She never quite got the breaks and vehicles that vaulted her into major stardom, unlike her daughter, Gwyneth Paltrow, who enjoyed the sunburst of *Shakespeare in Love.* Meryl Streep was a proficient technician, but Danner had the lyrical splendor of a Margaret Sullavan, a delicacy of touch and inflection that didn't seem mentally penciled in beforehand. She was radiant in the uneven *Lovin' Molly,* an adaptation of a Larry McMurtry novel that took a poison dart to the neck when McMurtry published an article in *New York* magazine just before the opening railing against the film for coarsening and low-browing his original work. Pauline resented how all the effort by the cast and crew got mud-spattered by a disgruntled author, giving audiences an excuse to stay away. Onstage, Danner had poise and projection, unlike a Madonna (in David Mamet's *Speed-the-Plow*) or even a Julianne Moore (in David Hare's *Vertical Hour*), both of whom stood glued as if they had lost the use of their arms, which hung dead. After the play we ran into a top editor at *Newsweek* and his wife, who invited us back to their Manhattan town house for drinks. Dominating the living room was a huge rectangular glass coffee table with sharp edges, ideal for splitting your head open to bleed to death after a fall. The long couches on which we reclined had such a steep slant that Pauline and I had to dig in our heels so as not to slide under the glass table and become specimens, like characters in *The Glass Bottom Boat.* The only item, or rather the only prominent item, placed on the glass plate was a copy of Joan Didion's then-latest novel, *A Book of Common Prayer.*

"So what do you think of it?" asked Pauline during a conversational lull, conversational lulls being rare when Pauline was around. The editor reached for the novel, held it up as if it had healing properties, and pronounced: "It's full of resonance." Thinking he was kidding, I almost snickered, having been an expert snickerer since high school, biting the inside of my mouth when I realized he was in earnest. I didn't dare exchange glances with Pauline, for whom Didion was full of something, but it sure wasn't resonance.

"I didn't realize editors actually talked that way," I said once we were outside.

"The ones in nice offices do," Pauline said.

"Maybe he was trying to provoke you, given what you think of Didion."

Reviewing Frank Perry's screen adaptation of *Play It as It Lays,* Didion's austere autopsy of sun-whitened anomie and depraved indifference along the intestinal freeways of Los Angeles, Pauline had not only panned the movie but had the audacity to make fun of Didion's epigrammatic, ivory-mask prose, which she called "ridiculously swank," the writerly equivalent to designer chic, "the sparse words placed in the spiritual emptiness of the white pages." Lines so many book reviewers had caressed as talismanic for our times— such as the opening chord, "What makes Iago evil? some people ask. I never ask"—gave Pauline a hoot, and she got a bigger hoot out of a pull quote from an interview with Didion where she laid bare, "I am haunted by the cannibalism of the Donner Party." Every day for Didion was the dawn of the dead. By pinning the bony tail of Didion's pretensions, Pauline's mockery shook the foundations of Didion's literary pedestal—like those of Sontag and Joyce Carol Oates, Didion's mystery cult was so without humor that it didn't know what to do when humor came knocking. A lifelong antipathy was the product of that review, with Pauline deprecated by

Didion and her husband, the novelist, screenwriter, and journalist John Gregory Dunne, as a hopeless outsider peddling inside dope. Dunne, who did the dirty work in the marriage in the scores-settling department, launched a counteroffensive against Pauline with a piece in the *Los Angeles Times Book Review* ("That may have been the review," Pauline told me, "where they used a drawing of me that looked like something out of *Der Stürmer*") that opened with her holding court in front of the TV at an Oscar night party, "in a Pucci knockdown and orthopedic shoes," bad-mouthing winners and losers alike. Dunne also disclosed that he had it on good authority that Pauline didn't content herself with heckling *Play It as It Lays* in private, she also gave free concerts for the public: "Wilfrid Sheed had reported her reading it aloud derisively on the beaches of Long Island." Despite that, Dunne professed personal fondness for Pauline in the untidy flesh, to borrow a phrase of Gore Vidal's, but lamented that she embarrassed herself sexually by rhapsodizing over "entertaining rubbish" such as *The Godfather*. Oh, *that* entertaining rubbish.

So, I hypothesized, by holding up *A Book of Common Prayer* as if it could ward off evil, the editor with the glass table was razzing Pauline—giving her the business, as they used to say on *Leave It to Beaver*.

"No, he's not that Machiavellian," Pauline said, "Machiavellian" being a dirty word in her vocabulary, the paw mark of mendacity. "There was nothing ulterior going on. He was quite sincere."

(An episode that reminded me of something Pauline later said about the revelation she had after moving to New York from San Francisco:

Before I came here, when I used to read the papers and magazines and *Partisan Review* and the film journals, I used to think that there was all this intellectual corruption in publishing that explained why so many mediocrities were given the big push and so many gifted, trickier talents treated like bums. I thought people in publishing and so on were smarter than what they were praising and promoting, that there was a hidden adoption scheme that explained how we got custody of Arthur Miller. But once I started talking to writers and editors and publishers, I realized there was no cultural conspiracy at work, apart from conformity. They weren't Machiavellian or evil, they were just so cut off from their responses that their brains rolled downhill. And they were more provincial than you thought possible from how they pretended to such sophistication in print. I'd mention Satyajit Ray and you would have thought a flying saucer had landed on the roof. Intellectuals were the worst, some of them stupider than you thought possible.)

On another occasion Pauline invited me to an evening of one-acts written by Wallace Shawn, one of William Shawn's sons, whom I imagined having grown up inside a grandfather clock, thick carpets muffling every other sound. (The other son, Allen, is a composer and the author of a study of Arnold Schoenberg and memoirs about his agoraphobia and his twin sister.) This was early in Shawn's career, so early that he didn't as yet truly have a career; his rebellious incursions against his father's cloak of reticence and soft persuasion in *Aunt Dan and Lemon*, *My Dinner with André* (his conversational duet with André Gregory), and *The Designated Mourner* (the film version of which Pauline thought was a supreme feat of self-portraiture on Mike Nichols's part, revealing his calculating worminess) lay ahead, along with those gnomic appearances in everything from *The Princess Bride* to *Clueless* to *Gossip Girl*. The playlets were not well received. The audience was seated on long wooden benches, designed for maximum puritan discomfort, and the monologues were so vacuum-sealed and off-putting—a fireman baroquely boasting about items he had stolen from arson sites ("That's a terrible way to libel firemen, as a bunch of scavengers, the volunteer department here are total sweeties," Pauline said), and, in another, a hospital patient ruminating aloud as if already dead while a mute nurse attends to duties—that one by one, then in accelerating numbers, audience members began bailing, too impatient to wait for intermission, the benches scraping loudly as we maneuvered our legs and buttocks to let the defectors pass. What kept us in our seats was the knowledge that, unbeknownst to the audience, Wally himself was seated several rows back, witnessing the exodus. Pauline felt bad for him, even though the one-acts weren't to her liking either. "He does have talent," she said afterward, "that's the damned thing." Talent wasn't the great exonerator, but it needed to be defended, in Pauline's view, because everything was arrayed against it. Regarding Hollywood, she would say, "Never underestimate how much those in power resent those with talent—talent being the one thing they can't buy for them*selves*. But they never tire of fucking with it, that's *their* talent."

"Is she expecting you?" asked the editorial receptionist at *The New Yorker* when I visited Pauline at her office in the afternoon.

This may have been the receptionist whom Pauline referred to as Morticia, a chalky apparition with a remarkable ability to misplace phone messages or relay them after they were useless, to whose desk older male writers and editors were drawn, attracted to this inviting mixture of Pre-Raphaelite muse and sitting duck. In time, Morticia would write an erotic memoir of the married and single men she bedded with at *The New Yorker* ("bedded" being an inclusive verb, since some of the erotic action had taken place on the carpet), racking up an impressive scorecard for someone so inanimated. After enough visits qualified me as a semi-regular, she stopped asking if I was expected, simply buzzed me through. Whatever male writer or editor she was talking to would pause until I was safely out of range and then resume his erudite sales pitch.

"Hi, c'mon in," Pauline would say, standing half-in, half-out of her office door. These were the days when *The New Yorker*'s offices were on West Forty-third Street and, in their beige palette, faint melancholic air of apathy, and stoic indifference to having the uphol- stery repaired, were usually compared to the faculty department of a small agricultural college or an insurance firm down on its luck. History may have haunted the halls, but it didn't haunt the walls, which were bare of framed magazine covers or awards plaques that might be interpreted as showing off for visitors, institutional boast- ing. Ostentation was considered poor form and vulgar taste, with noise the rudest intruder of all, the sound of unmoderated laugh- ter a breach of monastic protocol that would have the church mice poking their heads out doors and then retreating to add another link or two to the paper-clip necklace they were assembling. Some of this irritation was directed at Pauline because hers was one of the few writers' offices that welcomed visitors and hosted conversa- tions conducted at normal human volume instead of the rice-papery whispers that kept everybody's tongues on tiptoe. Some hall mates resented having their quiet concentration broken, even though it was quiet concentration that had them in a cement headlock. There were offices occupied almost every weekday by staff writers whose typewriter keys almost never clacked. I once asked Pauline about a staff reporter with an elegant byline who always seemed to be pos- ing in profile, even in the elevator, and whose output was pristinely small. She always seemed to be in her office with the scenic view, pensively, decorously not writing—what does she *do* all day? "She thinks beautiful thoughts," Pauline said.

Pauline didn't have the luxury of Wordsworthian contemplation, not with her pressure-cooker schedule, a vicious cycle of deadlines that had her meeting herself coming and going. She did her writing on the second floor of her house in Great Barrington, Massachu- setts, bent over at a drawing table facing light-flooding windows looking out on her long, descending lawn to the road below. She wrote in pencil with a rubber thimble on her thumb, her phenom- enal concentration pouring from the point of her pencil across the page as she followed the line of argument wherever it led, keeping every circuit open. In his memoir-meditation *Sontag and Kael: Opposites Attract Me*, Craig Seligman recalls sitting on the veranda of Pauline's house, staring vacantly, when Pauline asked him what he was doing. "Thinking," he replied. "I only think with a pencil in my hand," Pauline said, a bit of overstatement, but what it was overstating had a core validity; the pencil point was the drill bit that drove through surface resistance, releasing unconscious energies and correspondences. She scorned reviewers who outlined their pieces in advance, executing a blueprint, saying of one such practitioner, "That's why his pieces read like term papers." She wanted the writing to read like one long exhalation that would seize the reader from the opening gunshot and then drop him off at the curb after a dizzy ride. The first draft was given to her daughter, Gina, for typing, and then corrections were made on the typescript. Pauline would then be driven to the city, where by day the piece would go through *The New Yorker*'s fanatically fly-eyed round of copyediting and fact-checking while at night she would catch screenings of the movies she would review for the next column, returning to Great Barrington to write over the weekend and then back again to the city, a rapid turnaround that could have devolved into a repetitive grind for someone simply filing copy. But Pauline was still riding the crest of the crescendo that was *Deeper into Movies* (1973), the collection of reviews that stamped her name as the most important and embattled film critic in America, her championing of *The Godfather, McCabe and Mrs. Miller, Cabaret,* Steven Spielberg's *Sugarland Express* (when most critics preferred Terrence Malick's *Badlands*) helping augur the seventies resurgence of American cinema that left us such beautiful scars and drizzly haze. It was the feudal age of film criticism too, when criticism retained the ability to make readers mad in both senses of the word, angry-mad and crazy-mad, with popular opinionists such as Judith Crist and Rex Reed and deep-dish ponderers such as Vernon Young (the *Hudson Review*), William S. Pechter (*Commentary*), and Charles Thomas Samuels (an academic freelancer whose mentor was John Simon, then at the unpopular height of his Dracula impersonation) making every major studio release or prestige European import a debatable proposition, the basic terminology setting a dividing line. "[John] Simon's brief for insisting on 'films' instead of 'movies' reminds one of two monks chaffering over the word 'consubstantiation'—no mean issue in its day," wrote the novelist and critic Wilfrid Sheed from his own shaky vantage point as an unallied observer. "Movies means popcorn, double features, and coming in the middle: democracy. Film means, well, at least chewing quietly, no talking (a rule Mr. Simon has been known to break in person), the seriousness one brings to the other arts: aristocracy." Pauline, a movies person, found it absurd that "film" should be accorded such fancy airs. Asked for the ten thousandth time why she preferred "movies" to "film," she said, "Film is what you load a camera with." Simple as that.

As I enter Pauline's office, she clears a place for me on the couch if there's no spot to perch, moving aside scripts she's been sent, stacks of newly delivered books and galleys, unsolicited manuscripts, manila folders with news clippings, and whatever else has come through the pipeline. On her desk lay the latest set of *New Yorker* galleys, undergoing extensive surgery. Although Pauline wrote fast and was accused of being more impressionistic and free-associative than rational-analytical (an accusation laced with a sexism with which she was wearily familiar, the implicit and sometimes explicit assumption that a woman critic was more at the mercy of her hormones, mood fluctuations, and monthly cycles than a marble bust of judicious decorum such as the *New Republic*'s Stanley Kauffmann or a sprightly carnation such as Vincent Canby of the *New York Times*), she was meticulous with her copy, as fanatical a tinkerer as any fussbudget from the E. B. White elf academy. It was the aim and direction of her perfectionism that were different. She didn't pursue evenly smoothed embalmed non-reflective-surface perfection. She sanded down the jagged edges of her reviews to piercing effect. She was slangy the way *New Yorker* writers were slangy in the thirties, before excess propriety and hallowed obeisance to the fine-toned points of craft outfitted writers with clerical collars. Rather than camp behind the fine-mesh scrim of mandarin prose or adopt the chummy manner of *New Yorker* critics past (such as Robert Bench-ley, Wolcott Gibbs, Dorothy Parker, and her predecessors on the film beat, among them John McCarten, John Mosher, and Brendan Gill), she filed battlefield reports from the front line of the back row, writing for the ear as much as the eye, one of the few critics (to borrow a locution from Seymour Krim) whose words were capable of matching the speed of our minds. In his book, Seligman quotes one of Pauline's editors at *The New Yorker,* John Bennet, describ-ing the complexity of her creative-destructive grid work. "Balzac, madly revising at his most caffeinated, Proust at his most hypoder-mically caffeinated, had nothing on Pauline when it came to cross-ing out, writing all over the margins, taping extra sheets of paper to the margins to make even more revisions—revisions of revisions, inserts inside inserts." Entire paragraphs were x-ed out and new ones inserted, sentences were transposed within paragraphs that them-selves were moved around like modular furniture, commas delicately planted by *The New Yorker*'s notoriously comma-promiscuous copy department (resulting in sentences that resembled a higher plane of constipation, bogged down in late-period Henry James particular-ization) were plucked out and em dashes liberally thrown like left jabs. Even without the benefit of literacy, strictly as an eye exam, her pieces looked more *alive* on the page than those of anyone else (save for Donald Barthelme and his typographical Monty Python circus). Nearly every cut and addition she made was to foster idiomatic verve, direct contact, and acceleration, the hum of a live broadcast.

Having made her name as a film reviewer for a Berkeley radio station, Pauline was an advocate of reading work aloud to make sure that it "played." She would sometimes read me reviews or par-tial reviews over the phone, not to toot her own horn (though she loved it whenever a line got a laugh), but to have a sounding board, a preview audience. It was a way of pinpointing false notes and dead spots, lopping the branches off of sentences that went on so long that her voice ran out of wind before the finish line. On rare occasions she'd call because she was "stuck" (she would read up to the point the piece hit a blank wall, trying to figure out how to push through), but more often she wanted to know if she "went too far" this time "going after" a certain movie or actor or director, knowing that by execrating the latest Neil Simon or some meretricious bagatelle from Mike Nichols ("God, the shit he gets away with"), she was blaspheming everything the *New York Times* Arts and Leisure section held hallow. It wasn't that she was looking to cotton-pad her opinions; it was that she didn't relish another round of aggravation from the aggrieved and wanted to settle in her own mind that animosity hadn't gotten the worst of her. "I want to be fair to the son of a bitch," she said once, cleaving to the belief that every filmmaker was capable of redemption, even Ken Russell, though that might be pushing it (she once said he deserved having a stake driven through his heart, if they could find it). Sometimes the fear of going "too far" went in the other direction—Pauline would seek confirmation that she hadn't snapped out of earth's orbit by hailing *Carrie* or *The Warriors,* two pulp smashers considered garish and low-pandering not only by most fellow critics but by many of *The New Yorker*'s readers, whose nerves couldn't take all this noisy ruckus. Such movies, they were enough to tip over one's gondolas.

I once was witness—a student co-pilot—to a master class in Pauline's instant power-on of articulation, where every phrase quivered like the handle of a knife whose blade had just lodged in the tree bark. It was a pilot for a talk show hosted by David Susskind's wife, Joyce Davidson, who had already established herself as a TV name in Canada and was looking to expand south. David Susskind, for those who need escorting into the memory vault, was an adventurous, high-strung, phone-juggling, devoutly, almost stereotypically Jewish urban liberal (back when the *New York Post* was the tabernacle organ of middlebrow, middle-class Jewish liberalism, home to columnists such as Max Lerner and Dr. Rose Franzblau). He was the producer of socially conscious dramas such as the TV adaptations of *Raisin in the Sun* and *Death of a Salesman,* and the groundbreaking, gritty-vérité original drama *East Side/West Side,* starring George C.

Scott as a social worker contending with slum conditions, child abuse, drug addiction, racial discrimination, and the bureaucratic coils of the welfare system, and the host of a weekly two-hour Manhattan-based talk show that was part seminar, part encounter group, part freak show, and part celebrity séance, with Susskind rattling his papers and stammering questions as if trying to make sense of the madness pitching the deck of his once stable world. With his white hair and Mr. Magoo eye pouches, Susskind was a monochromatic man made dizzy by the kaleidoscopic swirl of the sixties. Unlike on the *Charlie Rose* set (Charlie sharing some of Susskind's befuddlement but exuding a far stronger sense of varnished ease in the international brotherhood of media moguls and the permanent political class), guests weren't expected to be on their best behavior when they convened in the Susskind studio. Some of his most famous installments were barely contained uproars, such as the reunion of the Andy Warhol superstars that turned into a queeny uprising over the vile influence of Paul Morrissey over Andy; a debate about feminism in which Germaine Greer squashed the book reviewer and culture critic Anatole Broyard like a presumptuous grape; a discussion of "radical chic" in which guests of Leonard Bernstein's fund-raiser for the Black Panthers vented against an absent Tom Wolfe over his caricature of them in his infamous *New York* cover story (illustrated with a photograph of supposed uptown socialites making a black power fist salute to the camera); and the classic "How to Be a Jewish Son" support group featuring Dan Greenburg, David Steinberg, and Mel Brooks at his most hilarious-spontaneous.

One visual sip of Davidson's Chardonnay chill and it was clear her talk show was going to be a classier affair than her husband's, no rolling around on the floor or raised voices. The guests for the pilot episode were the actor Ed Asner, Gore Vidal (a frequent guest on the Susskind show, whose entire two hours were devoted once a year to Vidal's "state of the union" reflections), Pauline, and myself. It was an impressive lot, apart from me, a relative nobody. I was there because Pauline suggested me to the producer in my role as a TV reviewer for the *Voice* and because, I think, she wanted company in the rental car that ferried us to and from the studio, which I remember as being outside of Manhattan. Connecticut? Long Island? I don't remember, only that we passed a lot of trees.

What I do remember was my first meeting with Gore Vidal, who was then, as now, quintessentially Gore Vidalish—"in character," as it were. We chatted beforehand while Pauline was elsewhere, perhaps in makeup, about the literary feud ablaze between Lillian Hellman and Mary McCarthy, which one wag compared to the gunfight between Joan Crawford and Mercedes McCambridge in *Johnny Guitar,* only less butch. It was one of those spats that escalated into a rift that divided cocktail parties into two opposing camps glowering at each other with frosty eyebrows. The fracas uninnocently began when McCarthy, a guest on *The Dick Cavett Show* (during its PBS iteration), rendered a verdict regarding Hellman's veracity as a memoirist, declaring with a leopardess smile that had claimed many a victim before: "Every word she writes is a lie, including 'and' and 'the.'" That Hellman's relationship with the truth was a rather smoky romance with a lot of room for mythmaking and revision was not a controversial notion. Pauline, for example, had pegged the heroic saga of *Julia* as a phony from the get-go, a suspicion vindicated when the real Julia—Muriel Gardiner, who shared a lawyer with Hellman—surfaced to reveal that Hellman's memoir was a self-glorifying fiction, a form of identity theft. And those in the liberal anti-Communist camp were almost admirably agog at how Hellman had managed to misty-watercolorize her Stalinist past, repackaging herself as a doughty heroine—a thorny survivor—for a new generation of feminist readers for whom the iridescence of Anaïs Nin had lost its lozenge effect. But the forest-clearing *sweep* of McCarthy's dismissal—executed with such blithe condescension ("tremendously overrated, a bad writer, a dishonest writer, but she really belongs to the past")—was like flaunting a red flag in Hellman's face, if I may mix metaphors with mad abandon, and Hellman retaliated not with a poison-dipped dart of her own but with a lawsuit upside

McCarthy's head. She sued not only McCarthy for defamation but Cavett and the Educational Broadcasting Corporation too, asking $2.25 million in damages. The cost of defending the suit threatened to impoverish McCarthy (Hellman was far wealthier, in part due to the royalties of the Hammett estate), and the spectacle of two writers dragging their war of words to court was abhorrent even to many of those who felt Hellman had been wronged.

Vidal was dispassionate, viewing this folly, like so many others, through a long lens. He understood what motivated Hellman to persevere, and it wasn't a sense of injustice. "When you reach a certain age," he philosophized, "sometimes there's nothing that gets you out of bed in the morning with more zest than a nice juicy lawsuit." (It only occurred to me later that Vidal must have had more than his share of zippedy-do-dah days, given his headline-making lawsuits with William F. Buckley Jr. and Truman Capote.) I mentioned that Norman Mailer was playing the unlikely role of truce maker, referring to an article Mailer had done for the *New York Times* appealing to Hellman and McCarthy to drop their gloves and call off the legal hostilities. "Ah, yes, Norman," Vidal said, "he always has such a vital role to play, being our Greatest Living Writer, as you so often remind us in the pages of the *Village Voice*."

Boy, did I feel swatted! And yet thrilled too. Here I was, low person on the totem pole, being put in my place as a Mailer fanboy by Gore Vidal in his inimitable epigrammatic manner, his irony at my expense proof that he had been reading me at the *Voice* and was aware of my existence as a writer, however irksome. Vidal knew who I was! That he found me egregious was secondary. I had, in some small, meaningless, minuscule way, arrived.

The taping began. The first guest was Ed Asner. It took him only a few minutes to sink the pilot and send Davidson's hopes of an American career nosing to the ocean bottom. I thought—assumed— that Asner the talk-show guest would be like his *Mary Tyler Moore Show* alter ego, Lou Grant, a gruff ball of ornery no-nonsense. If only. He began by asking if the microphone attached to his shirt (or was it a sweater?) was picking up his stomach gurgles. No, he was assured, first by our host, then by the stage director. But Asner was not assured, returning to the issue of his growling stomach and the distraction it might cause. "Maybe they can edit this out of the tape later," I whispered to Pauline, who said, "We may want to edit ourselves out of the tape later." "Why don't they just start the taping over? It's not like this is going on the air tonight." I was hushed by a sidelong look from someone connected with the production. Giving his stomach a rest as a topic, Asner then began talking honestly and sincerely, earnestly and devoutly, about how therapy had helped him as an actor, gotten him over some hurdles. The last of our curmudgeonly hopes were dashed. It was like listening to a testimonial at a 12-step meeting, euthanizing the show before it had had a chance to perk up its ears. "*Actors . . . ,*" Pauline quietly groaned, as if despairing of their entire race. The interview finally tapered to an end, and Pauline and I were ushered onto the set for our segment, the bright studio lights beating down and blocking out everything beyond the island rim of the stage, our butts making those crucial last-minute adjustments to achieve comfort as we were wired with mikes.

The subject of our segment, the reason we were there, was a new sitcom called *United States,* an unpeeling portrait of a marriage in close captivity starring Beau Bridges and Helen Shaver. Influenced by the unsparing domestic glumness and eruptive psychodrama of Ingmar Bergman's *Scenes from a Marriage,* whose original five-hour version for Swedish television had been compressed into a powerful depressant that was released into U.S. art-houses in 1974 and hailed as a landmark study of intimate warfare, *United States* was the first series created and written by Larry Gelbart after the success of *M*A*S*H.* It was greeted as an artistic growth spurt, solemnized by many reviewers much as Woody Allen's forays into mirthless seriousness were lauded for their "growth" and "maturity." In those days before the arrival of the prestige cable series (no *Sopranos,* no *Wire,* no *Mad Men*), *United States* was one of the rare shows that smart people felt a semi-obligation to have an opinion about, to adopt as their own.

Also, male critics by the carload had major crushes on Helen Shaver, whose gravelly voice was a seductive warm-up act for Demi Moore's.

Pauline and I hadn't rehearsed or vamped anything ahead of time, not wanting our comments to sound canned. So when the first question came about *United States,* directed at Pauline, I was interested in what particular points she would make, the tack she would take. Then, you know, we'd chat, compare notes. Instead, it was as if everything fell away as Pauline's voice, almost independent of her person, began to screwdrive into the show's aspirations and pretensions, articulating everything that was wrong with its format and execution with a lucid, methodical, almost *lilting* precision that was like a mini-tutorial in criticism. So rapt was I by Pauline's analysis that I forgot I was supposed to chip in too as I sat there fascinated at this fencing display of *formal rigor,* not wanting to break the flow. It wasn't just the brilliance with which she took the series apart cubistically; it was this palpable sense of criticism as a higher power, something that made you lean into the pitch, not just a series of opinions beading a target board, but a liberating force that lit up the top floor of your brain and cast out fear. After leaving nothing standing except a few support beams, Pauline was asked by the host what the show revealed about its creator, and she said, as if slamming shut the car door, "It's the work of a man with a lousy marriage." Rather more candor than Davidson anticipated, judging from her frozen-parfait expression. Not for nothing was Pauline a fan of Thelma Ritter, whose classic line from *All About Eve* about Eve Harrington's contrived tale of woe—"Everything but the bloodhounds snappin' at her rear end"—was one of Pauline's favorites. (Her favorite line reading may have been Jean Hagen's nasal sublime "Ah cain't *stan'* it" from *Singin' in the Rain,* which I once heard her emulate when asked her opinion of William Styron—"Ah cain't *stan'* 'im.")

Months went by, the pilot wasn't picked up, and, most irksome, we were never paid the fee we had been promised. "I figured they'd find a way to forget us," Pauline said. "Well, I blame Ed Asner," I said. "He ruined it for everybody with his stomach growls. I wonder how Vidal's segment went, though." We had left after our segment.

"Don't worry," Pauline said. "Whatever he said, he'll be sure to repeat it on some other show."

After a messenger picks up the latest set of galleys Pauline has notated, she slides the pile of correspondence to the action part of her desk: a paper-clipped stack of fan letters, film scripts, forwarded news clips, nitpicky corrections, three-page dissertations explaining the throbbing urgencies of the latest Fassbinder she hadn't reviewed, anti-Semitic diatribes (although it's hard to imagine anyone who made less of her Jewish background in print than Pauline, she somehow attracted the wrath of Jew haters who seemed to subscribe to *The New Yorker* for the sole purpose of sending her periodic harangues—with every phrase you could practically hear hot cinders heaving through their nostrils as they blamed her for making Barbra Streisand and Elliott Gould possible), and insistent pleas for Pauline to stop squandering valuable space in the magazine on movies that appealed only to the most violent, primitive tastes—why dignify and encourage such cultural Visigoths? (It was a question floated by Pauline's colleagues at *The New Yorker* as well, some of whom trooped off to a movie she personally recommended only to emerge with a cultural crisis of faith that cinema had come to this.) Occasionally, Pauline would slide over a letter from a reader that was so flecked with rage and personal invective that I would ask, "Why don't you just toss it in the trash? It's got to be bad voodoo having all this hostility hanging around." "No," she said, "it's just to respond and acknowledge their existence, otherwise they'll just keep writing." So to the correspondent who expressed his detestation as if he had scorpions dictating his sentences, she would dash off a courteous "Let's just agree to disagree" response on *New Yorker* note cards that were designed for elegant brevity and to discourage further elaborations. It was with a deeper sigh that she moved on to the weightier correspondence that (unlike the scattershot nut mail) descended from some loftier altitude of intellectual pretense, printed on fine stationery (who knew there were so many subtle shades of cream?) and bearing the professional letterhead of a professor or, worse, psychotherapist or, worse still, heaven spare us, a *married* pair

of Ph.D.'s who had drafted a joint communiqué intended, after dol-
ing out a few olives of praise, to set Pauline straight. Like Norman
Mailer, Pauline was more exasperated by leechy, well-intentioned
liberals trying to set everything in proper order than by outright
antagonists. She trailed a finger along the italicized title of the film
about which Pauline had so fallen short.

"Oh, God, not that one," I said. Pauline read:

"As long-time readers and devotees of your *New Yorker* columns . . ."

"—*who are about to viciously turn on you,*" I interjected.

". . . we looked forward, as we always do . . ."

"—the two of them, waiting by the mailbox . . ."

". . . to your review of *Seven Beauties* by the Italian director Lina
Wertmüller, which in its broad, intemperate disregard for the dark
comedy that infuses Wertmüller's vision . . ."

Not a movie whose mention today lights the black-mass candles
of Nazi-kink nostalgia (displaced by Liliana Cavani's *Night Porter,*
where sadomasochistic decadence was represented by the ravishing
desolation of Charlotte Rampling's Euro-goddess bone structure),
Wertmüller's *Seven Beauties* was a major honking controversy when it
was released in 1975, a black comedy set mostly in a concentration
camp where Giancarlo Giannini, to save his cowardly hide, submitted to sex with the obese commandant, played by Shirley Stoler,
their coupling filmed as if he were mating with a hippopotamus
or elephant, an obdurate, bestial, Diane Arbus bulk. Long before
the word "transgressive" became a journalistic crutch and Quentin
Tarantino a jacked-up marionette, *Seven Beauties* put viewers' heads
in a thunder-thigh vise. It might have remained a film festival/art-
house transient had it not received the grand push by the *New York
Times* ("*Seven Beauties* is Miss Wertmüller's *King Kong,* her *Nashville,*
her *8½,* her *Navigator,* her *City Lights*"), which awarded special dis-
pensation to any Holocaust-related work, its lead reviewer, Vincent
Canby, christening it as "a handbook for survival, a farce, a drama
of almost shattering impact." And the film brandished a feminist
sash because it was directed by a woman who, by pulling out this
hand grenade and juggling it with such bravura, was making a bid

for major-league status in foreign film as a female Fellini. (Fellini himself having gotten a bit run-down and recyclish.) Pauline found *Seven Beauties* a porky, pretentious wallow, as reflected in the title of her review, "Seven Fatties," a head that nowadays would have the beleaguered remnants of the copy department fretting that such phrasing might be construed as insensitive, weight-ist. I can almost hear Pauline's pithy, characteristic response: *"Tough."* (Which sometimes, depending on the situation, had a *"shit"* attached.) It was often what she said when someone expressed queasy apprehension on some point of possible offense, a retort that was made not with anger or defiance but with a snorty impatience for euphemism, false modesty, and weak-kneed equivocation as secondhand mode of shirking the truth, or, worse, killing a joke. Tender feelings were a fraudulent cover for larger failures of nerve. (Pauline agreed with Nabokov's contention that sentimentality and brutality were the flip sides of a subservient mind.) But with a film such as *Seven Beauties,* the background shadows of barbed wire and camp barracks made critics pro and con feel compelled to dress their prose in its Sunday best, which Pauline only did when true reverence was due (as, say, whenever the majestic prow of Vanessa Redgrave hove into view), and her pan of *Seven Beauties* was considered a slap in the face of the more sober-minded symposiasts. It was only after the psychologist and critic Bruno Bettelheim, a survivor of Auschwitz whose authority on the subject of the camps was unassailable, published a devastating critique of *Seven Beauties* in *The New Yorker* in August of that year that its high-minded defenders lightened up on Pauline, but letters still trickled in, furrowed with disappointment. The backlash over *Seven Beauties* proved to be light flak compared with the furor over Claude Lanzmann's *Shoah,* when Pauline was more cautious in her tone and respectful in dissent and fat load of good it did her, what she got in return was the plague, accusations of being a self-hating Jew.

After reading a passage from the duo's letter citing Günter Grass's *Tin Drum* and Jerzy Kosinski's *Painted Bird* ("to further my education, I suppose," Pauline said), she handed me the letter so that I could see for myself the closely packed paragraphs of reasoned dissent demonstrating that Pauline had missed not only the boat on *Seven Beauties* but the ocean, and the larger lesson of the Holocaust, not to mention the farcical dimensions of moral choice in a universe gone madly awry.

"I see that they urge you to see the movie again and reconsider," I said, hopping to the last paragraph, its decrescendo. "See it again through their eyes."

"My eyes are the only ones I have," she said. "And they're allowed to get tired."

Reconsiderations could wait until a lazier, more contemplative day, of which there were few on the horizon. It was Pauline's practice and principle to beam a movie into her brain once and move forward, believing that the first responses were the true responses and that repeated viewings gave rise to rationalizations, a fussy curatorship—a consensus-building exercise in your own mind full of minor adjustments that took you further and further away from the original altercation (although she did go see Robert Altman's *McCabe and Mrs. Miller* a second time, anxious to confirm her original feeling that it was a great shaggy melancholy beauty of a movie worth going to the wall for). She wanted the nerve endings of her reactions exposed, not neatly tapered and trimmed. She was amused by a *New Yorker* colleague who only watched old movies, "as if she can't bear to part with her black-and-white TV." Nearly the first question Pauline asked a friend in conversation was, "Have you seen anything?" Meaning: anything new, anything she should know about, anything exciting. So much was happening in the ragged advance of movies in the seventies that she craved reports from the front lines, confirmations that she wasn't crazily alone in her likings.

As Pauline edited her copy and winnowed the mail, a thin traffic stream appeared and disappeared at the door, not all of them *New Yorker* cast members.

"Hi, do you know Jim Wolcott?"

Whom did I meet in Pauline's office in those years? Piper Laurie, famously speared by the flurry of telekinetically delivered kitchen knives in *Carrie*. I interviewed Sissy Spacek, the star of *Carrie*, for the *Voice*, illustrated by a portrait of Spacek by the photographer James Hamilton that made every freckle look fetchingly spooky, not that I recall that actually coming up in our conversation with Laurie, since I don't recall our conversation, only the moment of hello. The screenwriter Ron Shelton, who would later direct *Bull Durham*, whose famous "I believe" monologue (". . . that the novels of Susan Sontag are self-indulgent, overrated crap"), delivered by Kevin Costner, seemed to chime with Pauline's tastes. Did I meet the writer-director-reprobate hyphenate James Toback there? It doesn't matter, because Toback is a universal application, his friendship with Pauline and her praise of his directorial debut, *Fingers*, one of the whacking sticks used against her. It wasn't enough that Pauline's opening sentence shot like a squirt of lighter fluid—"James Toback is trying to be Orson Welles and Carol Reed, Dostoyevski, Conrad and Kafka" (though Pauline said to me it wasn't as hyperbolic as it sounded: "I said he was *trying* to be them, not that he had achieved it")—but she also compared his flair for self-dramatization to that of the "young Tennessee Williams," though one imagines Toback's *Glass Menagerie* would be shattered by roughly obtained orgasms. Reviewing *Fingers* for *National Review*, John Simon claimed that Pauline's championing of Toback represented personal logrolling and "rather shoddy journalism," given their prominent chumming around, and the ugliness evolved from there. (Years later, following a screening of *Fingers* at the Museum of the Moving Image, Toback set the record straight in his rogue fashion: "John Simon actually wrote and implied that I was fucking Pauline Kael—that's why she wrote what she did about the movie—and then said it at UCLA at a big gathering they had. And they asked me about it on a TV interview after that and I said, 'I have fucked Pauline Kael the same number of times I've fucked John Simon.'") If it wasn't in her office that I met Toback, it may have been at a screening, it may have been anywhere, because he was everywhere then, just as he's everywhere now, and we'll be leaving for the screening soon, just as soon as Pauline polishes off a final query or two from the fact-checker, removes the rubber thimble from her thumb, dips a pair of fresh pencils one after another into an electric sharpener, and collects her things.

The phone rings. Mr. Shawn would like to speak to her now, if she's available.

"I'll be right there." Sigh. To me: "He's probably going to implore me to substitute 'posterior' for 'rump.' As if anyone has ever said, 'He gave her a smack on the posterior.'"

Pauline had regular tussles with Shawn over the years over the fine points of acceptable slang and vulgarity, generating a defensiveness within Shawn and a resentment on the part of the staff that Pauline was pursuing liberties that others had the good grace not to drag out of the locker room. They seem almost antique today, these battles over words for body parts and suitable euphemisms, when *The New Yorker* of the Tina Brown–David Remnick era publishes the humorist Ian Frazier's irregular series of Cursing Mommy routines ("Fuuuuuuuck! Ow! Jesus Christ! Fucking shit! I stubbed my fucking toe!") and its dance critic can casually refer to a plié as "the cunt-dip," but they were quite stressful for both parties at the time, a small-scale war of attrition that was a big wear-down. When it became too animated, Pauline was advised (by whom, she didn't say) that Shawn had been having heart problems and pressing him just might push him over the top. Pauline had been advised this so many times that she suspected it was a form of emotional blackmail, intended to make her ease up, and so whenever the issue of Shawn's fragile ticker came into editorial play, I would grab my chest and wave my arm in the air like Redd Foxx's Fred Sanford staggering backward, feeling the "big one" coming on. I was careful not to do this when anyone else was around.

"This shouldn't be long," Pauline says. "Here's the new issue of the magazine. Lore Segal has a wonderful story in it."

It's also a long story, so instead I go puddle jumping from cartoon to cartoon. Pauline returns in record time.

"Turned out he wanted to ask for some other change, and was so relieved when I just gave in without making an issue of it. It feels so good not to fight."

"That's what my parents used to say between bouts."

"We'll have to hurry now."

Pauline brushes her thin, neatly kept gray hair (the ripplier hairdo in the jacket photo of *I Lost It at the Movies* a historical curio), knots a scarf around her neck, assuming it's chilly out, which, let's stipulate, it is, slips into her brown suede coat, and grabs her carrying case by the handle. If it's heavy, I'll do the carrying, but this time it's not. Out her office door we go, passing the miniature satanic mills of Harold Brodkey's tireless genius, muscling out countless drafts of his Proustian epic that was provisionally titled *A Party of Animals,* then later retitled *The Runaway Soul* (an alteration that Edmund White called a catastrophic mistake), or perhaps it was a separate novella or story endowing the out-tray. I never met Brodkey in the transcendent flesh during my visits to Pauline's office. Our run-in would come later, at an Upper West Side book party, like the kind you read about in novels about the fast-fading Literary World, when I genially noted that Brodkey (who prided himself on his height, as he prided himself on everything) wasn't as tall as James Dickey, whom I had just returned from interviewing down in Columbia, South Carolina. To which Brodkey snapped, in one of the great impromptu non sequiturs ever to fly in my direction: "Dickey doesn't live in New York and put up with what I have to put up with." I laughed, assuming Brodkey was kidding about the invisible ceiling restricting the towering climb of his true full height (i.e., that he'd be a few inches taller if New York literary society hadn't stunted his growth), but a kidder he was not. It was an incident that would oil-spill into print, in the pages of the *New York Observer* to be precise, but Brodkey is gone now, the monumental presence he thought he was permanently casting eaten by sunlight.

Down the hall Pauline and I go, past a long table sparsely piled with miscellaneous reading material and past the lobby desk, where Morticia hands Pauline phone messages she had taken that had somehow slipped her mind earlier, as if they were parking tickets that had collected under the windshield wipers. Pauline waits to read them in the elevator to see which important calls she has missed and which needn't be answered because now it's too late. Once an older gentleman entered the elevator with us and replied to Pauline's greeting with what sounded like a semi-monosyllable, as if he were withdrawing a word in mid-release. When the elevator deposited us in the downstairs lobby and distance was thrown between us, Pauline said, as if indicating a local landmark, "That's Joe Mitchell." Joseph Mitchell, whose reputation would be resuscitated and permanently restored with the publication of *Up in the Old Hotel* in 1992, was the legendary "fact" reporter of raffish dives and waterfront lore who had hit the unmerciful wall of writer's block following the publication of *Joe Gould's Secret,* where the secret was that Joe Gould, a Greenwich Village bohemian human scarecrow legend who claimed to be working on a diary that would be the masterpiece the century was waiting for, was a fraudster whose magnum opus was all gummy mouth. Mitchell, like so many in the Village, had been taken advantage of and taken in. (The cranky co-dependency of author and subject became the basis for a too-stately film starring Stanley Tucci as Mitchell and Ian Holm as the Greenwich Village John Aubrey.) Although Mitchell maintained an office at the magazine, he had not been published in its pages since 1964, his decades-long journalistic silence a phenomenon as pregnant with absent presence as J. D. Salinger's permanent sabbatical a'twidst the protective birches of New Hampshire. But while there were those who insisted that Salinger was diligently, monkishly scribbling away, fewer prospects were held that Mitchell was squirreling anything away for posterity. His garbage can was often empty at the end of the day, no bouquet of balled-up discarded pages left behind as evidence of frustrated effort. His muse seemed to have given up the ghost. It was after another round of throat clearing from Mitchell (this time in the lobby) that Pauline said to me, "I keep reading about Joe Mitchell the Southern gentleman. I've been saying hello to him for twenty years and all I've ever gotten back is a grunt."

We head to Sixth Avenue, along Forty-fourth Street. Picture blue-gray garbage-y streets, multilayered traffic tiered all the way up to Fifty-ninth, where Central Park begins. Most of the screening rooms are on the West Side, if not in the Times Square area, then higher up, approaching Carnegie Hall. If the screening room lies within reasonable walking distance, we'll hoof it; if not, we'll try to snag a taxi, always an adventure in midtown, especially in the seventies, when the most frequently spoken language from the driver's seat in the cab was surly, especially at rush hour. We catch one at Sixth, the driver grumbling after hearing we're only going a few blocks up and over. At night, when the traffic had thinned, the mood coming from the front of the cab might be more philosophical, more inclined to a *comme ci, comme ça* approach to the human endeavor, but now, the minutes ticking down to reach a 6:00 p.m. screening, f-words and car honks alternate as if *The French Connection*'s Popeye Doyle were bent over every steering wheel, boiling from the eyebrows up. Antici-pating the light going green, the cab hops forward, then brakes to avoid fendering a pedestrian of nonwhite denomination.

"Nigger got lucky that time," the driver says.

"Now, now," Pauline says.

The driver's elbow juts out his rolled-down window as the light turns green and he eases ahead. Detecting the note of reprimand in Pauline's words, he explains that he doesn't have a beef with all blacks, just the ones who make it shitty for everybody else.

"You may need to give the matter a little more thought," Pauline says, which doesn't stop him from further elaboration and clarifi-cation of his point of view. We stop at the screening address, and Pauline pays the fare, plus some.

"I didn't want him to think I was using his racist talk as an excuse to under-tip him," Pauline says as we make our way to the building lobby.

Upstairs, a young female publicist giving out press kits—back then, it was always a young female publicist, shiny with hope—hands one to Pauline and enjoins us to enjoy the movie, like a flight attendant welcoming us aboard. Perhaps a couple of Pauline's other invitees are waiting so that we can all go in together, or perhaps they're already inside, saving seats. It wasn't that Pauline wouldn't or didn't go to movies alone, or with a single partner; it's that she didn't see moviegoing as a solitary rite that required silence, devotion, and rapt communion. What she brought from San Francisco was an informal sociability that abjured pigeonholes and caste systems—all the trappings of Manhattan snobbery—in favor of a floating party whose membership was in intimate flux. Because she'd been forced to give up minor vices (allergies would later restrict her meals and activities), conversation was the one buzz left to her, and no wonder she responded with such kin affinity to the multilayered murmur and byplay of Robert Altman's ensemble films, those cloud maneuvers of subtle relations.

Sometimes we don't go straight in, instead waiting outside for the previous screening to end and the audience to vacate. Pauline told me once of a film she was seeing that was being shown in back-to-back screenings, she having arrived for the later one. The doors opened and one of her then protégés, now one of the few remaining prominent film critics with a paying job, came out with his usual facial arrangement of academic thoughtfulness. "So how was it?" Pauline asked.

Not much, he said. A few good scenes but mostly a mess. I'm not sure I'd bother with it.

"Well, since I'm already here . . . ," Pauline said.

The movie was *Mean Streets,* not Martin Scorsese's first feature, but the one that missiled his directorial career and that of its stars, Robert De Niro and Harvey Keitel, De Niro's entrance into the Little Italy bar to the sound of "Jumpin' Jack Flash" one of the great character intros in movie history, the rest living up to its kinetic promise, a film in which Catholic guilt earned its own dressing room.

So after that Pauline stopped trusting immediate eyewitness reports, assuming she ever did.

We take up mortar position in the back row. Pauline nearly

always sits in the back, often right beneath the projectionist's portholes, flanked by fellow critics on her squad, *New Yorker* fact-checkers and copy editors, a lateral entourage of friends and allies. (The auteurists—those ardent members of Andrew Sarris's Raccoon Lodge—tended to huddle closer to the screen, as if to meld mind and image into a blissful, shimmering mirage of Kim Novak with her lips parted.)

A few rows ahead, one of Pauline's protégés stands and adjusts his jeans, which seem to sag in the back no matter how tight his belt is notched.

"R. never did have any ass to him," Pauline observes almost wistfully.

R. removes the jacket he was using as a seat saver to make room for his date, a co-worker from *Newsweek,* who's running a bit late.

"R. will probably be bringing her along afterwards," Pauline says, "afterwards" referring to wherever we decide to go for the post-mortem.

"Oh, goody," I say, as Pauline gives me a light rap on the arm.

Another of Pauline's junior G-men arrives, ceremonially helping his date off with her coat with the Southern courtliness of a quality seducer. I can tell from his forlorn gallant wave to Pauline before he sits down that he's miffed he didn't arrive early enough to sit in the back row, forced instead to make do with a middle row far from the nerve center of activity.

The rustling in the seats subsides. Here we are, pencils and pens at the ready.

"Let us pray," Pauline says, as the lights dim in the screening room, hoping for the best that this movie might deliver. And as those lights dim, a silhouetted figure dips into a seat nearby, an apparent latecomer.

Without moving her head, Pauline registers the peripheral blur and whispers, "Spy."

In those days before blog reviewers who tweet insta-responses in mid-screening, the studios would have little birdies pop into the screening room to report back to headquarters on the critical reactions, as much as could be roughly measured in groans, laughter, irritable fidgeting, and silent pockets of bored indifference. (Sometimes the spy was simply a publicist doing double duty.) Given how much money had been invested in a production, it was understandable that the studio and the distributor didn't want to fly blind into a wall of hostile reviews. Even unequipped with a special swivel head and night goggles, almost any screening-room informant would have found Pauline an easy "read." When she was held by a film, her head was raptor-rapt, and the notes she took were few, her hand moving almost independently as if not to break the transmission chain. Laughter would lightly bubble up at the appearance of one of her favorite actors, anticipating that his presence meant we were in for a treat (her grin and George Segal's grin would almost meet in midair), and the laughter would be sharper, caught off guard by delight, when somebody new shot up the energy, whether it was Jeff Goldblum in *Next Stop, Greenwich Village* or Shelley Duvall in *Nashville.* When Pauline fell out of sorts with the film, she would rest her face in her palm and sometimes make a vague gesture at the screen, as if to say, It's a lost cause, or, They've lost their senses. Sometimes, she would give voice to exasperation, as during the screening of *Welcome to L.A.,* when Keith Carradine wrapped a blanket around a naked Geraldine Chaplin and Pauline said, quite distinctly, "That's the first decent act that's been performed in this movie." No matter how dire the movie was, professional obligation semi-dictated that Pauline stick it out for the duration, and of all the screenings I attended with her, the only time we walked out in the middle was during the eighties, the movie in question being Hal Ashby's inexplicable, unendurable piece of slop *Lookin' to Get Out,* remembered today only because it offered the first screen appearance of a little bundle named Angelina Jolie. I'm not quite certain why we bailed on that one, having stuck to the finish of films far worse, but I believe it was because, along with further evidence of Ashby's decay, Pauline found the artistic deterioration of the film's star (and Angelina's father), Jon Voight, so dismaying. She had heralded him for being so sunnily alive and vigorous as the rural teacher in *Con-*

rack, and here he was starting to show the self-conscious decay of a Michael Moriarty, whose film career she pretty much destroyed with her scathing mockery of his existential clamminess in *Report to the Commissioner.*

There was an occasion when I solo ejected from a movie, under what I thought was justifiable provocation, though at that point I might have seized upon any opportunity to devour daylight. The occasion was a special early screening set up for Pauline and her crew of Bernardo Bertolucci's *1900,* a pseudo-Marxist epic of oppression, decadence, and revolt that also revealed to the world Robert De Niro's penis in its raw, shy state of nature. Gérard Depardieu's too, though that may have been previously exposed. Given Pauline's streaking-comet exaltation of *Last Tango in Paris, 1900* arrived atop a moving pyramid of lofty expectations, its huge cast and histori- cal canvas suggesting an unholy trinity of Sergei Eisenstein, David Lean, and Luchino Visconti, a lush panorama bursting with cherry reds of downtrodden peasants who seemed to have sprung out of the soil and debauched aristocrats trained at the de Sade Academy of the Performing Arts. Having so publicly and passionately com- mitted to Bertolucci's carnal vision with her *Last Tango* rave, Pauline was pulling for him to bring off this symphonic opus and trying to extend every benefit of the doubt while I, feeling queasier with each cruelty served on a platter, slumped so deep into myself that I felt like a ball of wax with walnut eyes. And this was only the first half of the five-hour uncut version! There was going to be a break in the afternoon, followed by Part Two. As Part One neared its climactic end, one of the inbred decadents in the film—played by Donald Sutherland with all the dementia at his disposal, which was *a lot*— tied a wriggling kitten to the wall, and I said to Pauline, "If any- thing happens to that cat, I'm outta here." After a beat to build up a sense of apprehension, Sutherland bashed the kitten with his head, killing it. I'm sure the killing was faked, but that was enough for me, I'd had it, and I didn't return for Part Two. Pauline understood my squeamishness (she too let out a yip when the kitten was brow- hammered), but I also think she thought I was being silly, letting it get to me that much. She prided herself on being able to sit through something as brutally protracted and fecal as Pasolini's *Salò* with nary a qualm. Her review of *1900* would be an unwieldy teeter-totter straddle—acknowledging its grotesqueries while praising its titanic scope ("It makes everything look like something held at the end of a toothpick")—but once Bertolucci unburdened himself of the ludicrous *Luna,* starring Jill Clayburgh in a near-career-killer role as an incestuous mom, she was unable to argue herself out of her disenchantment with Bertolucci.

Apart from *1900,* the screenings held especially for Pauline were the most enjoyable because we could chat among ourselves without heads snapping and shushes coming from scholars trying to concentrate. Even then there could be repercussions once the studio spies reported back to the brass. I recall a screening of *Bobby Deerfield* at which Toback was one of the invitees. Toback, not just a writer, director, and actor, but a gambler, storyteller, and heat-seeking sausage of hit-and-run legend whose pickup tactics would make him a familiar *Spy* target in the eighties, was the most conspicuous fireball in Pauline's orbit. (Not that he didn't have a lot of other orbits in which he moved, as a friend and collaborator of Warren Beatty's—Toback did the screenplay for *Bugsy*—and a disciple of Norman Mailer, whose improvisational bad-vibe weekend-party pseudo-documentary *Maidstone* he had covered for *Esquire.* Toback went even more white Negro than Mailer dared, playing Jewish-intellectual sidekick to the football great Jim Brown, his personal guide into the vectors of soul power and black studhood. In *Jim,* Toback's "self-centered memoir" of his friendship with Brown, they end up in a big bed with a couple of hot chicks, balling in bonding syncopation.) It was easy to see what Pauline saw in Toback as a person, what all of us did: his glistening presence, radio hum of energy, self-deprecating humor, constantly refilling trove of jaw-dropping anecdotes about Hollywood trespasses, and ebullient outgoingness—a high-voltage extroversion that made those of us who stuck to the word trade feel like fabric samples. He was out there banging while the rest of us played spectator, or so it seemed. As the opening credits of *Bobby Deerfield* began to roll, Toback supplied a running commentary on the names presented on-screen, supplying capsule descriptions such as "useless," "totally useless," "completely pathetic," "former Teamster," "drug addict," "Warren slept with her once," "I thought he had retired," "completely unacceptable," "met her by the pool once," "what's he doing here?" and, as Al Pacino's Bobby Deerfield emerged, an immaculate placard of focus and integrity in a motorized circus of competitive uproar, the greeting "Nice jacket, Al." The churchly, hunting-dog nobility of Bobby Deerfield only liberated Toback even more, his sit-down stand-up routine more entertaining than anything on-screen, until eventually he too became subdued by the leaden import of the tedious plight of a race driver's conscience and church mice we all became. But word got back to those concerned, as it would later when a small knot of us dared take Alain Resnais's *Providence* (a meditation on death and creativity endorsed by Susan Sontag, swinging her incense ball) less than solemnly, and, finked out by someone in the projection booth, we found ourselves publicly chided in the press for sullying cinema.

Screening chatter didn't entirely run into negative territory. That wasn't the norm. Once Pauline invited me to tag along to a screening of a movie that the studio didn't seem to know what to do with, set in Baltimore, 1959, and featuring a large, shiny cast of mostly unknowns. Mark Johnson, who, I believe, lived near Pauline in the Berkshires (or perhaps his mother did), was one of the producers of the film and hoped Pauline could rescue it from being dumped at the dog pound, should she have any enthusiasm for it. Since I had grown up near Baltimore, conversant with its local customs and dialect, Pauline figured I'd be interested in the film and could serve as tour guide. The movie was, of course, *Diner,* directed by Barry Levinson, an ensemble scrapbook in which the memories seemed slightly blackened at the edges, vignetted by the passage of time. The movie seemed weirdly ajar at first, with a car accident staged as a prank that made Pauline wonder aloud where this thing was

heading, but when the male buddies took up their familiar posi-
tions in the diner booth and began razzing each other, exchanging
insults and riffing like a handful of young comics after hours, Steve
Guttenberg and Daniel Stern sparring as if they were going to be
doing this for the rest of their lives until they ended up on parallel
cabana chairs in Miami Beach, Pauline was helplessly laughing, and
in thrall. "What's that they're pouring on the French fries?" she
asked as the camera panned the diner counter. "Gravy." "They put
gravy on French fries?" "Oh, yeah, beef gravy. Though chicken gravy
is also an option." The classic diner that I had gone to as a teenager at the corner on Route 40 (banally replaced by a McDonald's)
served gravy over fries, and I just assumed growing up that it was
the national custom. I filled Pauline in on the supreme importance
of every particular regarding the Baltimore Colts—who Gino was
(Gino Marchetti), and what made the play-off game with the Giants
so epochal—and the mythic tackiness of the Strip, where so many
of Maryland's young men had lost their innocence and wished
they could get it returned, along with the money they had wasted.
"Where did she come from?" Pauline wondered in amazement as
Ellen Barkin bared her first crooked smile, and Mickey Rourke, who
had shone in a small, instrumental part in *Body Heat,* proved he had
the murmurous charm and insinuation of a romantic, applying little
touches to his scenes with Barkin reminiscent of Brando trying on
Eva Marie Saint's white gloves in *On the Waterfront.* Pauline wouldn't
be the only critic to praise *Diner,* but her going to bat for it before
anyone else had seen it kept it from being bottom-drawered as just
another coming-of-age film, a nice try. Absent that screening, *Diner*
would have died an obscure death, rediscovered for its qualities only
after its rediscovery was too late to do anybody any good.

On another occasion a screening was set up for Pauline of a film
that was causing much deeper jitters for those concerned, one that
was far more unpeggable and unsynopsizable; she assembled a larger
posse for this sneak peek because she thought it would be fun. It
didn't start out fun. A severed ear in a grassy field, where the ants

seem to be having a picnic. The deceased owner of that missing ear tied to a chair, the squawk of his suddenly come-alive walkie-talkie making everyone jump in the screening room. A ritualized sado-mazzy episode witnessed through the bright crack of a closet door. Given how pre-chewed every movie is now, with scripts leaked to the Internet and bootleg footage popping up on popular sites, enabling bloggers and tweeters to condemn a film as DOA even before baptism, it's difficult to convey the dread, drawing-in power of a film about which you know nothing in advance, which belongs to no genre (though it would inseminate its own genre), where you have no idea where the next scene is going because you have no idea what's yet to unravel in the scene still playing. To be a *Blue Velvet* virgin was to have your consciousness porously flooded with invasive forces that subsequent audiences were slightly spared, having read the reviews and having had the violet nightscape prepared for their arrival. We were unprepared, which elated those who loved the film and pummeled those who were less intoxicated, me being in the latter camp, the sight of a naked, bruised Isabella Rossellini staggering across the lawn crossing a line into exploitation, as if she were meat that had climbed off the hook. But unlike at *1900*, I questioned my own squeamishness more here, and shared the transporting moment of Roy Orbison on the soundtrack, his skying lamentations part of the soundtrack of my youth, a portal into a higher plane. Pauline's response was pure elation spiked with relief and vindication, since she had been instrumental in David Lynch's getting hired as director of *The Elephant Man*, perhaps the most tender exploration of Otherness, of the spark of divinity embedded in even the most deformed, ever achieved on film. It was a freak show that panned up to the firmament, at the forgiving stars, which may have been more than reviewers and audiences expected, given their grudging responses. After the garish disarray of *Dune*, which I saw with Pauline and of which I remember mostly giant worms and warts, *Blue Velvet* proved that Lynch hadn't lost his idiosyncratic eye and nerve. Once we were out on the sidewalk, reacquainting ourselves with reality after being held lidded inside the warped glass of Lynch's strawberry preserve jar, Pauline said, "It might make a wonderful date movie. I wonder what was in Dennis Hopper's inhaler."

"Insecticide," said Veronica Geng, a *New Yorker* humorist and editor who was scarily, sexily talented and thinky, an electrical storm waiting to happen.

We repaired to wherever we repaired, and afterward, back at her hotel room, Pauline let the film's publicist know how much she loved the film. Later the phone rang. It was the publicist reporting that she had told Lynch of Pauline's reaction and Lynch had said, like Red Skelton signing off on his variety show, "God bless."

Instant feedback didn't always produce abundant thanks. I remember sitting with Pauline through *The Savage Is Loose,* a Robinson Crusoe tale of primitive survival with an incest angle that was directed by George C. Scott, who shared campfire duties with his real-life wife, Trish Van Devere, whose name reminded me of silk slippers skipping down the foyer and whose demure beauty and dimples seemed designed for ingenue comedy. Unfortunately for her, us, and anyone else watching, Lubitsch humor had no place in this Darwinian allegory that was like *Gilligan's Island* goes *Lord of the Flies;* Scott suffered, Van Devere suffered, we all suffered, the movie a loud, grueling lecture-demo where each apprehension you had about the plot and characters was fulfilled on schedule with a thud. Afterward, we were worn-out, eager for the solace of something poured into a glass over ice, when a publicist approached Pauline before we reached the hallway to the elevator. It was a violation of protocol to waylay Pauline or any reviewer immediately after a screening to pry out a response, but the young woman obviously had her instructions.

"Miss Kael, Mr. Scott is eager to know what you thought of the picture. Is there anything I can tell him?"

"Tell him to bury it," Pauline said without hesitation or glint of hostility, the bell-like chime of her voice more damaging than any wrecking ball.

The publicist smiled, pricklings of panic at the corners of her eyes, as if her mind were checking to make sure she had heard right. One did not envy her task. It would not be fun playing messenger and telling General Patton that he was being advised to cut his losses and dig an unmarked grave. But Scott had invested too much blood, guts, sweat, and tears (especially sweat) in this personal statement to submit meekly to such drastic counsel. Instead of burying the film, he propped up the corpse and kept it up for public viewing. He rented a movie theater on East Fifty-eighth Street that showed *The Savage Is Loose* for months, an expensive gesture of defiance that failed to germinate a cult but may have salved his ego, who knows. I would sometimes walk by and see the ticket taker staring out into the street, there being no tickets to take, the box office an Edward Hopper exhibition of marooned human mannequins.

After a screening we would often decamp to a restaurant where informality, elbow room, and a tolerable decibel level made animated conversation possible.

"Let's go for a drink, like civilized people," Pauline would say.

One favorite destination was Un Deux Trois on Forty-fourth Street, where you could doodle and write on the paper tablecloths with crayons like carefree Picassos. The downside of Un Deux Trois was that it could get too loud when the theater crowd made like an anvil chorus, laying on the gusty laughter and drowning our nifty comebacks to each other as soon as they left our mouths. So it was usually to the Algonquin that we mended, which was conveniently across the street from the Royalton, where Pauline stayed when she was in town. Before its Ian Schrager–Philippe Starck minimalist makeover in 1988 (ah, those waterfall urinals), after which the staff was costumed in sleek-fitting ninja black and the dining room became the unofficial commissary for Condé Nast (with Tina Brown queen-beeing it at one of the power tables), the Royalton had a history of being a haven for *New Yorker* writers who couldn't afford rooms at the Algonquin. Robert Benchley, a founding member of the Algonquin Round Table, maintained a small suite at the Royalton. (And Pauline, as I recall, only stayed at the Algonquin when the Royalton was full.) We favored the Algonquin not for its

Round Table lore but because of the unpretentious, unobstructed open-airiness of its main room, with its islands of couches and tiny tables with bells attached to summon a waiter. Or at least that was the wishful idea. It was William Shawn, whose delicate stomach restricted him to a regular diet of warm milk and shredded wheat, who had immortally said with a sigh: "You ring and ring, but no one ever comes." So Samuel Beckett! Pauline was less orphaned, one or two of the waiters greeting her with a kindly "What can we get for you, Miss Kael?" but there were times when the button would be pressed and the bell wouldn't sound, as if the ringer had been removed. This, too, added to the existential tone. If anything, service was even more Samuel Beckett–ish in the Blue Bar, which was then a small, dark cove located to the right of the main entrance, so dark that it was difficult to see the James Thurber drawings that hung on the walls even after one's eyes adjusted to the mole light. It was a room that seemed to be designed for bourgeois adultery befitting a Cheever or John O'Hara story, and Pauline mentioned spotting a prominent literary critic nesting in the corner with a woman not his wife who later became his wife after the woman who had been his wife got wise and cut the cord. In the Blue Bar there were no table bells to ring, leaving you sitting stranded, making little hand wriggles to attract the attention of waiters who struck neoclassical poses at the bar like chipped pieces of statuary, to borrow an image from the novelist Anthony Powell. Once drinks did arrive, however, a sense of sanctuary unknotted all tensions and concerns, the outer world kept at bay.

But the Blue Bar was most suitable for only two or three conspirators at best. So let us imagine that the main room of the Algonquin has couches to spare, enough to accommodate a squad of us assembling to talk about the movie or, if the movie was hopelessly humdrum, to chat about everything else, or nearly everything. In my memory, one topic that never came up was money. The seventies were the last decade in which money with a capital *M* wasn't party to every conversation, ready to prey. Everyone apart from Pauline was renting, so real-estate prices were also a non-preoccupation. This freed up so much head space to devote to the things that mattered. In her recent memoir, *The New Yorker Theater and Other Scenes from a Life at the Movies,* Toby Talbot presents a vivid home movie in words of what Pauline was like in the early sixties, having arrived east with Gina, a collection of Tiffany lamps, and a dog named Corgy, holding forth in the living room of the Talbot household: "Pauline, at five feet, was larger than my Naugahyde sofa. *Gutsy, gusto, gumption* are words that come to mind—along with salty, unsentimental, bawdy, brash, jazzy, feisty, passionate, ecstatic, scornful." Affixed to the sofa, Pauline held forth like a bohemian intellectual trying to make herself heard over the din of Dwight Macdonald: "Pauline, with her usual bourbon in one hand, cigarette dangling in the other, took alternate sips of bourbon and puffs on her cigarette. Her arms flailed in excitement as we heatedly discussed—was it *Hiroshima Mon Amour?* As the bourbon decreased, the ash on the cigarette slowly mounted until, with one grand sweep of her arm, it *fell* on our Naugahyde sofa. Its pristine surface got marked with a *hole for life!*"

This rootin' tootin' double-shootin' Pauline, alternating from cig to sip in a torrential outpour of words, was not the Pauline alighting at the Algonquin. She had given up both cigarettes and alcohol for health reasons by the time I knew her, and conversation was now her chief outlet for release and decompression. *We* were her way of unwinding, the bull session between the leaning-back intensity of viewing a movie and the leaning-forward intensity of reviewing it.

Who makes up the revolving cast? Other reviewers, protégés of Pauline's; non-reviewers, who were friends of Pauline's. Let's say it's a winter evening, since Pauline's six-month alteration with Penelope Gilliatt annually began in autumn and ended in spring, and so we are all unbundling ourselves as we make ourselves comfortable. Although the Algonquin had a dress code, requiring jackets for gentlemen, it was laxly enforced, although there was one evening when a waiter, perhaps under heat from management, informed us—me, mostly—that our attire wouldn't do. The hotel kept jackets handy for just such embarrassing occasions, and the waiter brought out a pair of blue jackets that appeared roomy enough to fit anyone short of a sumo wrestler, the long sleeves hanging down to my knuckles.

"It's like a Jerry Lewis routine," Pauline said.

"What did you think of *The Nutty Professor?*" someone says.

Pauline: "Stella Stevens was so scrumptious in that film, you think she'd have had more of a career."

"She wasn't bad in *Cable Hogue,*" someone else says.

"No, she was quite touching. But her character was oversentimentalized, which wasn't her fault."

"You wouldn't believe how much lint there is in these pockets," I said, fishing around.

"We'll take your word for it," Pauline said.

Others brought dates to the after-screenings. Me, never. Partly because I've always operated on a "need to know" basis, preferring my personal life to be a phantom subplot rather than an open secret—a bit of a mystery, even if nothing much was going on, which was, in the early seventies, often. (Though I did tell Pauline once about a date I took to see Alfred Hitchcock's *Family Plot* who, sitting back in her seat like Gidget or Patty Duke, hissed at the movie to express her feminist displeasure. "Well, it was a truly terrible movie," Pauline said.) When something *was* going on, I wasn't interested in entering my girlfriends into competition, submitting them for inspection. Not that there were that many girlfriends to shield with my Zorro cape—I was a serial monogamist, not a compulsive pollinator. But I felt, rightly or wrongly, that introducing a serious girlfriend into Pauline's court risked a spillover that could spoil everything. It wasn't that Pauline was a scary matriarch, putting young women in their place with an ice dagger of disdain, or that the other male critics would start verbally pawing some unsuspecting cutie as if she were the bride in Peckinpah's *Ride the High Country,* in danger of being passed around to the groom's mangy brothers. But there was an air of audition whenever a new ingenue was introduced to Pauline, some of Pauline's guys seeking her approval and hoping to impress the other studs. I didn't go in for sexual shoptalk, swapping tales being a one-sided trade since I didn't divulge any particulars about anyone I was dating.

I felt myself becoming a prim prune when a film critic who aspired to the patriarchal status of Irving Howe or Moses the Lawgiver, apropos of nothing, began regaling me with how M., a former girlfriend whom I had met when they were still an item, had a pussy that was always piping hot—"she's like an oven down there," he said, "or an active volcano." That was rather more vivid than necessity required, and I had nothing to offer in response, not wanting to imagine his frankfurter being grilled and having the uneasy sense that he was nudging me to take a temperature reading myself. Another member of the fraternity, let's initial him S., was equally expansive about a woman who was one of my editors then, marveling over the milky slopes of her flesh, which was far more firm underneath than you anticipated from seeing her clothed. She had the muscles of a belly dancer, he said, and again I felt as if I were being encouraged to test the slopes myself and report back to my buddies at the lodge. Yet another offered me his girlfriend's number before he moved to Los Angeles to pursue his dream of being the next Robert Towne, screenwriter-shaman-sage-seducer extraordinaire, saying I should give her a call. "She's really into helicopter sex," he said. "That's when the woman wraps her legs around you while you're dicking and you swing her around the room." I had seen a similar scene in *Five Easy Pieces,* with Jack Nicholson giving Sally Ann Struthers the whirlybird, but I couldn't see myself calling a stranger based on so specific a recommendation. So I demurred and of course kicked myself about it later, during those 3:00 a.m.'s of the soul when you know there's a lot going on in the untamed night and you're not doing any of it.

Some reviewers traded off girlfriends, or the young women in contention themselves decided to switch partners, which in itself was not unusual—similar roster moves went on in the rock-critic world, but rock critics, surprisingly perhaps, seemed less partial to anatomical shoptalk than the film critics I knew, who were more engaged in competitive jousting while showing off for Pauline. Pauline wasn't a snob about intellect, nor did she crave yea-sayers; the young women she enjoyed were those who were pretty, sparkly, animated, pixieish—H.'s new girl is "darling," she would say, or R.'s new girl was "such a doll." But the dolls and darlings didn't stick around long, replaced by other passing lights until the fella had acquired himself a serious girlfriend, which didn't preclude bringing other new faces to screenings, a turnover that entertained Pauline because she liked new faces and seemed to get a spectatorish kick out of the rakish complications. Also because the Serious Girlfriend often became a serious drag, excess cargo, especially if matrimony ensued.

It wasn't as if Pauline disapproved of every girlfriend and spouse. She was keen on Susan Cahill, the wife of Tom Cahill, who would go on to best-selling success with *How the Irish Saved Civilization*, and championed Susan's Catholic schoolgirl novel, *Earth Angels*. She got a kick out of Joan Ackermann-Blount, the then wife of the humorist and Southern prodigy Roy Blount Jr., a neighbor of hers up in the Berkshires. Joan was an athletic spitfire who went on to become a playwright (*The Batting Cage*) and TV screenwriter (the HBO sports comedy *Arli$$*), and she and Roy would later divorce. But whenever there was trouble in Tahiti, to borrow the title of Leonard Bernstein's suburban operetta, Pauline tended to fault the girlfriend/wife as the guilty albatross. "She's a *clog dancer*," Pauline said of one critic's wife, whose folk dancing she considered culturally stunted, and would refer to another protégé's wife's penchant for spangly bracelets and peasant skirts as if she were a refugee from a gypsy caravan who had gotten him under her witchy spell. In her review of *West Side Story*, she talked about the unendurable vexation of dating someone whose movie tastes you didn't share. "Sex is the great leveler, taste the great divider," she wrote. "Boobs on the make always try to impress with their high level of seriousness (wise guys, with their contempt for *all* seriousness). It's experiences like these that drive women into the arms of truckdrivers—and, as this is America, the truckdrivers all too often come up with the same kind of status-seeking tastes." Truck-driving aesthetes being in short supply in New York, it was college-educated women whom Pauline perceived rightly or wrongly to be prisses and conventional-minded cultural pretenders, more inclined to gentility. (Pauline admired the intelligence and stately poise of the film critic Molly Haskell, the wife of Andrew Sarris, but thought Molly was corseted by her fear of anything unruly and new, stuck in a potato sack race with her husband's fogy tastes.) So when Pauline spotted slippage in one or another of her single protégés, small failures of nerve or lapses of taste that took the edge off his fastball, she would some-times attribute his wayward slide to his current choice of girlfriend. "H. really seems to have lost his way since he started dating P.," she would lament, to which I replied, "I know—he could have been the next Dr. Kildare!" Which made no sense but made Pauline laugh, and for me then there was no happier calling than making Pauline laugh. (I ran into another ex-girlfriend of H.'s years later who told me, "I think Pauline cooled on me after I told her I didn't like *Yentl.* In retrospect, that was the Beginning of the End.")

Pauline had female protégées, such as the tall, husky-voiced, meticulously perceptive Lloyd Rose, who wrote for *The New Yorker* and the *Atlantic* before becoming theater critic for the *Washington Post* and then jettisoned criticism to write paperback novelizations of *Doctor Who,* and the even taller Polly Frost (epic-scaled women amused Pauline—they had a storybook quality), a California export who published humor pieces in *The New Yorker* of quirky, elliptical, scattery unclassifiability that would find no place later under Tina Brown's more utilitarian regime. But it was the male rowing team with whom she most identified. She already had a daughter, Gina—film criticism gave her a raft of sons. Male energy and bra-vado provided a hum that appealed to Pauline's iconoclasm, with her refusal to make pretty or put up with soppy sentiment; tem-peramentally, she was very much of the thirties, when wisecracking rough diamonds played by Joan Blondell, Ginger Rogers, and Jean

Harlow sized up a man or a scene with one measuring glance. (She was an immediate fan of *Sex and the City,* considering Kim Cattrall's Samantha the trophy heiress to the screwball-comedy legacy of lewd sass.) A fellow writer at the *Village Voice,* who knew Pauline in San Francisco, said she would walk into a party and size up the weight of a man's balls in the cup of her hand. I assumed she was speaking metaphorically—I really should have asked—and this was not the Pauline I knew, and my balls never met her scales of justice. But she did derive a vicarious kick from the company of men on the make, renowned studs, seducers, pickup artists, and passive-aggressive victim-magnets such as Beatty, Toback, Towne, and the aforementioned helicopter pilot (who, after moving to L.A., told me of being caught in bed with a friend's wife and sternly lectured, "D., it's bad enough, your fucking my wife, but I really resent you thinking that gives you the right to borrow my fucking bathrobe"). Toward the exploits of a number of her tomcatting protégés, she also adopted a lenient policy.

Pauline once related to me the travails of a rakish writer of our acquaintance who had contracted a sexually transmitted disease from a partner in a one-night stand. The problem was that Rakish Writer had a steady girlfriend, and when he told her about the STD, how he had gotten it, and why she needed to get herself tested, "she didn't react very well," Pauline reported with a sympathetic sigh. "She was awfully hard on him." Pauline thought the betrayed girlfriend should have been a little more understanding, at least until the test results came back. Pauline knew RW was in the wrong, but that's where her sympathies tilted, with the guy who couldn't resist a scoring opportunity. Pauline could sometimes excuse male appetites with rationales that won points for originality. Although she disapproved of the goings-on at Roman Polanski's clubhouse, based on firsthand reports from Towne (the screenwriter on *Chinatown*), she thought too much fuss was being made over the underage-sodomy incident that sent the director into exile. "It's not as if he could physically hurt those girls," Pauline said. "Have you ever seen Polanski?

He's quite tiny and slight, about the same size as those girls they're talking about. They're on an equal scale." But he's still so much older than they are, I said; he's the adult here. "Oh, I know, I know," Pauline said. "Gina doesn't agree with me either." It was clear she thought Polanski deserved clemency, a view that was shared by critics who otherwise shared few opinions with Pauline, such as Andrew Sarris. A director's prerogatives got a lot more leeway back then.

When not wishing she could tear certain relationships down the middle along the dotted line, Pauline would play matchmaker, the unlikeliest fairy godmother imaginable. She would drop ten-ton hints to pry a little interest and initiative from my direction. Of Veronica Geng, she remarked in her office one day, "Have you noticed, Veronica's got the cutest figure." I had noticed, not being insensible, but never thought of Veronica as girlfriend material because her dance card, to use an antediluvian phrase, seemed filled, and temperamentally, psychologically, aesthetically, Veronica was a quadratic equation way beyond my ability to comprehend. I got a huge charge whenever we ran into each other—Veronica was incapable of conventional responses, the crook of her smile presaging some darted observation or madcap disclosure. ("This guy I like is coming to New York this weekend—I better start doing some *leg lifts.*") But I also knew that she could click off on people who had displeased her as if they had never been born. Suddenly they de-existed. But Veronica, sprite with a bee stinger that she was, made more sense than another of Pauline's date suggestions, a lanky, tomboyish writer-editor whom we'll call Stacy. "You really should ask her out," Pauline said. "You'd make quite a pair."

"I thought she was a lesbian."

"Oh, that. So what. Aren't you up for a challenge?"

"No. Are you sure you're talking to me and not H.?"

(H. was always giving women he scarcely knew neck rubs to "loosen them up.")

"It's just that your senses of humor are so much alike," Pauline said. "Anyway, it's worth considering."

And then I found myself up in Pauline's hotel room with one of Pauline's friends, whom I'll call Madison. In the realm of pulp fiction Madison would have been known as a man-eater: slender, dark eyed, her gaze direct and appraising, long, thick brown hair—an urban Jane ready to swing from a vine and carry a man off to her bachelorette tree house, where she would ravish her prey between tidbits about the latest movies or art shows she had attended. Not the worst way to spend an evening, if you could keep up with her quick costume changes of mood. She was unique in Pauline's circle for her lightning lack of hesitation to sass Pauline or shoot down innocent bystanders until smoke poured from their fuselage and sent them plashing somewhere in the Pacific. She could be breathtakingly rude, like Lauren Bacall in the backseat of a limo, casting aspersions that carried the whap of a slap; yet she could be tremendously tactful and generous, too, returning from her travels with the perfect present, often a rare edition of a book that the recipient had mentioned in passing but Madison had entered into her case file. Her tastes and Pauline's often clashed because her taste seemed so whim-driven. "She's a snob who likes everything," someone said, but the snobbery came across as brattiness, not as the pinched anality of someone awaiting Susan Sontag's next encyclical. Her sexual forthrightness was the flip side of the pickup-artist swagger Pauline found so amusing, and here she was, seated on the edge of Pauline's bed in the Royalton, looking up at me with licky eyes, as if I were that night's barbecue special, or was that my tropical imagination? And was Pauline stage-managing this moment? I pretended innocence just this side of stark insensibility, suspecting that whatever might transpire between Madison and me that night or any other night would be broadcast to Pauline, and I simply didn't want Pauline knowing my business, not like she seemed to know that of so many others. Much as I adored her, I didn't want the godmother to have total jurisdiction.

Although the seventies had a lot more going on at groin level than the decade that followed (when whoring for fame earned its

racing stripes), it would be an error of my own emphasis to leave
the impression that Pauline's loyal band was primarily libido-driven,
a nest of *Les Liaisons Dangereuses* swingers trading "biting repartee"
without benefit of painted fans and snuffboxes, as Pauline occupied
the center of the silken web, eating the flies we brought her. The
erotics at play were less those of the flesh than those of yearning,
striving egos—an erotics directed toward recognition. The motoring force at work as we sat there in the glorified drawing room of
the Algonquin was the drive for approval and attention, Pauline's
approval and attention most of all (the larger world's acceptance an
amplification and ratification of hers), which was won and held not
by being smarty or fawning or doctrinaire but by being receptive
to whatever might be coming around the corner, willing to play
the tricky carom. She couldn't stand "stiffs," whose tastes were fully
formed, rigidified, and stuck in the petrified forest of the past, and
those of us sitting in the Algonquin were on the upswing of our
careers, just starting our scouting missions. These were the years
of encouragement. Some would stray off target, disappear into the
reeds, defect from criticism under the pressure of unfulfilled expectations and career frustrations, or simply find something more frol-
icking to do, Pauline being more ambitious for them than they were
for themselves. In a sense we all would fail Pauline because none
of us would surpass her defiant nerve, her resounding impact. But
tonight, we're modestly in character, the future only extends so far,
and Pauline is sipping tea from a cup, having brought her own tea
bag. H. is there, looking Southern courtly as his words seem to
roll down his tapered wrists, like beaded droplets. R. is there, leaning forward, avid, his date poised on her chair as if it were a lily
pad, choosing each peanut from the peanut bowl with premeditated
care. Madison presides from her corner of the sofa, giving a Tallulah
Bankhead performance. As for me, there I am, just a few years after
leaving college, sitting at the Algonquin with the greatest film critic
then or now, part of the gang, wearing jeans that probably need
washing and nursing a Coke, the only thing I ever ordered. And

Pauline—she listens, she laughs, she passes along nuggets ("I asked Peckinpah why he made —— look like such a dumb cow in ——, and he said, 'Because that's what she *is*'"), but she doesn't hold forth, she doesn't make pronouncements, she doesn't pontificate, and she doesn't traffic in absolutes, like Ayn Rand holding an indoctrination séance. "Let's order a last round, like civilized people," she says, and rings the bell.

A waiter miraculously materializes, as if emerging from the carpet.

It gets late, eleven thirtyish, the hotel guests have levitated to their rooms, only a few rendezvousing couples occupy the corner tables, and Pauline has galleys to tackle the next day. She rings for a waiter, the bill is brought, and Pauline pays the tab. Pauline always paid the tab, though some chipped in. A couple of us accompany her across the street to the steps of the Royalton, where we say our good-byes. The air rings with cold. "I have a screening tomorrow night for *The Last Tycoon,* so let me know if you're up for it. It's hard to imagine Elia Kazan and Fitzgerald being a good match, but you never know."

And with that, a wave as if given to a departing train, and up into the marble lobby of the Royalton she goes.

PART III:

Punk

It was like seeing my own ghost, the Spirit of Punk Past.

I was home, dawdling across the cable-TV dial, when I was arrested by the sight of a host of once-familiar faces, a few of them sporting incongruous New Year's Eve hats and leis. Incongruous, not because it wasn't New Year's Eve, but because of the lean, lunar faces jutting under the hats. These were not faces normally associated with holiday mirth. Fervent intent was usually more like it, furry heads and furrowed brows. I identified the bleached-out footage as being shot along the bar at CBGB's, some of the faces belonging to Tom Verlaine (sitting on an actual bar stool, like a normal person), Richard Hell, Richard Lloyd, Billy Ficca, John Cale, Deborah Harry, Chris Frantz, Tina Weymouth, the journalist Lisa Robinson, and Lenny Kaye. And then, a flash of light and gone, there I was: me—the me I once was, one of the milling crowd, part of the scene. Chatting with someone at the only place where my memories are three-dimensional, a hologram in my head that still feels like a crummy home movie. The film—run on the Independent Film Channel—was Amos Poe and Ivan Kral's *Blank Generation,* a music documentary shot mostly in the loose bowels of the Bowery, its title taken from a song by the sun-glassed poet, mouth-grimacing virtuoso, and inadvertent style setter Richard Hell, whose torn T-shirt bearing the inviting plea "Please Kill Me" proved to be one of the period's most enduring fashion statements, along with laced-tight bondage gear tricked out as smart evening wear. Filmed in black and white with no live-synced sound (the songs draped over the images like a scratchy, patchy carpet), *Blank Generation* jerked along like a home movie even back then and today looks like an archaeological find, a kinescope discovered in a salvage yard recording the last known sightings from that prelapsarian age when un-trust-funded artists still coyoted the streets and, be it ever so humble, every hovel felt like home. I had forgotten I was in *Blank Generation,* however fleetingly, and seeing myself again as if for the first time didn't make me mourn Lost Youth, that not being my preferred form of masochism; it made me smile. It was like a college yearbook come alive. Here were my fellow classmates, the old alma mater in its midnight glory.

Arabian swelter, and with the air-conditioning broken, CBGB resembled some abattoir of a kitchen in which a bucket of ice is placed in front of a fan to cool the room off. To no avail, of course, and the heat had perspiration glissading down the curve of one's back, yeah, and the cruel heat also burned away any sense of glamour. After all, CBGB's Bowery and Bleecker location is not the garden spot of lower Manhattan, and the bar itself is an uneasy oasis. On the left, where the couples are, tables; on the right, where the stragglers, drinkers, and love-seekers are, a long bar; between the two, a high double-backed ladder which, when the room is really crowded, offers the best view. If your bladder sends a distress signal, write home to your mother, for you must make a perilous journey down the aisle between seating area and bar, not knocking over any mike stands as you slide by the tiny stage, squeeze through the pile of amplifiers, duck the elbow thrust of a pool player leaning over to make a shot . . . and then you end up in an illustrated bathroom that looks like a page that didn't make [Norman Mailer's] *The Faith of Graffiti.*

—from my *Village Voice* piece "A Conservative Impulse in the New Rock Underground" (August 18, 1975)

My admission into the orphanage began as an assignment like any other, a pop-in/write-up of eight hundred words. The year before, the *Voice* sent me to review some poet-chick fronting a drummer-less rock band, a setup I pictured as some macrobiotic Beat type with bird's-nest hair declaiming her lyrics from loose-leaf pages while a lot of noisy noodling went on in the background. How I drew this mental sketch on the basis of near-zero actual familiarity I can't recall, although I did see the poet Anne Waldman read once in the East Village, standing on one leg like a stork as her voice ascended into incantation. What I can recall is that there was some pro and con among those with actual working knowledge of the downtown scene as to whether this rock-poetess was a true original talent, a magpie on the make, or something betwixt, a combination of thin-lipped calculation and burning vocation, like Bob Dylan after he had outgrown his Woody Guthrie britches and began playing his personas like a cardsharp. Shortly after entering below the awning of a bar and club with an initialed name, a place I'd never been to on a street that still looked like a Robert Frank photograph of raw, spilling night, I gingerly installed myself for a bar-stool view of the stage, which was stationed left of the aisle and barely large enough for a barbershop quartet. The atmosphere was most unmagical, worthy of a cheap paperback set on skid row. It had a palpable texture, this prosy ambience, a bit of World War I trench-warfare leftover aroma of dung, urine, and damp carcass, but it was the seventies and not a time to be picky. Then I saw this visage, this vision, shark-finning the length of the bar, and I knew this had to be Her. A scarf was knotted around her throat, and her hair was raven; her chin cocked directly at her destination point, doorward.

Patti—one of those performers whose first name alone was enough to spell it all—projected star quality, had willed it into being and possession with a bite of hauteur. What Madonna would master and Lady Gaga after her would embellish into jeweled armor, Patti Smith flashed like a blade: the crowned awareness that to become a true star is to act like a star from the moment of self-conception and let the world play catch-up. Even when chewing gum, she seemed to be chewing it for the ages. Patti looked formidable and imperious until she grinned, the sort of equine grin Pauline Kael treasured in

Lily Tomlin but goofier, like a latch that allowed her whole body to hang loose.

That grin was retracted before Patti's first set under a game face of gunslinger intent as she took the stage and wagged around, wiping her nose now and then with a sawing finger, while her musicians tuned up as best they were able. Her lead guitarist, who shared Patti's sapling thinness, was Lenny Kaye, he of the Yeshiva-student spectacles, whose name was better known to me than Patti's. I had been reading his articles for years in *Hit Parader, Creem,* and *Rolling Stone* (where he reviewed *Exile on Main Street*), and every rock cultist had a copy of *Nuggets,* his influential, indispensable double-album compilation of psychedelic hits and rarities, many of which sounded like garbled satellite transmissions from the weird beyond. On bass was Ivan Kral, on piano the nimbus-curled Richard "DNV" Sohl, one of those fallen angels with more room to fall. (He would die of a heart attack at the age of thirty-seven.) As soon as the band revved its engines, it was clear that this wouldn't be bop prosody set to a bongo beat; the opening number, the Velvet Underground's "We're Gonna Have a Real Good Time Together," came out of the corner punching, Patti hitting the word "shoot" in the Harlem heroin stanza—"Everyone shoot shoot shoot"—with a right-left combination as if the mike stand doubled as a sparring bag. (Patti's brand of calisthenics would find its musical anthem in "Pumping.") What other songs were in that first set? "Space Monkey," to be sure, "The Hunter Gets Captured by the Game" (a Smokey Robinson cover in which Patti substituted "junta" for "hunter"), her tender tribute to her sister, "Kimberly" (how many songs then, before, and now have been dedicated to sisters?), "Redondo Beach" ("where women love other women"—a song and a descriptive phrase that led many young women of lesbian or bi inclination to believe Patti belonged to their sorority), "Piss Factory" (her first single, a prole lament and lyrical gesture of defiance), "Birdland," and the expansive version of "Gloria" that seemed to camera-pan across the wide-screen horizon on galloping hooves. (It would provide the climactic set piece to her *Horses* album.) The band wasn't as tight and motoring as it would become (especially after Jay Dee Daugherty joined on drums), but it also wasn't the Fugs futzing around, and Patti already had her stage persona pencil-sharpened into a self-conscious, couldn't-care-less wild child, playing with her zipper like a teenage boy with a horny itch, pistoning her hips, hocking an amoeba blob of spit between songs, scratching her breast as if addressing a stray thought, and, during the incantatory highs, spreading her fingers like a preacher woman summoning the spirits from the Père Lachaise graveyard where Jim Morrison and Oscar Wilde were buried to rise and reclaim their former glory. It was one of those nights when the invisible partitions between you and the performance dissolve and you realize, This is something, even if you don't know what that "something" is yet. There's a knock at the door that you have to answer.

One thing I learned from Pauline was that when something hits you that high and hard, you have to be able to travel wherever the point of impact takes you and be willing to go to the wall with your enthusiasm and over it if need be, even if you look foolish or "carried away," because your first shot at writing about it may be the only chance to make people care. It's better to be thumpingly wrong than a muffled drum with a measured beat. Now, Patti didn't need me championing her in the *Voice*—it wasn't a rescue operation, like Pauline going to bat for *Bonnie and Clyde* after Bosley Crowther clubbed it in the *New York Times;* Patti's breakout probably would have been able to hop from pony to pony no matter who supplied the initial press boost—but I needed to feel that I could write about something new and still forming that mattered, something that I could help *make* matter. Readers and fellow writers get a mean rise out of demolition work of overblown popularities or grandiose follies, but it's the trail-scout discoveries that a critic cracks into daylight that make the difference after all the balloons have popped, whether it's Edmund Wilson's championing of his brother Princetonian F. Scott

Fitzgerald or Randall Jarrell's rescuing Robert Frost from the hayloft
of platitudes and Yankee pith to which his poetry had been consigned; a critic remembered only for his damnings, however brilliant
and left bleeding his victims, has failed, leaving behind little more
than a patch of crabgrass with a few Easter eggs scattered around.

. So, leaning on the throttle to hurry up the future, I reviewed
Patti's performance in the *Voice* (accompanied by a photo of what
looked like Patti in a white Communion dress) with all flags flying:

> She's a knockout performer: funny, spooky, a true off-the-
> wall original. Like the character in Dickens, she do the police
> in different voices. One moment she's telling an agreeably
> dopey joke about kangaroos (". . . and Momma Kangaroo
> looked down and exclaimed, 'Oh, my pocket's been picked!'")
> and in the next she's bopping into the scatological scat of "Piss
> Factory."
>
> Because of her notorious poetry readings, her reputation
> is largely as a crazy-as-birds stage speaker, but it's clear she's
> going to be an extraordinary rock singer, maybe even a great
> one. Not that her voice has richness or range—there might
> be 200 female rockers with better voices—no, Patti possesses
> a greater gift: a genius for phrasing. She's a poet of steely
> rhythms—her work *demands* to be read aloud—so language is
> her narcotic, her lover, her mustang.
>
> And her body is as eloquent as her voice. Scrawny and angu-
> lar in repose, it becomes supple and expressive when the music
> sways. Dressed in black jeans, black coat, and loose T-shirt,
> she dances with a smooth sassiness, her boyish hips tenderly
> pistoning, her bamboo-thin arms punctuating the air for
> emphasis. The performing area at CBGB is as tiny as a bath-
> room tile so it'll be interesting to see her hit her stride on a
> larger stage.
>
> . . . Rock fans are going to be enraptured making all the
> allusive connections in her work; one of the best songs—

which begins with the entrance of the four horsemen of the Apocalypse and ends with a burial in the horse latitudes—is a surreal fusion of rock mythos and horse/heroin imagery.

So would it be too awful to say that Fame is her steed if Patti Smith chooses to mount? Well, the horse might be the perfect emblem for her career. "I ride the stallion thru the dust storm" is the way she begins a poem entitled "Mustang." "Get off your mustang, Sally, is what the women told her at the Piss Factory." But Patti didn't listen, Patti said screw it, and skinny schizzy Patti is on her way to becoming the wild mustang of American rock.

Okay, true, granted, I slapped a bit of mustard on that fastball, especially in the last sentence ("schizzy" was a pure Pauline-ism). But it was the last great hurrah period of rock-crit tell-it-from-the-mountain epiphanies, and few of us were immune. Only a year earlier a pop music critic high on the totem pole named Jon Landau had pronounced, "I saw rock & roll future and its name is Bruce Springsteen" (Arise, ye faithful!), and when Springsteen (with Landau now serving as his record producer and horse whisperer) went on to make the covers of *Time* and *Newsweek* the same week, an unprecedented coup, I muttered to myself at the newsstand: "I have seen the future of rock, and now we're stuck with him." It wasn't that I disliked Springsteen—how could you dislike a scrappy car mechanic of a singer-songwriter-showman so driven, enthusiastic, passionate, embracing, and earnest? It'd be like ragging on Thanksgiving. But it was his very earnestness, his eager-to-serve sincerity, that dulled the tips of my nerves even when I was riveted by one of his legendary performances at the Bottom Line in 1975, the stint that has lived in the annals of Bruciana. I remember checking myself during one of his big rousers with the question, "This is incredibly exciting, so why am I not excited?" It just seemed too smoothly assembled from every rock fan's dream kit of salvation. Eight hundred years later, he's still never awakened me, his husky voice intoning like something chiseled on Mount Rushmore now, an august chunk of Americana.

When my review hit the pages of the *Voice*, Patti was happy, the band was happy, her manager, Jane Friedman, was happy, CBGB's was happy, I was happy, everybody was happy, and it was nice not feeling like the bad guy in print for a change. Normally, I would have pocketed that happy outcome and moved on to the next target spot, but I kept returning to CBGB's to catch Patti's sets, sometimes two a night, chatting with Patti and Lenny, the neon beer signs lined above the bar, the click of pool balls, and the smell of wood, beer, urine, sweat, mop water, and time ill spent reminding me oddly, fondly, of the American Legion hall where my parents did so much of their drinking while I fed the pinball machine. A former Hells Angels hangout, CBGB's still hosted the occasional Angel or three. Word was that the owner, Hilly Kristal, and the Angels had an arrangement in which they could drink for free and in return wouldn't kill any of us, which seems fair and reasonable. Their arrivals and departures were still intimidating, in particular the entrance of one glowering, fur-bearing boulder who wore his leather vest over a wide-load body that spurned bathwater and soaping those hard-to-reach places as intrusions of civilization. You could smell him coming and you could smell him going, his pungency notable even in this tramp steamer: he had reached the stage when only a fire hose on full blast would help. "Do you think he knows how bad he smells?" one regular asked, to which another dryly replied, "I dunno, you could always go ask him." Which of course would have resulted in a horizontal ride to the emergency room. The Angels were not to be trifled with, theirs was not a sporting manner. One of the scariest early moments I had in New York was when I was sharing a crosstown taxi with a former teacher of mine from Edgewood High who had temporarily moved to Manhattan to do graduate work at New York University's theater department. The cab stopped mid-block in the East Village at a red light. "Jesus, look at that fat slob," my teacher said. It was a hot summer evening, the cab windows were rolled down, voices carried, and the fat slob in question resting on his gut was a Hells Angel squatting on the steps of the Angels' clubhouse on East Third Street, the same clubhouse where a woman had been thrown to her death from the rooftop by one of the members. It was unclear whether the Angel on the steps had caught the exact phrasing of the exclamation from my teacher, but his head turned in our direction and his eyes twitched, the shift of his buttocks indicating he was about to rise to his feet. The light was still red, two or three cars were in front of us, and then it turned blessedly green, the cabdriver easing forward so that it wouldn't seem he was hurrying guiltily away. "Sorry," my former teacher said, his voice overlapping with the driver's saying, "Man, don't ever do anything like that again."

If nothing else, the seventies in New York taught me situational awareness, a vital attribute for every slow-moving mammal prone to daydreaming. Like so many who came to see Patti, I would sometimes glide backward to the street when the opening band began tormenting their guitars after tuning up on each other's nerves for five or ten minutes. It wasn't like cooling your heels out on the piazza. Bottles would be dropped from the Palace Hotel men's shelter above CBGB's, their green and clear glass smashing on the sidewalk, some of them exploding with pee, the contents recycled from the beer or Thunderbird that the bottles formerly contained. It wasn't a nightly occurrence, but it happened often enough to keep you limber. Scraggly panhandlers who didn't bother to work up an inventive line of patter to go with their outstretched palms would pester anyone stationary, even though CBGB's customers themselves were the very portrait of slim pickings and linty pockets. Abuse was shouted from passing cars, on general principle, not for anything in particular, and the occasional curiosity-seeker or casual-date couple would serenade by, open the front door for a peek, and get a faceful of inchoate racket blasting from the stage—all the deterrence they needed to keep moving to find a different lovebird destination, assuming they weren't eaten by cannibals before they got to Canal Street.

One night after Patti finished her first set, she stopped to say hi at the bar and leaned in with a pointed suggestion: "James"—she always called me "James"—"you should stick around for these guys. They're really amazing, you've got to see them up close."

It wasn't too much to ask, given that it was said to be two of the members of Television, Richard Lloyd and Tom Verlaine, who had convinced Hilly Kristal to book them there on otherwise empty Sunday nights, a band that hardly conformed to Hilly's original concept as musical host, the full initialed name of the club being CBGB & OMFUG: "Country Bluegrass Blues & Other Music for Uplifting Gourmandizers," a mirthful mouthful. Inside and out, CBGB's looked like a hick joint, a misplaced honky-tonk, an impression fortified by Hilly's flannel shirts. So, in retrospect, Television's guitar duo were the Romulus and Remus of American punk. It didn't occur to me until then that my skipping the band's set after the first song or two might have been noted as a shade insulting, given that I had rapturized Patti and looked as if I were giving her regular openers the brush-off. It wasn't that I was a significant presence in the room but that the funky birth canal of CBGB's was so tubular it didn't take binocular vision to spot a regular beating an exit. Patti's request was also an allusion to the fact that I usually stationed myself at the back. This was a pattern that began in grade school, when we were seated alphabetically and I nearly always ended up against the back wall, helping forge an identity of being the classic wise guy in the last row, the classroom's color commentator. And it continued with my comradeship with Pauline, who, as mentioned before, favored the last row of the screening room, the film projector's beam raying directly above our heads. But this hanging-back business was more than precedence and habit. It betrayed my reluctance, my fear of getting too close to anybody or anything; my preference for maintaining detachment, distance, for avoiding involvement and allowing myself a quick escape route from wherever I found myself. I wanted to take everything in, from safe afar, through a panoramic lens. But that night I did as Patti beckoned and positioned myself closer to the stage for Television's second set.

It took them forever to tune up, but then it always took them forever to tune up, bent over their guitars like car mechanics over a tricky transmission. Then Verlaine, relatively satisfied, would nod, their name would be announced to scattered applause, the lights would come up, and Tom would open with a little joke. It was always the same little joke, the same lame little icebreaker. It was about asking a flower seller on the street about buying some flowers for his sweetie and the seller giving him one rude brush-off after another before squawking: "Listen, pal, stop bothering me—can'cha see I'm trying to sell these flowers?" It was not a joke that got funnier in the retelling, and the fondness Verlaine held for it would always be inexplicable, like so much else about him. He was and would remain an unbreakable code. After the punch line died a small, swift death came the siren-whine of guitar as Television began "Fire Engine," a cover of a 13th Floor Elevators song whose cover-appeal was also elusive, so Tinkertoy was its construction, no matter how gussied up the guitar attack. Up close was better than the back, but I still wasn't getting the gnostic gospel message. But at some point in the set, perhaps it was "Venus de Milo," perhaps it was the gorgeous "Judy" (which the band never recorded, a sin, a crime, though it has surfaced on bootlegs, like a plaintive cry retrieved from the ruins of Atlantis), Verlaine lifted his face to the light, eyelids closed, and I could see that he was beautiful, the light striking his Antonin Artaud cheekbones like a close-up in *The Passion of Joan of Arc*. (One of Patti's favorites, and I could see now how Verlaine was Artaud to her Falconetti, not a comparison that rose naturally from seeing them hold hands like sweethearts between sets at the rear of CBGB's.) The imploring death rattle that was his normal singing voice didn't matter, because it was meant to sound constricted, his eyelids fluttering like exaggerated REM sleep or pained rapture. As the songs became longer and the virtuoso soloing of Verlaine and Richard Lloyd wove intricately, passionately upward in a double helix without spiraling off course and descending into doodling, as drummer Billy Ficca kept jazzy order in the backseat (instead of pounding rhythm like a heavy-metal humpster), I felt a religious conversion coming on without quite being sold, despite the bravura finish (the first of many bravura finishes) of "Marquee Moon," which planted the summit flag on the set. Because although there was dynamic dissonance to Television's performing and the discordant jabs that testified to the influence of free-form improvisationalists such as Albert Ayler and John Coltrane, two of Verlaine's favorites, there was also an underlayer of discombobulation.

Or, rather, a side pocket.

Flanked on Verlaine's right was Television's bassist, Richard Hell. Hell was not only the band's bass thumper but also a singer and songwriter and a longtime friend of Verlaine's, the Paul McCartney to his John Lennon, ideally. (Verlaine once told me that one of the best things about the Beatles was the way they could shout out harmonies and make them seem intimate.) They had met at boarding school in Delaware, a couple of matching misfits named Tom Miller and Richard Meyers who hopped the fence to hitchhike to Florida together, only to be stopped in Alabama, not the most welcoming place for strangers, and sent packing home. But the two of them had gotten a gulp of the fugitive kick of busting out of the regiment and didn't intend to take their boring slot in the employment line. New York was where they had to be, the cockroaches welcoming them with waving antennae. They eventually adopted alter egos together, shedding their everyday humdrum names for legendary French *poète maudit* personas—Verlaine deriving from Paul Verlaine and Hell from Arthur Rimbaud's *Season in Hell*—dissolving their former identities by dropping acid together to invite visions and synesthesia, knocking down the partition walls of selfhood. They also gender-bender-blended, adopting a mutual drag persona in print, that of the floozy poet Theresa Stern, a Puerto Rican prostitute working the streets of Hoboken and the author of *Wanna Go Out?* ("Wanna go out?" was what hookers asked in the seventies of any man who caught their eye, the predecessor to the later invitation "Wanna party?") The author's photo for Theresa Stern was a composite shot of Verlaine and Hell wearing wigs—a blurred sister persona. (Though it would be Hell who kept up the Stern impersonation solo in print, giving interviews under her name.) It was seeing the drag-happy New York Dolls at the Mercer Arts Center that clicked Hell into realizing there was much more sexy fun to be had playing rock than pecking at the typewriter keys like a trained chicken.

Photographs of the test-run incarnation of Television called the Neon Boys reveal the pouty preening of so many rockers dabbling then in David Bowie's and the New York Dolls' makeup kits, going for that androgynous, washed-ashore, fuck-me-I'm-pretty look. But by the time Television was double billing with Patti, Verlaine had adopted the nondescript tee or the thrift-shop bargain shirt that actually buttoned for those special non-festive occasions, dissolving the barrier between street clothes and stage wear and spurning the theatricality of glitter and glam droogies like the Dolls and their imitators. It was a taste choice, Verlaine being a master of high-visibility low profitability, but it also reflected a recoil from the train-wreck legacy of the Dolls, whose members buckled from too many drugs and reeled off the road, regrouping and forging ahead but never again with the runaway splendor of their legendary perfor-mances at Mercer Arts Center, where the lead singer, David Johan-sen, and the guitarist Johnny Thunders augured to be the Mick Jagger and Keith Richards of the East Village cockroach kingdom. (As was remarked at the time, David had the lips and Thunders the licks.) The commercial flop of the Dolls and their inability to break out beyond their cult following (though their influence in England was incalculable, the Smiths' Morrissey being their number one pin-ing fan), coupled with their casualty toll and reliable undepend-ability, made it that much harder for newer New York bands to get signed. I mentioned this once to Bob Christgau, saying that some of the younger rockers felt the Dolls had blown it for those coming up after them, to which Bob shot back, "Well, if that's how they feel, fuck 'em." He wasn't going to coddle a bunch of ingrates.

Hell's look was his own—like Edie Beale, he inventively made do with whatever was near at hand and served his whims—but his Cannes-starlet bare-shoulder T-shirts and sunglasses and color palette clashed with Television's first-thing-picked-off-the-floor anti-fashion indifference, its muted choice of cuts and fabrics, which sent a different message statement: it's the music that counts. Not visual flash and certainly not pose-flexing showmanship, which Hell also had on tap. Unlike the archetypal rock bassist forged in the medieval ironworks, Hell didn't hold his sentry position as the unmovable pillar in a cross-fire hurricane, bolted to the bass and rooted to the floor in the classic stoic stance of the Stones' Bill Wyman and The Who's John Entwistle. He got buggy onstage with a popcorn-popping battery of head-wagging, moue-making, and hair-raking, with a few Pete Townshend jumps thrown in that had rather less liftoff than Townshend's, but then Pete was the more practiced catapulter. Perhaps Hell made a minor spectacle of himself in self-defense to distract from his bass playing, which fell a bit below minimum requirements even by garage-band standards. "Close enough for rock" went the jokey catchphrase, but Hell wasn't close enough to get close enough for rock, often seeming to lose his place on the bass. What he brought to the stage was louche charisma and the authorship of the future punk anthems "Blank Generation" ("I belong to the blank generation and/I can take it or leave it each time") and "Love Comes in Spurts." But even these assertive numbers were rudimentary pumpers compared with the topographies Television was intent on exploring; friendship or no friendship, it never would have worked out. There was room for only one vision in Television, Verlaine's. Hell would soon vacate the crew, his corner filled by Fred Smith, who defected from Blondie and conformed to the Wyman-Entwistle model of unassuming sentinel safeguarding the beat. Hot-chick interest peeled considerably after Hell left the band, but he wouldn't be gone from the CBGB's stage for long, returning with a sound that went every which way, like bullets careening off steel drums with a slow-death heartbeat in the background of something big about to keel over.

Patti was the first draw at CBGB's and the first to break out of

the pack. I interviewed her in her studio apartment a block up from
St. Marks Place, which looked as if it had been tossed by narcs given
a bad tip on a drug stash and not bothering to tidy up afterward.
It was hot, as I recall: no air-conditioning, Patti tugging on a bra
strap that seemed to be chafing. In the sink a Lone Ranger mask
floated in a glass of water. Before we went up to the studio, I met
Patti at a coffee place in the East Village where, prominently on
the table, was a brick-heavy copy of a dictionary of symbolism. I
got the impression that she used it to interpret the symbols in her
own lyrics, explore the Jungian range of their profundity, and when
I mentioned this reference book being displayed for my benefit to
someone later, he found it posey and pretentious. I found it the
opposite. A truly pretentious artist would have disavowed any schol-
arly knowledge or curiosity about the symbols in his or her work,
regarding them as mysterious effusions from the etheric realm that
it was up to each listener to unriddle—oh, don't ask me to explain,
it's up to you to explore the ambiguities while leaving my precious
artistic integrity intact. "We murder to dissect," and all that. Patti
didn't treat her creative apparatus as a tamperproof black box with
a secret password. Patti was an unabashed autodidact. That was one
of the most admirable things about her. In a decade with so much
fatalistic derision stocking the pantry, her hero worship was unfash-
ionably uncool, her faith in the pantheon unshaken. Our idols are
our instructors, and revelations without knowledge are just pieces of
dreams with no assembly kit. William Blake, William Burroughs,
Allen Ginsberg, Rimbaud, Edie Sedgwick, Isabelle Eberhardt (who
dressed as a boy and adventured in Arab lands, her memoir one of
Patti's touchstones), her friend Robert Mapplethorpe, Robert Bresson, Carl Dreyer, they constituted the geometric points of the con-
stellation she aspired to join. I was present when one of her cryptic
idols paid a call, and I wrote it up for the *Voice* as if witness to a
superpower summit:

A copy of *Witt* was slid across the table to Patti Smith.
"Would you sign this for me, please?" "Sure," said Patti, "what's

your first name?" He told her. "Like in New Jersey?" Patti asked, and he said no—with a z. "Well, I'll draw you a map of Jersey," and so on the inside page Patti scratched its intestinal boundaries, in the middle labeled it Neo Jersey, signed her name, and passed the copy of *Witt* back to Jerzy Kosinski.

The night before, after the second set at the Other End, the greenroom door opened and the remark hanging in the air was Bob Dylan asking a member of Patti's band, "You've never been to New Jersey?" So, all hail Jersey. And in honor of Dylan's own flair for geographical salutation ("So long New York, hello East Orange"), all hail the Rock and Roll Republic of New York. With the Rolling Stones holding out at Madison Square Garden, Patti Smith and her band at the Other End, and Bob Dylan making visitations to both events, New York was once again the world's Rock and Roll Republic.

Patti Smith had a special Rimbaud-emblematized statement printed up in honor of Stones week, and when her band went into its version of "Time Is on My Side" (yes it is), she unbuttoned her blouse to reveal a Keith Richards T-shirt beneath. On the opening night she was tearing into each song and even those somewhat used to her galloping id were puzzled by lines like, "You gotta lotta nerve sayin' you won't be *my* parking meter." Unknown to many in the audience, parked in the back of the room, his meter running a little quick, was the legendary Bobby D. himself. Dylan, despite his wary, quintessential cool, was giving the already highly charged room an extra layer of electricity and Patti, intoxicated by the atmosphere, rocked with stallion abandon. She was positively *playing* to Dylan, like Keith Carradine played to Lily Tomlin in the club scene from *Nashville.* But Dylan is an expert at gamesmanship, and he sat there, crossing and uncrossing his legs, playing back.

Afterwards, Dylan went backstage to introduce himself to Patti. He looked healthy, modestly relaxed (though his eyes never stopped burning with cool-blue fire), of unimposing physicality, yet the corporeal Dylan can never be separated from the mythic Dylan, and it's that *other* Dylan—the brooding, volatile, poet-star of *Don't Look Back*—who heightens or destroys the mood of a room with the tiniest of gestures. So despite Dylan's casual graciousness, everyone was excitedly unsettled.

And there was a sexual excitement in the room as well. Bob Dylan, the verdict was unanimous, is an intensely sexual provocateur—"he really got me below the belt," one of the women in the room said later. Understand, Dylan wasn't egregiously coming on—he didn't have to. For the sharp-pencil, slightly petulant vocals on *Blood on the Tracks* hardly prepared one for the warm, soft-bed tone of his speaking voice: the message driven home with that—Dylan offhand is still Dylan compelling. So with just small talk he had us all subdued, even Patti, though when the photographers' popping flashbulbs began, she laughingly pushed him aside, saying, "Fuck you, then take *my* picture, boys." Dylan smiled and swayed away.

The party soon broke up—Dylan had given his encouragement to Patti, the rest of us had a glimpse from some future version of *Don't Look Back* (but with a different star)—and the speculation about Dylan's visit commenced. What did his casual benediction signify?

Probably nothing, was the reasonable answer. But such sensible explanations are unsatisfying, not only because it's a waste of Dylan's mystique to interpret his moves on the most prosaic level, but because the four-day engagement at the Other End convincingly demonstrated that Patti and the band are no small-time cult phenomenon. Not only was Patti in good voice, but the band is extending itself confidently. Jay Daugherty, the newly acquired drummer, provides rhythmic heat, and Lenny Kaye has improved markedly on guitar—his solo on "Time Is on My Side" for example moves Keith Richards riffing to Verlaine slashing. The band's technical improvement has helped revivify the repertoire: "Break It Up" is now more sharply focused, "Piss Factory" is dramatically jazzy, and their anthem, "Gloria," ends the evening crashingly. Missing were "Free Money," and "Land"—the Peckinpahesque cinematic version of "Land of 1000 Dances"—which is being saved for the forthcoming album.

Something is definitely going on here and I think I know what it is. During one of her sets Patti made the seemingly disconnected remark, "Don't give up on Arnie Palmer." But when the laughter subsided, she added, "The greats are still the greatest." Yes, of course! All her life Patti Smith has had rock and roll in her blood—she has been, like the rest of us, a fan; this is part of her connection with her audience—and now she's returning what rock has given her with the full force of her love. Perhaps Dylan perceives that this passion is a planet wave of no small sweep. Yet what I cherished most about Patti's engagement was not the pounding rock-and-roll intensity but a throwaway gesture of camaraderie. When Lenny Kaye was having difficulty setting up his guitar between numbers, Patti paced around, joked around, scratched her stomach, scratched her hair—still Kaye was not quite ready. "I don't really mind," she told the audience. "I mean, Mick would wait all night for Keith."

Keith was a frequent comparison point for Patti, who once lamented that she had to go onstage and perform even when she had her period—"Keith doesn't have these problems."

I actually left the sanctity of studio apartment and black cat to catch Patti on out-of-town appearances, at a time when audience reception for a New York poet-rocker was a roll of the dice, the dominant bands being mega-hair arena rockers who bombasticized everything they flagellated and drew upon what the poet Philip Larkin once derisively called the "myth kitty," invoking the combination of Nibelungen, Camelot, and Satan's barbecue pit that Spinal Tap would turn into a tacky arcade. By contrast, the Patti Smith Group looked like a scarecrow outfit with aspirations that would barely form a bicep—abjuring the Nietzschean hard-on of heavy metal and scratching an artier, jazzier upward path, "arty" and "jazzy" being what so many mid-seventies rock fans most wanted to avoid when they went out at night to get laid and wasted, as hormones and Kiss intended. But by now the Patti Smith Group had added a drummer, Jay Dee Daugherty, and acquisitioned its own rogue force and demolition expert, albeit with impeccable avant-rock credentials: the grinning volcano that was and is John Cale, whose mood swings you didn't want to get in the middle of. A classically trained musician born in Wales who had once taken part in an eighteen-hour piano performance with John Cage, Cale was a founding partner of the Velvet Underground with the singer-songwriter-scowler Lou Reed, his viola sawing away moodily on the Velvets' "Black Angel's Death Song," a shredding, assaultive La Monte Young dissonance and groaning industrial drone that seemed to rise from the bowels of the subway system. He also played keyboards, his electric organ propelling the Velvets' improvisatory epic "Sister Ray" like a runaway calliope. He and Reed had an unamicable parting, unamicable partings being one of Lou's specialties, and he recorded a number of solo albums with literary-minded song titles ("Hedda Gabler," "Graham Greene") and others of savage candor, such as the cuckold's tale of "Guts," with its pulp-novel opening. He also produced albums, including the desolate masterpieces by his fellow Velvets castaway, the imperiously beautiful and opaque ice sculpture Nico (whose handbag rattled wherever she walked, holding a bootleg pharmacy), and he was chosen as producer of Patti's debut album, *Horses.* He and Patti's manager, the shortcake Jane Friedman, were living together, and Cale would join the band onstage for their encore cover of the Who's "My Generation." He also was billed as a solo artist in concert appearances in which Patti headlined (sandwiched between Television and

Patti on one halcyon occasion), injecting songs with a haunted-sanitarium psychodrama punctuated by primal screams that out-did John Lennon's on his Plastic Ono Band album—Cale's had more grizzly volume, less sinus infection. Crooning Elvis's "Heartbreak Hotel," he would miserabilize, "I get so lonely/I get so lonely I could . . . *DDDDDIIIIIIIIIEEEEEEEEEEEEEEEEEEEEEEEEEEEEEEEEEEE!!!*" That woke up the dead. It was common info that the recording sessions for *Horses* had been "stormy," and Cale was capable of generating thunderclouds even without a lot of ego friction in a collider chamber like the recording studio.

Drinking brought out his daredevil demons, as if a concert pianist suddenly Incredible Hulk–ized into Oliver Reed. Once at a club date in Washington, D.C., that I attended that already had its surreal aspects—a double bill with Garland Jeffreys, who wore masks onstage as racial signifiers and Brechtian devices—and joining Patti and crew onstage for the "My Generation" finale, Cale was possessed of the whim to poke out one of the overhead stage lights with the spear end of his bass; he thrust the neck of the bass upward, missed by inches, and the momentum carried him over the lip of the stage onto a table that overturned, creating an interesting cascade. A couple of Patti's bandmates, along with a roadie or two no doubt, carried Cale backstage like one of the wounded warriors from the rugby field in David Storey's meaty spectacle *The Changing Room*. As they carried him backstage, they passed Jeffreys, who may have been wearing one of his voodoo masks, at least that's how it's been lacquered into memory all these years. "Lucky he missed the light," someone said of John backstage—"he might have been electrocuted."

I flew once to San Francisco, my first visit, to see Patti perform. I must have had money and time to burn, though I don't recall it. After the encore Cale laid his bass on the stage floor near an amplifier, and a foghorn roar of feedback was the result. A stagehand, presumably doing what he would have done under all similar circumstances, zipped from the wings and moved the instrument away from the amp and set it upright on a stand, as if tidying up. He failed to factor in that to an avant-gardist of the research-and-development wing of rock, droning feedback was a design element, one of the votive sounds in the church of noise. Irked in the extreme by this intrusion, Cale bit the helpful roadie on his jeaned butt. No damage, but he got the point across. And these were incidents I witnessed firsthand. There may have been others. Once, after Patti returned from an out-of-town appearance, I asked Jane Friedman how John had behaved. "He was great," she said. "G-r-a-t-e."

I had my own run-in with Cale's wolfman side one night at CBGB's when I offered to buy him a beer. What kind? I asked. "Mossuh," he said, the word hard to pick out from the din coming from whoever was playing. What? I asked. He raised his voice, but somehow what came out of his mouth managed to be even less decipherable. "Moses?" I asked. And his hands were suddenly around my throat and he barked, *"MOLSON!"* With exquisite dry irony, Merv the bartender said, "John's requesting a Molson's," as he proceeded to uncap a cold bottle, John's considerable grip receding from my throat now that his request had been properly translated. I didn't take it personally, and there was no repeat performance. In fact he was unfailingly genial and chatty whenever I ran into him, and his presence on the scene, despite the sporadic aggro-surges, cast a more generous corona than that of his former co-pilot, Lou Reed, whose cool-as-shit sarcasms seemed to come out of a private loop of Bob Dylan's surlier moments from *Don't Look Back* projected on the inside of his sunglasses. Lou was an infrequent drop-in at CBGB's, likely preferring the familiar discomforts of Max's Kansas City—the Algonquin Room of Andy Warhol's Factory—but perhaps he acted disgruntled there too, his look of disgruntlement being the little parasol he carried wherever he went. The first time I saw Lou at CBGB's he parked himself at a table in the back; at the table directly in front of him were a couple of rock chicks who were acting a trifle feisty. One of them, the more lubricated of the duo, began clapping along to whatever song was being played with the floppy enthusiasm of the temporarily uncoordinated. It was mildly annoying but also amusing, as so many things are in life, but Lou was not amused, his public amusement expressed mostly by a smile on a tight leash, easily mistaken for a sneer. "You're clapping off the beat," he told the girl, who paid him no never-mind, too far gone into the woolly interior to register a reprimand, even one from one of the founders of our country. "Clap on the *beat,* cunt," Lou said, as she persisted in clapping as if trying to kill a fly in midair. Curiously, "cunt" didn't come across as an offensive slur when Lou said it; it had the flat tone of an impersonal insult, just another nail he happened to be hammering. And CBGB's wasn't like the *Village Voice,* where the wrong word could set the entire playground into Balkan upheaval; a former hangout for the Hells Angels didn't lend itself to an atmosphere of heavy self-policing, language- or otherwise. Thwarted in his efforts to make the girl desist in her infernal flapping, Lou left the table like a diner who flings his napkin on the table and exits in a huff, only Lou and his huff didn't leave, simply shifted to another table, conceding this round to an oblivious amateur.

He fared no better in a later run-in with a more lucid adversary. One night Lisa Robinson, rock journalist extraordinaire, came up to me with the winged-Mercury enthusiasm of someone with some really good gossip to share and asked: "So did you hear what just happened? Verlaine just confiscated Lou's tape recorder. Went up to him and demanded he fork it over." Which Lou did, like a shoplifter surrendering a pack of cigs.

Such a heartwarming display of lèse-majesté by Verlaine, putting Lou on notice that his seniority and status didn't count, not in this saloon, not in Verlaine's musical jurisdiction, not where Television and its signature riffs were concerned. Verlaine must have suspected in advance that Reed was packing, foraging for inspiration, unless of course Lou was flaunting the handheld recorder in full view, making the recording-angel rounds like Warhol, who carried his around like a little air freshener. Then again, suspicion was slivered deep into Verlaine's nature, which was flecked with paranoia. Wariness seemed wired into the very tilt of his head, the angle at which he appraised whoever approached him.

(Even when Verlaine got angry, he was methodical. I remember once watching him destroy an uncooperative amplifier during a performance at a bar called Mother's. Most guitar heroes would have made a big *Rocky Horror Picture Show* of equipment wreckage, but Verlaine simply began tilting the amp forward and knocking it into the wall as if it were a vending machine that hadn't dispensed the candy and wouldn't give him his money back; interrogating it with his hands, as if trying to shake out information, until it was clear he wasn't going to get anything out of this holdout and polished it off for good. It was a set I remember well because for some reason Patti, sitting next to me, had been reading about the Mormons and the name Brigham Young seemed to rebound off the wall as Tom gave the amp what for.)

Although Verlaine was also not one to court the press or any other species, he and I got along fine, he wincing with irritation only if I rattled on too fast as if the curtain had just been pulled off my parrot cage, which I didn't take any more personally than I did Cale's death grip, since Verlaine winced at every speed jabber. Offstage, his sense of humor had a touch of the gallows. Once I was standing on a subway platform, leaning slightly forward to check if the twin lights of an approaching train were coming around the tunnel bend, when a hand pressed into my back, as if to push me onto the tracks, then gripped my jacket to prevent just that. I whipped around and it was Verlaine, cackling with amusement. Just his way of saying hi.

At CBGB's, rough democracy reigned. There were no separate tables for press seating (unlike at the Bottom Line), no backstage VIP playpen, no caste system, no dress code, everything informally in flux, not even any strict restrictions on entering and reentering the club, which allowed everybody to circulate, spread their germs.

The one checkpoint that had to be crossed was Roberta Bayley's station at the front of the club. (It was probably she I was talking to in my mini-moment in *Blank Generation*.) Reddish haired, pale white, thin, beautiful, smart, quick, Roberta was (to put it in *Mad Men* terms) the Joan of CBGB's, the goddess gatekeeper who had the authority of decree, the power to banish. I always marveled at how Roberta could accelerate in mid-sentence to spin someone around without touching him or her. "Joey was here earlier but I haven't seen him [dopey-looking dude appears in doorway]—*I told you you couldn't walk in here with a bottle take it back to the street and if I have to tell you again*—[dopey dude sheepishly disappears] so he might still be at Phoebe's." When the Runaways—that hotsy-twatsy jail-bait band put together by the West Coast impresario Kim Fowley whose first hit, "Cherry Bomb," established their truant image—played CBGB's on a special-event night, there was more press frenzy than I'd ever seen at the place, proof of how the horniness of men drives news acreage, at least then. As I and a few others entered with expressions perhaps a trace too shiny and eager, I heard Roberta say as we trampled past, "You should all be ashamed of yourselves."

I stopped and said, "Well, you know, I'm here strictly in my role as a reporter."

"Well, try to remember to take notes while your tongue's hanging out."

Roberta was also a no-fuss photographer, her cover shot of the Ramones for their debut album one of the most representative debris-imbued images of the period. It was the Warhol Factory aesthetic, aiming the camera straight ahead and not dicking around with technique, pricey state-of-the-art equipment, masterpiece aspirations. Record the moment and never mind the mess. One of my favorite photos of Roberta's, one of the most snapshot-y, caught the sweet incongruity of the *Punk* magazine mascot and interloper, Legs McNeil, wearing a Ramones T-shirt, chatting with Norman Mailer, who, after seeing the Ramones onstage disturbing the peace, had proclaimed, "They're heroic!" This, from the man who thought the Rolling Stones' "Sympathy for the Devil" was overrated and anticlimactic, was no small endorsement.

In the beginning they were more Bowery Boys than Braveheart.

One night I was at CBGB's to catch the Ramones, who were top-billed. I had seen them before but was laughing so hard the first time that much of their set blurred. Headlong blur was their objective. Their sets were blessedly, blazingly brief, setting land-speed records for most songs in the shortest span, each song launched with a 1!-2!-3!-4! count as if dropping the go flag on a Thunder Road drag race. At first the Ramones looked like a novelty act, as cartoonish as the Archies, but instead of gee-whiz varsity sweaters they were rigged out in matching monikers (Tommy Ramone, drums; Dee Dee Ramone, bass; Johnny Ramone, guitar; Joey Ramone, lead singer), leather jackets, hole-poked jeans, flat-soled sneakers (Keds they looked like, or Converse), mop-top haircuts, and, as if to complement the Beatlesque bangs, Joey's lispy Liverpudlian accent, which resembled Ringo's on the Saturday morning Beatles cartoon series rather than the real-life item. The arch enunciation of Joey's vocals defused the belligerency of lyrics about beating on the brat or the clenched warning of "Loudmouth" ("You're a loudmouth, baby/ You betta shut it up/I'm gonna beat you up"), especially since the spindly Joey, holding on to the mike stand as if for support, as if it were a sturdier spinal column, looked so much like an awkwardly assembled praying mantis that one couldn't imagine him throwing a punch that wouldn't completely creak him out of alignment. They saved their antagonism mostly for each other, like feuding brothers. Johnny and Dee Dee looked like the genuine reform-school sluggers, often barking onstage at each other before, during, and after numbers, looking as if they might have a throw-down right then and there, using Joey as a pike to thwack each other. (Tuning up at CBGB's became its own subgenre of psychodrama for the Ramones, as if they were taking batting practice before swinging aggression outward.) The uniform persona and unison attitude, the slashing zoom of their chords and lyrics, the ritualistic formalism of each set—"It's like a set of karate stances," Albert Goldman later observed with his customary cackle. *Kiai!* The intensity of the Ramones, the relentlessness of their chain-saw attack and paroxysms of anger that erupted whenever that attack was interrupted because a guitar strap snapped loose, was the intensity of a methodical strike force that didn't want to waste a second or a note or a needless word. The mark of mission accomplished for a typical Ramones show was looking pissed off as they left the stage, the exchange of well-done grins and tired beams of satisfaction having no place in their pit-crew operation. (I remember seeing Dee Dee backstage after a New Year's Eve concert where he was slumped against the wall, a model of exhaustion. I asked him about his holiday season. "Gonna take a few more days off," he said, "then it's back to writing those hits." I thought he was kidding, being self-deprecating, given that the Ramones hadn't had any real hits yet. But, no, irony wasn't the language he spoke. This was simply the work he had waiting for him at the assembly plant in his head.)

Even then, in howling embryo, the Ramones were a tough act to follow and a tough act to precede. Whoever opened for them might as well have been setting out the paper plates on the picnic table, so innocuous would they look by comparison. The band that opened for them that night looked innocuous even without anything as contrast. A trio, two smoothie-faced young men in preppy Izods or Polo tops and a young woman with short strawberry blonde hair who strapped on her bass as if donning a white lab coat, took the stage, looking as if they had wandered into the wrong campus bar. Or Pop-Tarts that had popped out of the same toaster. They didn't seem to belong in a Bowery dive where the very air seemed sometimes to be ovulating with amoebic dysentery, and yet they threw off no awareness or discomfort that they didn't belong, and so slid right into a slot that was theirs for the slitting. The lead singer, whose voice sounded as if perpetually about to break, his Adam's apple working like a baby's rattle, introduced the group: "The name of this band is Talking Heads, and the name of this song is 'The Girls Want to Be with the Girls.'"

"These people call themselves Talking Heads," I wrote in the *Voice*.

Seeing them for the first time is transfixing: Frantz is so far back on drums that it sounds as if he's playing in the next room; Weymouth, who could pass for Suzi Quatro's sorority sister, stands rooted to the floor, her head doing an oscillating-fan swivel; the object of her swivel is David Byrne, who has a little-boy-lost-at-the-zoo voice and the demeanor of someone who's spent the last half hour whirling around in the spin drier. When his eyes start ping-ponging in his head, he looks like a cartoon of a chipmunk from Mars.

They were strange, but straight-strange, a collegiate facsimile edition of a set of bland-seeming Warholian ironies about everyday objects, brand merchandise, and candy-pill colors bestowed on its citizens by a big, shiny, bountiful milkshake-machine America. "Don't Worry About the Government" went one song title, a sentiment that cut against the paranoid grain of the post-Watergate era, when *The Parallax View* and *Three Days of the Condor* sent their heroes into furtive phone booths to make desperate calls and Gene Hackman's Harry Caul in Francis Ford Coppola's *Conversation* ripped his apartment apart like an archaeological dig in a futile effort to locate the electronic bug. But this pose of benign acceptance, like Warhol's, laid a curved sheet of glass over a grid of nervous tremors, putting the aesthetic on a minimalist feed:

When the Velvets made their reputation at the Balloon Farm, they were navigating through a storm of multi-media effects; mirrors, blinking lights, strobes, projected film images. Talking Heads works without paraphernalia in a cavernous room projecting light like a television located at the end of a long dark hall. The difference between the Heads and the Velvets is the difference between phosphorescence and cold gray TV light. These people understand that an entire generation has grown up on the nourishment of television's accessible banality. What they're doing is presenting a banal facade under which run ripples of violence and squalls of frustration—the id of the vid.

There was also a TV-kiddie-show rinky-dink troubadour echo of the influential cult band the Modern Lovers, whose lead singer, Jonathan Richman, who went solo, once did three encores of "Ice Cream Man" strolling up and down the bar aisle of CBGB's, strumming his acoustic guitar as if leading a campfire sing-along. What I didn't know, watching the Heads for the first time, was that David Byrne, Chris Frantz, and Tina Weymouth had all attended the Rhode Island School of Design, where experimental artiness and eccentric presentation were encouraged rather than roughed up in the hallways, as happened at lesser institutions where jocks and unaffiliated louts committed acts of unsportsmanlike conduct upon those suspected of sissy aspirations or other faun tendencies. Not that there was anything fey about Talking Heads, or that it would have mattered much if there had been, the New York Dolls having broken up that stigma for scrap metal. But in the hobo boho jungle preserve of the Bowery, the dilettanti were given a thorough surface inspection, and the collegiate clean-cutness of the Heads was regarded with skepticism until they played enough sets (it didn't take long) for the regulars to recognize in Byrne a fellow misfit weirdo. His vocals, interspersed yips, head jerks, and boogie-down hip action suggested Norman Bates hitting the disco, and as soon as he began strumming the opening to "Psycho Killer," his certification seemed complete. "David Byrne sings tonelessly but its effect is all the more ominous," I wrote in the *Voice*. "The uneasy alliance between composure and breakdown—between outward acceptance and inward coming apart—is what makes Talking Heads such a central seventies band."

And then there was Tina Weymouth, about whom nothing appeared haywire. My crush on Tina was instantaneous. It was the only correct way to respond. Everyone got a crush on Tina, apart from those who preferred their rock women in a gaudier state of disarray, more lip-licorice-ish and torn-stockinged, a downtown Anita Pallenberg type fished out of a Dumpster. Those Dutch-boy bangs, those blue eyes that crystal'd through the swimming murk of CBGB's, the smile that broke mostly offstage, when her bass duties didn't require her monitoring David's every ostrich move—Tina was sexy precisely because she wasn't striving to be sexy, her not-trying coming across not as a feminist statement or a de-gendering decision to function as a unisex tablet but as an efficiency model that any young woman could look cool emulating. Female rock stars were rare, the codpieces and princely egos still ruled, but female instrumentalists functioning as equals onstage were rarer. Tina was a small revelation. That (everyone soon learned, with a deflated sigh) Tina and drummer Chris Frantz were girlfriend-boyfriend made the crush even nicer to let slush around in the mind since that knowledge kept infatuation on a happy, unattainable plane, fancifully out of reach.

Later, Tina and I even went on a couple of movie dates, one of the art-house choices being Rainer Werner Fassbinder's *Fox and His Friends,* a homosexual-pickup social Darwinist morality tale about a carnival worker (played by Fassbinder himself, without his Fu Manchu mustache and usual gunnysack slouch) who wins the lottery and attracts a new host of buddies who proceed to peck him until their vulture beaks have picked him clean and he dies in the subway, a couple of punks (the old-definition no-good kind) stopping by to rummage through his pockets. A feel-bad diagram of sexual-economic predation that made *The Boys in the Band* look candy-hearted, *Fox and His Friends* was one of the world's worst movie-date ideas for any male-female pairing and proof that ulterior motives weren't working any levers when it came to movie selection. Unlike some others, who gnawed the insides of their wrists over the unfairness of it all (why him? why not me?), I wasn't jealous of Chris, even when Tina stage-whispered to him one night in front of CBGB's about something special being on the menu later that night, and she didn't mean food. Unlike some bandmate boyfriends one could mention from the underground scene, Chris was so obviously not a snake-weasel-leech piece of future deadbeat material, bitching over his favorite coke spoon being missing or some other domestic crisis staged on a floor mattress where sheets were optional. Moreover, Tina had sisters who were datable, not that I ever did.

It turned out that the Heads were sharing a loft on Chrystie Street that I visited with my then girlfriend. Reaching Chrystie Street, south of CBGB's and pointed toward Chinatown, was not a stroll undertaken in the midnight hours without all of one's bat faculties primed. The bordering Roosevelt Park was well stocked with furtive hands ready to reach out for a rude gimme, and the nearby remaining Bowery flophouses, these remnants of the Depression with their last-stop Dreiserian stale aroma of defeat and spiritual malnutrition, drew panhandlers and derelicts to those cheerless streets looking for drink money if all the indoor cots were taken. The area also featured what Byrne would describe as the skankiest hookers in New York, though of course that's a subjective evaluation. But I had never been invited to an artist's loft before and was a total Heads convert when the invite came.

Loft living then wasn't the luxury alternative that it later became with the rise of SoHo and gentrification with a vengeance in Tribeca and beyond, as lofts became synonymous with airy storage units of flooding sunlight, gleaming bowling-alley hardwood floors, and quirkily amusing, slayingly chic art pieces chosen and arranged just so as tribal taste trophies, a photo layout of a setup perfect to raise a super-race of test-tube babies. Loft living in the mid-seventies was still in its pioneer post-factory, rat-haven phase, the elevators lowering and lifting like a large, groaning apprehension (as if operated by Marley's chain-hanging ghost from *A Christmas Carol*), the thick-piped plumbing still in its early Soviet phase, these industrial garrets too hot in summer, too cold in winter, but spacious enough to carry a bowling-alley echo. What I remember of the Heads' loft was the purposeful clutter of instruments, amps, tape recorders, and reading materials strategically stacked, with a rope hung down the middle to divide Tina and Chris's personal digs from David's, reminiscent of *It Happened One Night* without the curvy shadow-play peep show. Although they were artists from an art school living in an art loft, they weren't slumming, trying noble poverty on for size; they were making their place in the outdoor urinal of downtown as hardily as any glue-head fleeing the czarist oppression of Queens.

Even so, what wasn't clear from the Heads' fledgling performances was how much infantry stamina and pilot altitude potential they possessed, or whether they were future sugar dispensers, their encore cover of the bubblegum hit "1, 2, 3 Red Light" raising questions of how campy-cute they might go. (One of the three also expressed a fondness for "Chewy, Chewy," though I don't believe they ever pulled that molar-remover out of their candy box to perform.) Critics love dealing with raised questions, especially if they've raised them themselves from tiny qualms. I should have heeded—I later did—Pauline's great throwaway perception in her review of Mailer's cinema-verité Cassavetes-style police station psychodrama *Wild 90,* in which she compared Mailer's Renaissance ambitions with Jean Cocteau's multi-artistry as poet-filmmaker-novelist-designer. Mailer may be a two-fisted macho hombre, Pauline wrote, but those wiry cats like Cocteau are tougher than they look, making Mailer the moviemaker appear all blubber. No band or Symbolist poet wielding a Stratocaster below Fourteenth Street was carrying a blubber load, but compared with the cloudy turrets of the interior castles Television was climbing or the wood chipper the Ramones stuffed their sound into, the Heads could look deceptively light, a model airplane with an erratic flight pattern. But while so many others kept drilling the same woodpecker holes until their beaks bent funny, it was Byrne who would emerge as the Cocteau-esque Shiva figure—a visionary soundscaper (*My Life in the Bush of Ghosts,* his collaboration with Brian Eno), movie director (*True Stories,* which didn't receive its due and still doesn't), gallery artist, conceptual book designer, composer of string quartets and a song cycle about Imelda Marcos (with Fatboy Slim), America's unofficial ambassador to Brazilian music, and, his hair now holy white, an apostle of urban sustainability, globally light-footing-it through his blog and the travel collection it produced, *Bicycle Diaries*. Byrne's ambition was harder to spot at first because his voice broke like a choirboy's and his head was always bobbing or askew, not Fixed in Purpose or rapture-lost. He was as willful as Verlaine, but his willfulness wove outward, toward the honeycombed world, whereas Verlaine's narrowed to a shrinking portion of what he sought and fought to control. Byrne's very accessibility, his approachability, set him apart from Verlaine and (later) Patti, whose don't-bother-me-I'm-an-artist signs on their faces deterred those who might idly come knocking. One night a CBGB's regular named Valerie, a gorgeous speed freak whose chat accelerated into gibberish the longer she hung at the bar, said to me, spotting Byrne, "I'm going to pick him up and swing him around." "That I'd like to see," I said. As David headed toward the stage area, nodding his bashful hellos, Valerie grabbed him around the chest in a skilled grappling move and twirled him around, and as he spun, he said, "Whoa!" like a teenager on an amusement park ride, and when she stopped, he pretended to act a little dizzy, as if bopped on the head by a fuzzy hammer. Had she tried that with Lou Reed, he might have burst into mummy dust.

As a unit the Heads got tighter, tougher, and yet looser, their Tin Man joints lubed, Byrne breaking out some funky-chicken moves as Chris and Tina laid a deeper bottom to their sound. They held their own on a billing with any band, even bands that acted as if they came up from the gutter and brought the gutter with them. And there was a personal tension that ticked between Tina and David, captured cunningly in a YouTube video that cuts between their faces as they perform "Warning Sign," the dueling close-ups indicative, prophetic, of a hairline fracture building to something bigger. If I can pinpoint the moment the Heads burst through the attic and pointed north, it was the night when they introduced a new number, "Pulled Up," where the joy-whoop of "you pulled me up, up, up, *up, up, up!*" expressed a giddy, salvational energy that left Warholism behind like a toy-model village as Astronaut Byrne shed gravity and saw angels knocking around. Not Blakean angels, like Patti's, but Japanese toy ones.

The scene filled up, the club filled up, more and more of the sidewalk out in front of CBGB's being taken up between sets as the more bodies inside made greater the need to air out. With no flash-mob mentality or YouTube clip-load rushing everyone forward in random abandon, the slower pace of print and word of mouth allowed the scene to develop organically, roughly coalesce into what Brian Eno would call "scenius," the genius of a communal mind in group neurotransmission. There was a buzzy atmosphere of something happening but no bent ceiling of overriding importance or heavy expectation to suffocate impulses before they could give themselves a try. Rising to the moment can be overrated, unless we're talking fifth-set tiebreaker. CBGB's taught me that some of the most momentous performances occur when not much is on the line, nothing's immediately at stake, and the rest of the world dissolves until there's only us campfire girls gathered. Television's insomniac second sets, late into the a.m. after most had headed home—if splinters of Verlaine's solos don't flash before my eyes before I die, I'm going to feel cheated.

> Since this is *The Village Voice,* I will now insert my
> obligatory cross-cultural reference in record review (cf. past
> works of Messrs. Wolcott, Carson, Hull, etc.): Alfred Kazin
> said of Louis-Ferdinand Celine that . . .
> —Lester Bangs, "A Bellyful of Wire"

I knew Lester before I met him, talking to him on the phone long-distance in his role as one of the editors of *Creem,* the rock magazine located in Birmingham, Michigan, between the bicoastal, bipolar musical power points and yet exerting a journalistic-critical-cultural goofball influence as infectious in its parodic whammy as *Animal House* or Mort Drucker's movie parodies for *Mad* magazine. "Talking to him" is a slight misnomer, since Lester did most of the talking; he nearly always did the bulk of the dialogue, like an all-night DJ in a record-strewn booth with an inexhaustible bag of spontaneous bop and enough stimulants on hand to make it to dawn with mind and mouth still going. I did some reviews for Lester at *Creem,* including one that still makes me happy to discover tucked away on the Internet, a review of Eno's solo electronic album *Discreet Music,* its ambient sounds and its gentle wash of alpha waves not yet the New Age wallpaper for every yoga class, massage studio, and meditation enhancer. "This must be the first piece in *Creem* that quotes Balanchine," Lester said. I had cited Balanchine's Apollonian quip, "Some like it hot and some like it cold, and I like ice cream," and unlike so many other editors Lester didn't ask for references to be trimmed because the readers wouldn't "get it." (Today it's assumed the average reader won't get anything that isn't TV related.) *Creem* was a great place to write because they gave your enthusiasms galloping rein (pro or con), appreciated humor that ricocheted out of nowhere, and didn't fly-bugger every comma in your copy or try to get you to round off your opinion phrasings, "like those fuckers at *Rolling Stone,*" as Lester said.

But there was one oddity to Lester's nocturnal calls: he would sometimes repeat in successive conversations, once *three* times in a single week, anecdotes that he had told me the previous time we spoke. From distinguished old bores who had sat at many captain's tables, this might not have been unusual, but Lester wasn't old and almost never a bore, at least for the first hour. The initial time it happened, I just let him unfurl it as if I hadn't heard it before, figuring he talked to so many people he had simply forgotten. Then it happened again, and this time I thought it might be some kind of put-on, like an Andy Kaufman routine, testing how far he could take it. I didn't interrupt this time either, going along with the gag.

Only it wasn't a gag, it was some other inscrutable sub-modality of performance. All people repeat themselves, there are dreaded hostage takers who entrap a dinner party or casual get-together with the same vine-covered story they've told since Moses was beardless, but what was different was that Lester wouldn't stop even after you said, "Oh, yeah, you told me about that," proceeding as if he hadn't heard you and telling the story the exact same way he had before, with the same pauses, the same inflections, even the same anticipatory laughs as he relished the next bit in the story (as if they had been written as italicized cues adjoining the dialogue in a radio script) and sped up toward the payoff line. I would later know cokeheads who wouldn't brake their spiel even as I put down the phone, tiptoed to the bathroom, peed, washed my hands like a priest before mass, and then picked up the phone again as if I had been there the whole time. But it was never the *same* spiel, as if the playback button had been pressed. I filed Lester's repetition compulsion away as a minor interesting anomaly until he came to New York on a record-company junket, I believe, and a group of us visited him at the hotel he was being put up at and he entertained us with a boom box—a ghetto blaster was the parlance in favor then, until the term made liberals nervous in their service, to quote that distinguished theologian, Reverend Ike—which was loaded not with music but with a tape of Travis Bickle's mirror monologue from *Taxi Driver.* "You talking to me? You talking to me? You talking to me? Well, I'm the only one here." I can't say this was a speech that won its way into my heart when I saw/heard it the first time in the actual film— I've always thought it smacked more of an actor's improv audition than a prize scene to be set on the mantel next to Brando's wounded lament to his brother in *On the Waterfront* ("you shudda took care of me, Charley")—but even if it had earned a spot on my personal Oscar shelf, it wasn't something I wanted to hear replayed at DEAFENING VOLUME until each vowel cracked and splintered with static. It also made conversation nigh impossible, which may have been Lester's passive-aggressive intention, his perverse way of dominating a discussion even without having to say anything. Whatever the explanation, assuming there was one, it smacked of mind-fuck, though in fairness Lester never pulled anything like that again, at least in my vicinity.

It must have been later that year—1976—that Lester moved to New York from Michigan, ready to take the next ramp up in his career, one that led away from strictly rock reviewing and tour de force rampages (however fantastically baroque and comic a canvas he had made them for his paint-gun blasts, as in his much-beloved "James Taylor Marked for Death" and "Let Us Now Praise Famous Death Dwarves," in which Lou Reed was valentined, among other things, as "a panderer living off the dumbbell nihilism of a seventies generation that doesn't have the energy to commit suicide") into a dressier salon of journalism, where you weren't treated as an itinerant peddler. Lester had a much more difficult freshman orientation experience than I did, because I came to New York a nobody with no reputation to live up to, whereas Lester had a well-publicized clownish side that made fans anticipate/expect antics, of which he had a Santa bagful. Sometimes the hijinks bubbled up out of pure ebullience, other times it was the alcohol/cough syrup/whatever taking to the stage for a sweaty workout. This may have been no different from the way he behaved in Michigan or on press junkets. What was different was that in New York in general, the local rock scene in particular, and CBGB's in super-particular, he found the audience less receptive, and he in turn was less entranced by his newly adopted milieu: the recipe for a sour letdown. He would watch some band performing in the beery late hours and complain, "It's not exactly Iggy," meaning Iggy and the Stooges, and, true, no one onstage was rolling around on glass shards and flaunting Adonis abs for the greater glory of the sun god; likewise, he would compare some hard-charging unit unfavorably to the MC5. He would go on and on about how Television was essentially no diff from the Grateful Dead with their endless guitar ragas, a way of putting down Television without conceding a few points of originality. And it may have had more than a little to do with Lester's having bumped against Verlaine's bug repellent of fine-meshed, inviolable indifference, Lester's attempts to engage/amuse/mildly goad Verlaine (at least those I witnessed) deflected with a shrug and a James Dean drag of cigarette. Lester got along better with CBGB's rockers—members of the Dictators, for example—who appreciated his gags because they had their own humor routines going, a burlesque bombast that enjoyed strutting the wrestling ring.

Lester went into a self-described hermit phase his first few years in New York, a holing up many people do when they move to the city and don't have nine-to-fives. Lester's work habits worked against him in his efforts to turn total pro and escape the rathskeller of rock journalism, at least as a full-time address. It wasn't that he was lazy, anything but, but he wrote in key-clacking Kerouacian binges, cannonballing through the paper hoops of deadlines and then spilling more copy than they could use. He was less adapted or temperamentally suited for the sort of fine carpentry and assembly that a more structured piece required, too often winging it with hot-rod flames flying out of his ass and the streetlights rushing by, or so his prose read. It was said that he took the advance for a picture book about Blondie and buggered off the text in forty-eight hours, though some say he had sprinted seventy-two; whatever time ended up on the final clock, the result was a nonbook that didn't have the discursive, loose-thread-pulling comedy of, say, Geoff Dyer doing everything he diligently could to procrastinate on his D. H. Lawrence biography, or Nicholson Baker embarking on his Updike meditation despite having barely more than smidgens of Updike's industrious output, fiddling instead with all the silkworm ways Updike has infiltrated his brain. Even such serpentine paths take more discursive leisure than Lester had at his deadline-heavy disposal. Instead, the bigger the project, the bigger the noise-to-sound ratio, his glints of genius lost in the stew. Writing for Christgau at the *Voice,* Lester did superb, lively, often hilarious stuff, but it didn't get him an upgrade to the first-class compartment. As plum assignments remained out of reach, Lester decided he wanted to step away from the typewriter, seize the microphone, and make like the howling moon.

It was like running off to join the circus without having to run very far. Lester was already a performance artist on the page, an acrobat with crazy bounces, and there was precedence for rock writers getting into the act. Greil Marcus and co-conspirators had recorded a spoof bootleg album called *The Masked Marauders* in which a fake Mick Jagger blues'd it up on that modern lament "I Can't Get No Nookie," Lenny Kaye was a journalist and editor who bean-stalked into one of Patti Smith's transmission towers after Patti herself made the hop from print to poetry reciting to "Piss Factory," and Cleveland's Peter Laughner, a friend and fan of Lester's, wrote for *Creem* and played guitar for a number of bands, his early death of drug-related acute pancreatitis at the rotten age of twenty-four inspiring one of Lester's best pieces from the heart:

> Realizing life is precious the natural tendency is to trample on it, like laughing at a funeral. But there are voluntary reactions. I volunteer not to feel anything about him from this day out, but I will not forget that this kid killed himself for something torn T-shirts represented in the battle fires of his ripped emotions, and that does not make your T-shirts profound, on the contrary, it makes you a bunch of assholes if you espouse what he latched onto in support of his long death agony, and if I have run out of feeling for the dead I can also truly say that from here on out I am only interested in true feeling, and the pursuit of some ultimate escape from that was what killed Peter, which is all I truly know of his life, except that the hardest thing in this living world is to confront your own pain and go through it, but somehow life is not a paltry thing after all next to this child's inheritance of eternal black. So don't anybody try to wave good-bye.

(I had friendly hellos with Laughner, who was a big fan of Television, and was shocked during the concert intermission for something at the Academy of Music when I entered the men's room and a voice reverberated, "Hey, Wolcott!!!" issuing from someone unrecognizable. "It's me, Peter." "Oh, hi, sorry, you caught me off guard." What had caught me off guard was his smile, which was missing several front teeth since we last spoke, an almost hillbilly grin that hollowed out his cheeks and that I thought might be the result of heroin use, since junkies crave sweets like crazy. He seemed to be in a very jovial mood, though, joviality not being something most junkies display, so I didn't know what to think, my drug-addict knowledge being almost entirely conjectural.)

I don't want to accuse Lester of cynicism, because other people's motives are always a murky soup, but I do think there was a dollop of calculation in his decision to hit the CBGB's stage and unload both barrels, a decision partly derived from the carnival blur of seeing all these bands that he thought sucked to the rotting rafters grandiosely flailing around up there, figuring, "If these tadpoles can do it, why can't I? I've got as much gall as they do, maybe more." His boots were also following in the footsteps of Patti's ballet slippers in seeking to translate rants and reveries into shamanistic incantations, though where Patti massaged her spirit fingers in the air as if summoning the ghosts of everyone she had read, Lester seemed intent on being more of a barrelhouse bellower, a rough blueprint of the profane preacher-man Sam Kinison would uncork. Lester's rock-auteur itch fell somewhere between a lark and a headfirst lunge, and there wasn't the sense that he was willing to work at it—it was attention he seemed to crave, and a shot at asteroid impact. Lester's recording and performing phase is so well documented in Jim DeRogatis's *Let It Blurt: The Life and Times of Lester Bangs, America's Greatest Rock Critic* that I only want to mention an incident from that flurry that laid a lane divider between us.

It had to do with his obsession with Idi Amin, the vicious, dictatorial president of Uganda in the seventies, whose full name was Idi Amin Dada, which must have appealed to Lester's surrealistic humor, how could it not. Torture and genocide flourished under Amin, who was also rumored to practice cannibalism; in his insane caprices and delusional grandeur, Amin was like something out of an EC horror comic crossed with *Heart of Darkness*—a monster-buffoon. It wasn't that Lester *approved* of Amin—he would later bracket him with Hitler as a prodigy of inhumanity—but he would often start scatting about Amin, and the more he scatted, the more it became an impersonation, a tour of the palace of Idi Amin's babbling mind accompanied by beer burps. I never found this particular channel on Lester's radio band of funny voices a diverting romp, not because I was offended by its *Ubu Roi* shtick—I just didn't find it comical or satirical enough. At times Lester's voice veered into Bela Lugosi territory, not that anybody expected him to be Gore Vidal's match as a master of mimicry. This serves as the preamble to what happened after the first or second show of Lester's that I caught, when at some point during his set he started with the Idi Amin stuff, and even more grotesquely exaggerated onstage for an audience, his verbal blackface took on minstrelsy overtones that he may not have intended but served no put-on purpose if he had. Afterward, he asked me what I thought of the show, and I said something along the lines of "Not quite white enough," my admittedly maladroit, overly dry ironic way of suggesting he might want to tone down the Idi Amin rap. I should have been more plain and explicit, but he knew I didn't mean he should literally act more white onstage, as if he had ruffled my Valkyrie wings. The matter would have remained a minor nuisance between us if he had not written something for one of the rock mags quoting what I said, minus the context, with the requisite "sniff"—*"Not quite white enough," sniffed James Wolcott,* as if I had been nibbling a buttered scone or something. Well, such is journalese, of which I've committed plenty of my own infractions.

But it became a bit rich when Lester took to the pages of the *Voice* to pound horseshoes about the malignant racism he discovered behind the thin, sliced smirks of downtown hipsterdom and the punk scene. Called "The White Noise Supremacists," a muckraking title that evoked swastikas, skinheads, and a raised fist clutching a thunderbolt, the article peeled back the black leather jacket of punk to bare the scrawny rib cage of hip fascism. "This scene and the punk stance in general are riddled with self-hate, which is always reflexive, and anytime you conclude that life stinks and the human race mostly amounts to a pile of shit, you've got the perfect breeding ground for fascism." Although it scored some palpable hits with the scattering spray of its bird shot, the article won Lester few assenting allies in the punk scene and put off many more with its heavy icing of bad faith. In *Let It Blurt,* DeRogatis quotes some of the offending jokers cited by Lester, who felt he had taken something offhand and stupid they had said and hemstitched it into a damning exhibit, or mistook a mocking gesture for a genuine declaration. What truly riled people in the slag pits was Lester's preachy fervor about racism after running his own mouth off the road so often. He was a muckraker who had done more than his own share of mucking. He used the *n* word and similar felicities more than once in my presence, and although he may not have been the worst offender, I never heard anything comparable out of, say, members of Talking Heads or from the other rock journalists on the beat, apart from one who was a close buddy of Lester's. And although I heard the occasional anti-Jew comment at CBGB's, it didn't come from regulars but from boroughs kids trying to sound Scorsese-movie tough. As Steven Lee Beeber's book *The Heebie-Jeebies at CBGB's* (a valuable, invigorating history and eye-opener, despite its Halloween title) documents, CBGB's would have been inconceivable without the Jewish show-business tradition that traveled from Al Jolson to Tin Pan Alley to Lenny Bruce to Lou Reed to Hilly Kristal himself, the patriarchal founder. "Joey Ramone, a figure straight out of Kafka's *The Metamorphosis,* Richard Hell, a Jewish mother's worst nightmare, and Lenny Kaye, a kind of post-1960s Jewish mystic, rose up, ready to take over the world." Even punk outfits everyone assumed were Italian, such as the Ramones and the Dictators, were Jewish creations—parodies of guido swagger. So "a breeding ground for fascism" CBGB's and Max's Kansas City were not, despite a flaunting flirtation with transgressive Nazi chic by some, though not by punk's originators.

It wasn't that I disbelieved Lester's mea culpa over his own use of the word, though you have to wonder if his conscience wouldn't have been so stricken had he not been overheard. As he related in "The White Noise Supremacists": "I was in Bleecker Bob's the other night, drunk and stoned, when a black couple walked in. They asked for some disco record, Bob didn't have it of course, a few minutes went by, and reverting in the haze to my Detroit days I said something about such and such band or music having to do with 'niggers.' A couple more minutes went by. Then Bob said, 'You know what, Lester? When you said that, those two people were standing right behind you.'" But everyone knew he was given to passionate displays of big-heart declaration that he could reverse on a dime, blowing his horn in the other direction. He believed what he believed the moment he believed it, but his fluctuations were more jagged than those of most contrarians, depending on what was fueling him. And nobody appreciated the way he portrayed punk musicians and fans as a bunch of George Grosz grotesques whose defective anatomies flayed bare their twisted values. "So many of the people around the CBGB's and Max's scene have always seemed emotionally if not outright physically crippled—you see speech impediments, hunchbacks, limps, but most of all an overwhelming spiritual flatness." Expecting hills and dales of spiritual plenitude exuding from the patrons of late-night clubs is a losing proposition, and almost anybody can look like a bughouse freak when your eyeballs are soaking like a couple of martini olives.

Which is not to say Lester didn't have the capacity to change and climb out of his immersion tank of alcohol, cough syrup, and seaweed-choked moods. It's to Lester's credit that he did clean up his act and may have been on the road to recovery and perhaps eventual sobriety before his internal house of cards collapsed. The angel of mercy who presided over his makeover was a Southern woman whom I was dating during the period, a blue-eyed, fine-cheek-boned, auburn-haired sweetheart with a mild voice and a wild streak that didn't show itself in public. Within the slashy confines of CBGB's she couldn't have appeared more demure and self-effacing, as if she had taken a wrong turn on her way to the cotillion and ended up doing missionary work among the permanently hungover in the casualty ward. In DeRogatis's biography he writes that Lester became "a player in a love triangle" between me and the woman whose initials are the same as mine, but it wasn't really quite that way, it was hardly as *Jules and Jim* as all that, doesn't matter now. There's no question, however, that her velvet coaxings and grooming tips had a turnaround influence on Lester, a dramatic before-and-after effect. The next time I saw Lester was, appropriately enough, at CBGB's, where he no longer lumbered around as if having fallen asleep in the laundry hamper. Gone were the usual promotional rock T-shirt that had been through the Punic Wars and occasionally used as a table mop and the baggy jeans that helped inform an unkind article in the *Voice* (with incriminating photos) about Lester's slob-dom in which he was described as "a walking dirt bomb." Now he looked spruce, round cheeked rather than rubber faced, his hair neatly trimmed and his complexion unglazed with booze-damp, wearing a sweater—a sweater! in CBGB's!—that looked as if he were readying for a weekend at the lodge spent with the crackling of autumn leaves and fireplace logs. He looked a lot like me, actually, a cousin once removed. We exchanged glances that fell somewhere between sheepish and so-what, and that was it. I didn't intend this to be one of those years-long grudges so beloved by the more militant grievance-hoarders of the *Voice* (and later, *The New Yorker*—some of those passive-aggressive infighters kept the snubbing disdain in the freezer section for *decades*). In time we would have shrugged a mutual let-bygones-be-bygones and chitchatted like normal people comparing notes on the latest rock-scene follies; the woman we both dated was such a deft diplomat and tension defuser that at some point she would have maneuvered us into a peace settlement before our foggy egos could object. But that particular night, I just wasn't in the mood to be nice.

Moods aren't always the most reliable guidance systems to go by,

because that "next time" turned out to be the last time I would see
Lester. There was no way to know, but there's almost never any way
to know. I got a shaken phone call one day from J., who told me
Lester had been found dead, his body sprawled on the couch, as if he
had lain down to take a nap, except his eyes were open, his skin had
gone gray. The word "suicide" didn't flashcard in most of his friends'
minds. It didn't fit his state of morale. Even though Lester was prone
to dive-bomb depressions, nearly everything was looking up for him
now—new girlfriend, the prospect of decamping to Mexico to write
a novel without Manhattan jamming his frequencies. So an acciden-
tal overdose was the likely candidate, and yet that assumption didn't
make for a neat fit because Lester had made such strides in recent
months getting off the intoxicants and obliterators that had been
his faithful sidekicks for so many years. He had reversed the tailspin
that had sent Peter Laughner and so many others nose-diving. It
was Albert Goldman—who didn't know Lester personally but who
was a psychopharmacological wizard whose forensic premise was
that you couldn't fully comprehend any rock star's phenomenology
unless you knew what he was "on," what was in his tox screen—who
later explained to me how common such fatal setbacks were, the why
factor. The heavy-duty addict who's dumped the booze and drugs
from his system is in a weakened state that persists longer than he
anticipates, and is often most vulnerable when he's feeling better but
his system is still processing the slow-motion shock of withdrawal;
it's really a time to take it nice and slow and easy. However, the
addict's ego, that Gollum clinging to the rocks, tells the withdrawer
that after all the big-time stuff he's taken and the epic binges that
they still talk about wherever bearded sailors gather, having a taste
of this or popping a little of that is nothing he can't handle, no
big deal. Lester was especially vulnerable because for good or ill he
seldom did anything in a small way, using a mental measuring cup.

Goldman's snap diagnosis was confirmed (for me, anyway) when
DeRogatis's biography came out in 2000, detailing how on the
night before Lester died, the guitarist Bob Quine (of Richard Hell

and the Voidoids) visited his apartment carrying a tape of the new Voidoids album. "Lester emerged from the bathroom and swallowed a handful of pills. 'Valium,' he said when Quine inquired." The next day Lester rang up a friend named Nancy Stillman, whom he hadn't spoken with recently, and "she thought she recognized the higher pitch that Lester's voice assumed when he took Valium, and she asked him what he was on. 'Don't be my fucking mother,' he snapped." It was Stillman who found the body later that night. It wasn't Valium that ended up fingered as the primary suspect in Lester's death, but Darvon, a narcotic and analgesic that packed a much bigger risk of overdose. Whatever the final tab ("No one will ever know for certain whether Lester took two Darvons or twenty-two," DeRogatis wrote), Lester's death at the robbing age of thirty-three was a resonating heart-punch to everyone who knew and read him, though within journalism the resonation was confined at first to a small shock field.

In the obituary for Lester that ran in the *Voice* (May 11, 1982), Christgau wrote of Lester's problems bending the cage bars of rock reviewing and making his escape. "Although he was a more coherent, punctual, *professional* journalist than 90 per cent of the editors who considered him a lunatic, his autodidactic moralism, chronic logorrhea, and fantastic imagination rendered him unsuitable for the slicks. Anyway, rock criticism is below police reporting and horoscopes in the literary hierarchy, and while Lester wanted to write—and did write—about almost everything, rock criticism was what he was best at."

How low rock ranked in the literary hierarchy was played out for me just a day or so later, when I attended a cocktail party hosted by Mort Zuckerman, the real-estate mogul who bought the *Atlantic Monthly* in 1980 and wooed William Whitworth away from *The New Yorker* to be the magazine's editor in chief. I'm not sure why I was invited to the party. I knew Whitworth through Pauline—he was one of Pauline's editors, a model of tact and equanimity—and wrote for him at the *Atlantic,* but not every New York–based writer who contributed to the magazine under its new regime had been invited to this clambake, and I felt like a guest pass among a bevy of season-ticket holders. Since it was news in my universe, I mentioned to a couple of writer/editors there how awful it was about Lester's death, and it was clear I had flown right into the clouds as far as they were concerned, so few pigeon tracks did they have of who Lester was or what he did, apart from a front-page *Voice* byline or two that may have leaped off the newsstands. He was a distant rumble downtown that they were dimly aware of, though they agreed someone dying that young was awful. By the time I was introduced to Nora Ephron, who thanked me for something I had written about her recently (or was it for a dig I had taken against her former husband Carl Bernstein?), I had wised up enough to delete Lester's overdose as a conversation topic among guests aglow within the magic aquarium of Mort Zuckerman, his money, and what Mort Zuckerman's money would mean for the *Atlantic Monthly*. Besides, nobody likes a bringdown. At the end of our brief chat, at a loss for a suave way to take my leave, I inanely said to Nora, "Well, maybe we'll run into each other sometime soon." "I doubt it," she said, not curtly, but as a clipped fact of life, spearing my empty pleasantry with a fish fork.

And so it proved to be. I wouldn't run into Ephron until decades later on the opposite coast, where she and I were among those enveloped within the celestial orange cloud of the hospitality of Arianna Huffington, who was hosting at her Brentwood home a party for the *Nation* magazine in conjunction with the Los Angeles Times Festival of Books, then at the zenith of its luminariness under the impresario wand of the *Times*'s elegant book-review editor Steve Wasserman. The pheromones of success suffused the gathering even more strongly than they had at Mort Zuckerman's decades before. But then, success had become so much more successful since the seventies, a higher, richer, headier halation. I spotted Ephron from a safe distance; she formed a trinity with two other women, one of whom was the *New York Times* columnist and dark-stockinged, red-tressed femme fatale Maureen Dowd. "You should go over and say hello," my date for the evening suggested, but I declined, not wanting to interrupt this impromptu meeting of the Dorothy Parker Society. Gore Vidal was also in attendance, ensconced on a sofa (even in his late infirmity, nobody ensconces like Gore Vidal) as admirers, one after another in an orderly fashion, stopped to pay their respects, as if presenting themselves to a monarch in exile. I paid mine too, as was only proper, knowing much better now that we like-minded writers have to stick together no matter how much we defund each other's patience.

CBGB's wasn't a romantic-erotic rendezvous spot, a lovers' retreat with discreet corners for nuzzling and those more advanced favors provided in the balconies of Studio 54, say. It was not a place one went in search of a tender touch and molten glances. (Once when I asked the poet-rocker Lydia Lunch how things were going, she said, just fine: "My boyfriend and I spent the weekend drilling holes in each other's teeth.") Nor was it a slumming scene doused with the alley-cat stink of *nostalgie de la boue,* a dive where posh debutantes or downtown gamines in black leggings could find ravishment at the seam-ripping hands of a sensitive brute who worked at the Strand Bookstore by day, club-hunted by night, and knew how to weld. (Or perhaps there was too much alley-cat stink. I made the mistake of taking a date there once who prided herself on being a bohemian spirit, something she cultivated growing up in New Orleans like a rare orchid. She took one whiff of CBGB's, and if she had recoiled any harder, I would have had to catch her in my arms. And here I thought she would appreciate our little pissoir.) Personal charisma was sliced too thin in the punk scene to attract colorful moths. A lazy entitlement lolled south through the loins of those beyond-cool scenesters looking for something soft to lean against or into, as long as it didn't involve minimum-plus effort. One female friend, a fellow journalist who went on to direct films, nailed this type as the sort of charmer who, if you buy him a drink, might let you give him a blow job later. Falling asleep while receiving a blow job was not an unheard tale in those pioneer days, not the sort of thing to bolster a girl's confidence, though most sounded philosophical about it. Musicians scored at CBGB's (there was a sex chart in the ladies' room peter-metering the top contenders on the scene, a historical gem unfortunately lost to history—drowned under waves of graffiti), but musicians always score, in every musical field; they never go home alone (unless they already have somebody there waiting), from the classical violist to the jazz saxist to the most malnourished-looking rocker who at 3:00 a.m. can barely stand and hold his liquor without violent expulsion. When one of my former girlfriends, who traded in rock journalism for a folk-rock guitar, told Patti Smith that her latest fella had thrown up on her recently, Patti said, with the wise sisterliness of experience: "Oh, nearly all my boyfriends have thrown up in my lap at one time or another. A guy's not really your boyfriend until he's thrown up on you."

Punk, new wave, the underground scene, whatever handle was hung on what was happening downtown, it wasn't about hot-wiring the body, setting it into centrifugal motion under a flashing dome of lights with the bass thump rising from the floor like the heartbeat of a fertility god. When audiences stood at CBGB's, Max's Kansas City, or some unspecified fire-hazard club, it was usually to see better, and when they did instruct themselves to move, it was primarily back and forth from the waist, a metronomic trance that was a cross between an assenting nod and a Hasidic Jew shuckling as he reads the Talmud. Even Blondie—who would score a commercial success denied the Ramones and Television with a disco-inflected album whose diamond-etched production delineated the pop tunefulness of songs the band had muddled through for years onstage, like the cast of *Gilligan's Island* trying to build a boat—didn't unhinge their fans' hips and get them dancing, no surprise given that Blondie's phosphorescent chanteuse, Debbie Harry, teetering in high heels and flickering in and out of phase like a TV screen on the blink, couldn't get a groove going long enough for the other Mouseketeers to follow. It didn't help that her boyfriend and Blondie guitarist, Chris Stein, would sometimes sing harmony not by joining her at her mike but by hollering into her ear, which would throw off anyone's equilibrium. Whether Stein did this because he was being thoughtless or deliberately obnoxious, I was never sure, but this was a prankster who hit balls, so I tilted toward the latter interpretation.

What you wore mattered more than how you moved, and what you wore didn't matter much at first, until fetishism gained a steel toehold. Just as I never went hippie during the sixties (tie-dye doesn't look good on *anybody,* the one fashion dictum I hold absolute), I never went punk, sparing myself incalculable embarrassment in the future of photos surfacing on the mocking Internet showing me decked out like Jimmy Ramone, Boy Reporter, with my notepad flipped out, ready for action. Although I did buy a long brown leather overcoat with an almost military cut that had one friend concerned that it looked a little German officer corps, something retrieved from the Moscow retreat. I showed the label that marked it as American made from the sixties, but she still thought it might make people think of Field Marshal Rommel. To soften any such impression, I repaired a sleeve on the coat that was threatening to drop off like a severed arm with a ring of large pink diaper pins, which I thought was a nice punk touch (since safety pins were now all the piercing rage, stuck through fabric and flesh as if the two were interchangeable), with the baby pinkness adding a note of put-on, an anti-punk punk statement. It was without much in the way of using my brain that I wore this thrift-shop pink-diaper-pinned brown leather overcoat to my first meeting with William Shawn, the editor of *The New Yorker,* who, with a brown-egg composure as impossible to crinkle as a Zen master's, helped me out of it and hung it on the coat stand without a single comment or flicker of surmise, as if it were just another outer garment worn to ward off cold. As he led me into his office, I noticed a rip in the brown sofa that looked like a knife gash, itself a rather punk touch. I asked someone about it later, and she said, "It's been there for ages—so long the rest of us don't notice it anymore." Although Shawn said nothing about the coat and it didn't cost me an assignment from *The New Yorker* (a profile of a Las Vegas entertainment legend named Shecky Greene—a comedian renowned among fellow comics for his improvisational genius), I decided not to waltz that leather number out in adult society again unless I was sure of the company I was meeting. A true punk seditionist wouldn't have cared, but I started going to the ballet about then and knew so little about it that I wanted to look inconspicuous, if that makes any sense.

Punk fashion itself began to feast on its own lean meat as the "look" at CBGB's and similar clubs mutated into mutant *Clockwork Orange* aggro-wear baroque in its puncture-mark motorcycle-vampire detailing—a scavenger mix of Goth and garbage heap still venereally visible in what remains of the ungentrified East Village today (the punk equivalent to the historical restoration of the bonnets and shoe buckles in Colonial Williamsburg). This look reflected the transatlantic influence of English punk, which was far more radically tooled, piratical, politicized, defiantly, cawingly larynx'd, and media-provocateurish, and small wonder—London had all those "red top" scandal-crazed tabloids like the *Sun* and the *Daily Mirror* primed to have a sizzle-shit of indignation over the latest outrage from the obliging Sex Pistols. (THE FILTH AND THE FURY, barked the now-famous front-page headline of the *Daily Mirror* after the Pistols swore like parrots on live TV.) Meanwhile, here in our fair parish, the New York tabloids, the *Daily News* and the *Post,* had so many other five-alarm melodramas to cover (from the "Son of Sam" serial-murder rampage to the New York Yankees' Billy Martin–Reggie Jackson–George Steinbrenner axis of ego in the burning Bronx) that they weren't going to squander valuable outrage space on fish bait. Dominating the underground-rock-scene coverage in the daily press was John Rockwell, the chief rock critic of the *New York Times* and a friendly nodder to avant-garde aspirations, who accepted whatever sonic detritus might come jet-engining his way as if it were cousin to Stockhausen or La Monte Young banging on a treated piano. He wasn't going to fry bacon on his forehead over some skin-and-bones character spitting out curses onstage or off. Short of human sacrifice, offending Rockwell would take some doing.

(I once attended a party hosted by Rockwell in his loft to welcome Greil Marcus on a visit to Manhattan. Marcus, the author of *Mystery Train* and the future annotator of all things Dylanesque and Elvisiana, was based in California and considered the super-cerebral prince regent of the West to Christgau's East Coast suzerainty. He had the gritted zeal of a Marxist rhetorician with a deep-sea diver's quest for buried cosmology and gnostic scraps of "the old, weird America," wielding a different set of academic/analytical equipment from the majority of us ditchdiggers. In retrospect, the fact that I was invited to such a soiree marked an unofficial induction into the ranks of the fraternal order of rock critics, a sign that I wasn't considered just another freelancer dressing up the set. It wasn't only rock writers invited either. A *Village Voice* editor was engaged in such intense nebbishy flirtation with a *New York Times* writer, a petite, vibrant blonde who looked as if she were always up for a game of volleyball, that he came over to us and nervously said, "I mean, suppose something happens tonight, suppose we go back to my place, or her place—I don't know, I mean, she writes for the *Times*," italicizing the last word aloud. He was reassured that he would be able to acquit himself—"It's not as if you're going to bed with the building." He nodded, though you could see he was still mentally nibbling on the daunting task ahead like a squirrel working a nut. It was the age of *Annie Hall* and everyone played his or her part.)

But at some point the shock of the new wore off until bigger shocks were needed to keep everything twitching. Punk was an after-dark pursuit, but the darkness doubled, to quote a Television lyric, and acquired a taste of blood in its mouth and the oral archery of letting fly with saliva and phlegm. The array of spit tricks that came to be associated with punk were a British import, Talking Heads and other New York bands returning from their first English tours full of battle tales about being saliva-bombed in a relentless bukkake while onstage; as I recall, Tina Weymouth was a favorite rain target of punk gobbers, being spat on cited as a welcoming gesture of acceptance, like the Hells Angels pissing on an inductee's jeans as part of the initiation ceremony, then making him put them on. Coming offstage night after night and removing a dripping coat of spittle with a dry towel didn't foster a sense of belonging, however, no matter how favorable the subsequent reviews. Pogoing, too, was an English import, an indoor exercise perfect for tight spots, turning the pogoer into a hopping human exclamation mark. (Whereas disco demanded tons of hip room under the dome to set Dionysian centrifugal forces into motion.) Pogoing was compared to the hopping of the Masai, but the Masai hopped in unison, at least in the African documentaries and dubious colonial-war movie footage I had seen, whereas this indoor bouncing was closer to Whac-a-Mole with shaven and Mohawked heads popping up through the holes.

The droogier members of the English punk scene and the rock journalists who critically ransacked their way through the columns of *New Musical Express* (*NME,* as it was better known, a homonym for "enemy," as the Sex Pistols reminded us in "Anarchy in the U.K.") and Xeroxed fanzines with names like *Sniffin' Glue* and ransom-note layouts found much of the New York punk scene de-balled with artiness, affectation, and rhyming couplets, unwilling to wage militia battle against the deadwood holding insurrectionary energies down. While David Byrne seemed to be knitting a cardigan with his acoustic guitar and Tom Verlaine conducted a séance with the French Symbolist poets in some automobile graveyard, English punk bands such as the Damned had songs titled "Stab Your Back," and another band with a heavy rep was called the Stranglers, as if it had no need of sharp implements to inflict harm. None of the CBGB's punk bands were politically, militantly barricades-smashing like the Clash, a band Patti was the first to clue me in on and who seemed to have scoped out the field of fire for themselves. Unlike the Sex Pistols, whose cobra attack and anarchist cry, thrilling as it was, seemed too obvious a wicked potion whipped up in the manager-impresario Malcolm McLaren's Dada lab. A brilliant magpie with a knack for extracting the most delectable, usable bits, McLaren played his protégés and the press like a cross between Dickens's Fagin and Diaghilev, an exploiter capable of producing exaltation, although the corrosive charisma of Johnny Rotten—who always looked a little jaundiced around the gills—and the nose-bloodied insensibility of the bassist Sid Vicious proved more than even McLaren's mesmerist power could handle.

As English punk bands snatched the imaginations of New York rock fans by the scruffy balls and snub-nosed tits, the New York scene began to sling the drool around like sloppy seconds, and bands such as the Dead Boys became the house sensations. They were not subtle, the Dead Boys, jingling with Nazi regalia and flying a snot rag as their pirate flag, but they made for good copy and oodles of after-dinner conversation, taking romance for a spin with such numbers as "Caught with the Meat in Your Mouth" and "Flame Thrower Love." While their black leather look may have been borrowed from the Ramones (with Joey's blessing—he noodged them to move to New York), their stage exploits were more Iggy Pop–ish, each set a roller-coaster ride on a pain-pleasure sine wave. Pain was represented by the lead singer, Stiv Bators, looping the mike cord around his neck into a noose and hanging himself from the stage's light rig, his urchin feet dangling, like a suicide artist. Pleasure was articulated by the occasional blow job that Bators received onstage, the apple-bobbing of the young female volunteer sometimes simulated (judging by the overactive head action), sometimes not. I seldom threaded myself far enough up front and to the side to get a decent viewing angle to render a decisive verdict. Gary Valentine, bass player for Blondie, singled out the servicing of Bators's dangler onstage at CBGB's as the sign that "brain rot" had infiltrated the scene, attracting audiences addicted to sick tricks. The Dead Boys weren't the only sick tricksters out there, but they showed more variety and panache in their slapstick, such as lapping up a lick of their own vomit from the stage floor, blowing their noses into slices of bologna and then eating them (this was the guitarist Cheetah Chrome's showstopper), and, on one renowned occasion, pissing into the safety helmet of the previously mentioned bartender-bouncer Merv, a highly educated man who subscribed to the *Times Literary Supplement* and with whom I used to chew the fat about Kingsley Amis and Frank Kermode between sets. We both agreed that Kermode's critical style could do with a dash of pepper. It was never clear to me how his hard hat ended up in Bators's hands as a portable urinal, though it was difficult to believe Merv would have volunteered it as a prop. He was a tolerant man who had witnessed much behind the bar, but he was not an accomplice to shenanigans.

The Dead Boys didn't revert to mild-mannered personas when they were out in civilian daylight. In that they were consistent. I once saw Cheetah Chrome drop his cheetah-spotted pants in the middle of St. Marks Place, pivot, and moon someone walking toward him—his way of saying hi. Walking in the same direction at that moment was Karen Allen, the freckled delight with the root-beer voice from *Animal House* and the original Indiana Jones. So she got mooned too. Chrome probably wasn't aware Allen was sharing the same sidewalk as the friend he was hailing, but had he known, he might have dropped his drawers even sooner. He was, in his own fashion, a true vaudevillian.

So when the news came that the U.K.'s the Damned would be performing at CBGB's on a double bill with the Dead Boys, grisly anticipation gleamed from every Dracula fang. The Damned and the Dead—their very names told you they belonged together, competing for Gothic supremacy like rival biker gangs fighting over bragging rights over whose ass is hairier. (Such a contrast to the weekends when Television and Talking Heads double billed, more akin to watching twin rocket launchings set after set, each arc higher than the last.) The Damned were the odds-on favorite to triumph in this steel-cage Black Mass. They had been around longer and proven themselves in London and the rugged vomitoria of the

English provinces, and with a drummer called Rat Scabies, it was clear they weren't angling for debutantes, like Roxy Music, but trawling the Céline sewers. (Everyone eagerly awaited the *New York Times,* given its formal style, reviewing the band and keeping an institutional straight face as it referred to "Mr. Scabies.") The Damned also had a guitarist named Captain Sensible, whose name was a welcome whimsical stroke, like the fabulous ID of the lead singer of X-Ray Spex, Poly Styrene, the defiant, unbarricaded voice of the girl-power punk anthem "Oh Bondage, Up Yours!," each hoarse syllable hurled upward from the dungeon floor. The Damned were more a glued-together assemblage of shock tactics: Scabies's drums came hard down the tracks, and Dave Vanian's vocals nailed the staccato rush of "Neat Neat Neat" and "New Rose" like a rivet gun. Vanian wasn't a slurrer, unlike so many punk slingers. But the Dead Boys were newer, rawer, maybe a trifle leaner and hungrier, with home-court advantage. They had less to lose from this contest, more to gain.

And yet lose they did, not for lack of trying. Quite the opposite. They threw themselves into every song as if it might be their last (a reasonable assumption, given Stiv Bators's predilection for playing hangman's noose), and the Damned matched them in depraved dynamism, their dueling sets heading for a draw with no clear victor until Dave Vanian outfoxed everybody. He announced that the Damned's next set would be a tribute to boredom, and he performed not onstage with his bandmates but lounging at a table below, singing between bites of take-out pizza. It was a brilliant theatrical stroke, topping whatever tattered mischief the Dead Boys could do by adopting the pose of a slumming dandy who needn't bother demonstrating his superiority to these nouveau pretenders—rather than exert himself, he'd simply sit back and enjoy his own show, with a nice snack. By unilaterally disarming, Vanian converted the contest into a punk parody of patrician put-on—so British, so Peter Cook, so disdainfully droll. Not that any of this inspired the Dead Boys to question their tactics and hang a Brechtian frame around their trash pickups, but neither did it alter the mise-en-scène in New York as much as it did elsewhere.

It was on the other coast that the darkness went monochromatic and transgressive with a vengeance. Rival bands and factions in the New York scene did little more than exchange the sorts of half sneers and scowls indistinguishable from the dirty looks thrown around at the average book party uptown, back when they still had book parties that didn't look like Goodwill drives. But in Los Angeles in the punk seventies, the posturing ill will was enough to carve up a new Black Dahlia. "There's something unsubtle in the LA psyche," Valentine observes in *New York Rocker.* "Maybe it's the perpetual sunshine, or maybe it's living in a bunch of suburbs looking for a city. But the New York cool of Patti Smith, Television and Richard Hell didn't take. Safety pins, leather, chains and vomit—the whole UK thing—did." Once again the Damned were the ambassadors of this dystopian swan dive. As Valentine writes:

> In April 1977 with the Damned shows at the Starwood—a veteran rock club on Santa Monica Boulevard—life changed. Soon after, at a Punk Rock Invasion show at the Orpheum Theatre on Sunset Boulevard, the Dils played in front of a hammer and sickle flag, and the Germs' Bobby Pyn—later the ill-fated Darby Crash—ended their set by winning the Iggy Pop lookalike contest, covering himself in peanut butter while being whipped with licorice . . . Darby was making a successful play to become LA's comic version of Sid Vicious and Germs' fans later identified each other by the self-inflicted cigarette burns on their arms.

Three months later a new club opened on Cherokee Avenue called the Masque (presumably an homage to Poe's "Masque of the Red Death"), where this converted basement rehearsal studio became a punk rec room—or perhaps wreck room is more apt. "Its house rules were 'excess, excess, excess.' Graffiti blared FAGS IS NOT COOL and KILL ALL HIPPIES. Dress code demanded swastikas."

By the time Blondie was playing the New York punk clubs again after months of touring, blight had set in. "The Dead Boys and the Damned had made an impact, and the audience at CBs and Max's was mostly headbanging weekend punks, tumbling in from Long Island and Jersey. Excess and stupidity seemed on tap, and the whole scene started to take on a depressingly incestuous character." The trash-compactor smart-dumb of the Ramones was one thing—their lyrics, set to an engine roar, drew upon a drive-in double-feature schlock force that once doodled inside the skulls of so many gifted, stunted young male American misfits—but this was the real item, with nowhere to go but further down.

So, when Nancy Spungen and Sid Vicious took turns dying dismal deaths, she by a knife driven below her navel presumably by a zonked-out Sid in their first-floor room at the Hotel Chelsea, he by a heroin overdose following his release from Rikers Island, his ashes later scattered over her grave, it was only the Weegee garishness of the crime scenes that impressed. Their suicide-by-any-other-name obituary notices were already typed into their needle tracks. The final pressing of the self-destruction button was a foregone conclusion, Sid and Nancy leaning blearily on each other as they left CBGB's at night as if prematurely leading their own funeral procession, a pair of effigies. In a different decade, their lust for attention might have ensured their survival, a glimmer of self-interest staying his hand and diluting the heroin: the two of them pulling up just shy of death and entering rehab to co-star in a reality series upon their release from Dr. Drew's custody. But then they wouldn't have lived on in squalid legend, documentary makers three decades later still raising the question, "Who killed Nancy?," as if she were the victim in the punk pulp novel James Ellroy never got around to writing, with Sid the fall guy, a patsy held suspended by a single puppet string until that, too, snapped.

Not that there weren't macabre laughs to be had, even while so many on the scene seemed to wall-paint their moods a malevolent shade of black. As I wrote in the *Voice* in 1977:

"Love me," sings Lux Interior of the Cramps, hunched over on the CBGB stage, his hands dangling near his knees. "*Love me*," Lux demands, like a leper threatening tourists on the streets of Calcutta. He is flanked by guitarists Bryan Gregory, who turns his back and snarls over his shoulder at the audience, and Ivy Rorschach, who stands as sternly silent as a sentry with orders to kill. Behind them drummer Miriam Linna pounds away, her floor tom-tom propped on four empty kidney-bean cans. After his love begging leaves him empty-handed, Lux sings of the joys of strychnine and the torment of being a teenage werewolf ("with braces on my fangs"); later, they all don shades for "Sunglasses After Dark," and Gregory disdainfully tosses his plastic rimmed pair into the gallery.

—"Can the Cramps Loosen Up?"

The Cramps began getting noticed at CBGB's in 1976, it being hard not to notice a rockabilly band that was a cross between the Addams Family and inmates of a juvenile detention center, its lead singer named Lux Interior and the guitarist a Batman villainess called Poison Ivy, whose mushroom-cloud wig could cushion any fall, the five of them banging out a beat that lurched from side to side like skeletons swinging their bones. "I'm Cramped" may have been the band's personal anthem, but "Sunglasses After Dark" (about how wearing a cool pair of shades turns every night outing into an obstacle course) was the song fans adopted as their passport. The band called the Sic Fucks—whose backup singers, Tish and Snooky (the Laverne and Shirley of the East Village), dressed onstage in nuns' cowls and Bettie Page lingerie, were the entrepreneurial founders of the St. Marks Place landmark store Manic Panic—endeared themselves with such plainly felt sentiments as "St. Louis Sucks" and "Chop Up Your Mother," the lead singer, Russell Wolinsky, doing a hilarious running patter between numbers like some Catskills emcee, mocking punk pretenders and crusaders (he could be scathing about the Clash and their commando attitude), the scene having evolved far enough to burlesque itself. But even these laughs seemed to have been scraped off the crusty sides of the tension in the air, signs of a decadent phase.

It wasn't until the B-52s arrived from Athens, Georgia, like a megadose of vitamin D, that genuine smiles seemed to sunrise in people's heads unaccompanied by sarcastic critique. When they first took the stage at Max's and CBGB's, they were greeted by giggles and hollow whoops, the suspicion being that they were some kind of joke band, what with Kate Pierson and Cindy Wilson in beehive hairdos and the lead singer, Fred Schneider, apparently ready for a luau. But when they kicked into "52 Girls," their sound was more tight-meshed and shone like silver foil, and there were actual *harmonies*—so wondrously alien to our jackhammered ears—and when Fred rocked out during the instrumental bridges, he moved his arms and legs around until we recognized what it was: something known as *dancing*. Would marvels never cease? Patti Smith would every now and then do a Sufi twirl, if there was room, but breaking into an unembarrassed Frug seemed a violation of some local ordinance or tribal law. And when Cindy, beautiful Cindy, shouted the seemingly silly lyric "Why won't you dance with me?/I'm not no Limburger," her voice hoarsening into a grainy scrape of pleading, it was a needy cry so unlike the aura of invincibility that you expected from a band brandishing such upbeat Day-Glo colors and kitschy-kitschy coo. Ricky Wilson, the Bees' guitarist and Cindy's brother, would die of AIDS at the age of thirty-two in the mid-eighties, a victim of the devastation that extinguished so many talents of that young generation of gay men and left a permanent gray void, a lost kingdom of creative possibility, as symbolized by Ricky's grave site in Athens, Georgia, his headstone a miniature pyramid where visitors leave flowers and trinkets.

Sophomore jinx isn't just for baseball pitchers, and the second albums of both Patti Smith and Television got a more mottled reception than their rapturous firsts. *Radio Ethiopia* sounded like a clogged exhaust fan to some reviewers, especially its title track,

ten minutes of electronic dental flossing, and the opening lines of
"Pissing in a River"—"Pissing in a river/Watching it rise"—led to
wiseacre remarks about the huge holding capacity of Patti's bladder. Television's *Adventure* had some stunners—"Glory," "Ain't That
Nothin'," the tidal roll of "The Dream's Dream"—but the title song
sounded like a TV-jingle sea chantey ("Adventure/I love adventure"),
and *Marquee Moon*'s tight grip of tension escaping through a clenched
fist was missing, the curtain-parting sense of eventfulness dissipated
into too much immaculate musicianship. The critical reaction was
a shower of petals compared with the welcoming from the uninitiated. When Television toured with Peter Gabriel (the founder of
the group Genesis gone solo) to promote *Adventure,* they were met
onstage by a hard rain of objects hurled at them from an unappreciative audience that was unappreciative before the first guitar chord
was struck, that is, on ignorant principle. In theory, Gabriel fans
should have come from a more refined stratum of rock enthusiast;
in practice, they were just as happy as your subaverage heavy-metal
fan to exercise their throwing arms. With his analytical dispassion
exercised at a dreamy remove, Verlaine described to me what it was
like to be under grenade attack from an assortment of bottles, cans,
and small batteries. "There was no time to duck or react, because
the stage lights were so bright that you couldn't see what was being
thrown until it broke through that bright screen, materializing out
of nowhere, as if the darkness itself had thrown it." He might have
been an astronomer describing a shower of space debris, except that
this debris was fired on purpose with his name on it.

Patti, she fell into the darkness, a black hole just waiting beyond
the edge. Touring after the release of *Radio Ethiopia,* she was opening for Bob Seger in Tampa, Florida, when, during "Ain't It Strange,"
she danced herself off the stage and hit the concrete floor of the
orchestra pit fifteen feet down, breaking neck vertebrae and putting
herself out of commission for a year, which was preferable to some
of the alternatives. A fall like that could have been fatal. During
her recuperation I visited Patti at the airy apartment of Blue Öyster

Cult's Allen Lanier at One Fifth Avenue, where Patti was still getting used to swiveling around with a neck brace that seemed to hold her prisoner. She wasn't in bad spirits, considering, but each movement involved precautionary effort that you sensed her gauging inside her head, measuring in increments, which was sobering after seeing her spirit-glide in flowy half circles around the stage before. At one point she asked me if I'd seen anything lately I liked, and I went into a rhapsody about Twyla Tharp's dance *Push Comes to Shove,* starring Mikhail Baryshnikov at his most *Guys and Dolls* quick-cool, and after I described the stop-start vocabulary of Tharp's choreography with a rough-sketch demonstration, Patti said, as if informing me of a little fact I might have overlooked: "I do that onstage." A mild comment that jerked the reins of my insensitivity, snapping my mind awake to what my stupid mouth was doing: raving about erratic, eloquent, jazzy movement to someone with broken vertebrae in a neck brace having to hold herself as stiff as Elsa Lanchester in *Bride of Frankenstein.* Truth was, she *didn't* do that onstage, even when her chakras were uncongested, but she was determined to stick up for herself, not out of false pride, but because hanging tough is what divides the long-range dedicated from the dilettantes. It wasn't until my dumb feet were back on the sidewalk that I registered that she had used the present tense—not "I've done that," but "I do that." She hadn't let a chasm open in her mind between Before the Fall and After. It was all one continuum, something Buddhism teaches but hardly anyone ever practices.

Although CBGB's remained my main port of call, I hit other venues to see other bands as the underground/punk/new wave/neo-minimalist/post-punk/No Wave scene spoked off uptown and crosstown, to Danceteria and Hurrah and the Mudd Club, the latter having its own status strata and a more arty-boho attitude of enclosure than one encountered on the Bowery. (Though the rats that milled outside on the blocks adjoining White Street were, if anything, plumper and more capable of playing for the NFL.) As the bands I had first seen at CBGB's became irregulars now that touring had become their new mistress, my own visits became more infrequent, tapering off to nil once hardcore with its boots, stubbled heads, and mosh-pit crocodile feedings seized the banner as if it were a pikestaff with a head attached. Hardcore was too hortatory and single-minded for me, a power tool with only one fast speed. But each to his own bedlam.

After an absence of many years, during which I was introduced to adulthood, I made a little pilgrimage down the Bowery, part of a reunion tour. It was around midday. Rain spattered from a pouty, gray sky that had little to recommend itself, the rainfall light enough for the drops to make contact individually, though it was clear heavier reinforcements were on the way. The Bowery had seldom looked so indifferent to itself. And yet it was a warm occasion that brought me—us—here, a trio of former alumni. I was rendezvousing with Mary Harron and Fran Pelzman, whom I had met at CBGB's when we were young and pale and new to the show. Mary was more than pale, closer to spectral, as I discovered one afternoon when I ran into her on the street months after we had first met each other and did a double take. It was the first time I had seen her in daylight—she looked like something out of Henry James. Canadian by birth, educated in England, Mary imported a cool, accepting air of refinement to any room steeped in squalor, a probing curiosity attached to a deep appreciation for comedy that would come in handy in her role as *Punk* magazine's touch of class. Originally a print journalist, Mary began writing and directing feature segments for the BBC's *Late Show,* a cultural review show where we collaborated on a segment devoted to Martin Amis (during which we re-created his arrival at Oxford with a soundtrack choir of angels). When the *Late Show* and Channel 13/PBS co-produced an arts program called *Edge,* though public television being public television, whatever "edge" there was was soon filed away by the genteel overseers of caution under the Emasculation Proclamation that seemed to be PBS's primary directive. But before the bland-down began, we managed to do funny, imaginative visual essays on Norman

Mailer's *Harlot's Ghost,* the shock comedy of Andrew "Dice" Clay, and a never-aired visit to the luxury crypt overlooking Central Park South that was the diabolical lair of Albert Goldman, then at the height of his celebrity-defamation infamy, a mini-feature that was shot as an Expressionist horror film and never shown in the States, the corporate plug pulled on *Edge* before it could be aired. Mary went on to execute beautifully designed and comic outrages of her own as the director of *I Shot Andy Warhol* and the screen adaptation of Bret Easton Ellis's *American Psycho,* in which Christian Bale's cheekbones would be immortally etched as emblems of psychopathic yuppie evil.

Fran, who used to date Television's Billy Ficca, went on to write a guide to Cute Guys and later married the brilliant economics writer and *Barron's* contributor John Liscio, her life as a suburban mom sliced in two when John died of liver and kidney failure at the age of fifty-one, leaving her a widow with two children. She can be seen briefly in *Blank Generation* too, sitting at a table near the front. Fran and Mary weren't paying a nostalgic courtesy call to CBGB's; they were revisiting the shrine to research a possible film version of *Please Kill Me,* the oral history of punk that had become the *Paradise Lost* for those who ached for the gritty crucible they had never known, the train they had missed. (There was a young actor I thought would be perfect to play Verlaine, a guy on the TV series *Freaks and Geeks* named James Franco.) The Jungian analyst and author James Hillman once observed that some cultural moments and institutions exert an afterlife hold on the imagination through the anecdotes and incidents that accrue into a coral reef of true myth—or, as he put it in three little words, "all that lore." All that lore is what made CBGB's compelling long after it became a raucous shell, and what has kept the myth of the Algonquin Round Table alive, no matter how mid-range the achievements of Dorothy Parker, George S. Kaufman, and Robert Benchley appear today, or how downright dropped-off-the-map the names of Alexander Woollcott and Heywood Broun are. Same for the Beats—

they were a self-aware, self-promoting lore syndicate whose exploits still inspire hipster doofuses today, at least those who forswear irony. Lore is publicity that lasts long after there's nothing left to publicize.

Through the front doors of CBGB's we went, and there, sitting at his desk in the front, was bearded Hilly, as if he had not left his outpost since we had last seen him, the lone survivor of a deserted fort. The bar only hung with a contemplative weight of desolate quiet because it was early afternoon, not because it was closed for business, but we still felt a subdued piety because so many memories were held here in this living-dying museum that was once our skinny hangout. Hilly welcomed us sweetly, interrupting and then restarting a conversation with a contractor or inspector that had the Pinteresque aspect of missing parts in the dialogue that gave the bits we were hearing an occult quality, broken pieces of a ritualistic spell. We wandered around, so much as it was, but more so. The walls—they were like the drawings and inscriptions on the inside of a sacred grotto, layers upon faded layers of flyers for long-gone bands, rogue galaxies of graffiti, the Pompeian remains of the punk proletariat, so much more powerful than they appeared in photography books about CBGB's, more charged with presence and the absence of the hundreds of hands that had contributed every indecorous dab. I descended to the bathrooms downstairs, and they were just as Dantesque as ever, the stall-less toilet resting like a debauched throne, like the only thing left after a lightning bolt had blackened everything else to cinders and char. I experienced a tender awe amid this necropolitan splendor that had managed to be *left alone,* raising itself with minor supervision, as punk itself had.

When we reascended to join the surface dwellers, Hilly was still papa-bear-ing it at the front, his interlocutor gone. One of us asked about Joey Ramone, who was in the hospital with lymphoma, which had been taking it out of him for seven years. "I hear he's doing better," Hilly said. "Touch and go, but last I heard he was improving." It turned out to be the last rally before the final out, Joey dying not long after, on April 15, 2001, a year that had a lot more waiting for all of us. A stretch of East Second Street was later renamed in honor of Joey, the commemorative sign eventually raised twenty feet above ground level after having been stolen so often. That's where so much creative excitement ends up, with souvenir collecting. After years of Laocoön legal and real-estate tax battles, CBGB's closed for good in 2006 with a farewell performance starring Patti Smith, which was only righteous, Patti's birth star being where it truly began and now would snuff out. At one point she relayed a message from an absent Tom Verlaine: "Tom reluctantly sends his love." I laughed at home, listening to the live broadcast on Sirius satellite. It was the best use of an adverb since Hemingway's "magnanimously" in *A Moveable Feast.* I had been invited to CBGB's finale but decided not to go on the afternoon of the show, telling myself I was on deadline (I was, I always am), that it was too much of a drag to go that far downtown, that it would be a complete mob scene, all that. But I also think it was because I was afraid of how happy I might be to see everyone again after so many years, a coward when it came to unembarrassed joy and affection. I might have gone on a hugging spree, which is not how we did things back in those outlaw days.

PART IV:

Bodily Contact

A fiction writer friend of mine once told me about the exact moment she knew her marriage was sunk. It was the afternoon that she entered their East Village apartment and in the living room sat her husband and his brother, watching a porn movie together. That wasn't what unnerved her. What unnerved her was that they heard her come in, saw her standing there (the reaction on her face must have made for a classic close-up), and yet remained fastened on the screen action in the room, as if it were an NFL game, not even bothering to mute the groans or hit the pause button, perhaps not wanting to interrupt the "flow." For my friend, this was it, the final indignity. It betrayed such a down-deep disregard and disrespect for her feelings, such sofa-slug inertia and evolutionary back-dip, that "alienation of affection" was no longer a legalistic phrase but a palpable presence, a cold slap. It was right out there in the fuck-you so-what open, a form of infidelity so indolent it didn't even require another actual woman. I shared my friend's revulsion—I hadn't met her husband but had always assumed he was a snake, based on creditable hearsay coming mostly from her (she is now happily remarried)—but for me the real mind-boggler of the story was that this skink had been watching a porn movie *with his brother.* I have three brothers of my own, and I couldn't imagine settling in with a snack tray and watching a wankeroo with any one or any combination of them—how tarantula-crawling, the very idea. What if Mom found out? The very prospect made one crinkle inside. No, I maintained a more traditional attitude. As far as I was concerned, porn was to be enjoyed solely within the privacy of your own shame and guilt, or among strangers, unable to identify you from police suspect photos.

That's how the seventies raised me, one of the enduring values they instilled.

It was in the seventies that porn swamp-gassed into an atmospheric condition in culture and society, became part of the parlance, no longer treated as contraband or projected on a sheet in your weird uncle's living room. If in the sixties sexual liberation promised rainbow-arching orgasms that would melt the shoe buckles of puritanism and banish possessive ego to the bourgeois boneyard, that illusion was pretty much shot once the peace sign from the Summer of Love was bent into the swastika self-carved on Charlie Manson's forehead as the symbol of the decade. Porn was the prowler that made itself permanently at home, a movie projector beaming from the rear cave of the urban skull. Urban, because it was in cities such as Los Angeles, San Francisco, and New York that movie porn was produced, played in theaters, and available to choosy shoppers, the day of the local strip-mall adult distributorship having not quite blearily dawned. (In the better-stocked outlets along Eighth Avenue, you'd see guys going up to the counter with their arms full of shiny VHS cassette boxes, stocking up as if preparing for a long siege that might disrupt supply routes.) The Naked City conferred a cloak of anonymity, the opportunity to go undetected, unjudged. Even if one (and by "one" I mean me, and by "me" I mean a bodiless junior me delegated to revisit the past) decided to head-duck into a porn theater to catch a double feature of *The Filthy Five* and *The Promiscuous Sex* or some other inspired booking, it was considered discourteous to sit too near another patron, a buffer zone of two empty seats considered adequate, three exemplary, and choosing a different row altogether the truly gallant thing to do. Walking into the middle of a movie and asking someone to clarify a plot point—very poor form. Unlike gay men, whose porn-going was of a more active, participant nature, based on the recitals I've heard, straight men preferred to be left alone with their sunken thoughts in such situations without the chapel spell being broken, even those masturbating away as if to the beat of a Sousa march. In a memoir published in *The New Yorker,* David Denby describes attending a porn film with Pauline Kael, Pauline wanting to be up on the latest thing and perhaps throw a scare into William Shawn at the prospect of her turning in four thousand words on *The Private Afternoons of Pamela Mann.* Denby reports that Pauline's verbal captioning for the action on-screen was unwelcomed by those in the audience trying to concentrate and lose themselves in the beauty of the moment. "She was the only woman in the room. Onscreen, one of the studs melted for an instant and Pauline let out a loud, disappointed, 'Awww.' Men in black rain-coats sitting nearby rustled in their seats. After a few minutes, two rounded bottoms appeared, juxtaposed one on top of the other, and Pauline said, 'That's sort of sweet.' The raincoats turned and glared angrily in our direction; some of them stalked out."

Not every porn audience was as rapt as Antonioni fans trying to figure out what gives with Monica Vitti in *Red Desert.* Heckling voices were often raised during bad-dialogue scenes, of which there was no scarcity, voices that tended to belong to black men amus-ing themselves mightily and their fellow comedy fans. In one porn parody of a sci-fi epic, in which costumes and scenery owed pretty much everything to the crinkly versatility of aluminum foil, an actor so blatantly homosexual that he didn't bother feigning other-wise saucily informed the Empress Z'anna that he was going to ram his royal scepter deep inside her, to which a voice piped up, "Better ask your boyfriend first." Another time, when a porn stud sought to ejaculate on his co-star's face and overshot the landing area, hit-ting the pillow, someone chortled, "Y' missed, Robin Hood!" Such merry interjections were not the norm, however. Young and middle-aged couples would occasionally date-night at a porn film so that they could snuggle together and feel adventurously naughty, pre-sumably hoping to take away a few pointers that they could put into practice later, the cuties cozying into their seats for a bit of fun only to become uncomfortable with the sexual entrées being projected in proctological detail, their giggles and whispered asides drying up as the power plays between the characters on-screen got ugly, too forcibly overt and face-slapping for any ironic distance. As such couples slunk off in Napoleonic defeat, their bodies remained in a head-ducked semi-crouch all the way across the row and up the aisle, Groucho Marx–style, as if fleeing the scene of a bad idea. Some of them may be grandparents now, chuckling at the memory. Flickering shadows on the screen, migrating shadows in the theaters, and a Proustian forget-me-not bouquet flavoring the air—it is the sickly sweet reek of cherry disinfectant that conjures porn in the seventies for me, a candied aroma that imbued XXX theaters in Manhattan with a mortuary subduement, a certain consoling melancholy, like the bleak emptiness of a pizza take-out place at Christmas.

As with punk, my formal introduction into the porn funnel had begun with a *Village Voice* assignment. I was doing an essay on the eroticization and exploitation of young girls that puddle-jumped from Lewis Carroll's photographs to Lolita to Jodie Foster in *Taxi Driver* to Brooke Shields in *Pretty Baby* to wherever the last station stop in the piece ended up being. I needed to check out rumors that illegal underage porn was being openly sold in Times Square adult video stores and started scouting the aisles. It didn't take much scouting. The jailbait items for sale jumped out at you. It was there for peep-show viewing (peep-show booths, those Dr. Who telephone boxes for the sexually dispossessed), the footage imported from Denmark and other countries that didn't seem to care, vignettes involving young teens in student uniforms or Girl Guide outfits; likewise, bestiality films, also imported, judging by the peasant attire of the human participants on the packaging, the dirndls. I didn't want to imagine the sort of man who would linger too long at this county fair, because only a man would. Only a man would stage these things, film these things, watch these things. I was a man too, maybe not much of one yet, but enough of one to feel complicit simply knowing such things existed, maggot colonies of them.

I filed the piece, a responsible-toned cultural-reporting essay that avoided tabloid sensationalism and easy moralizing (it was not a subject suited for flippancies, that I knew going in). But after the article was printed I continued dropping in to Times Square (and by "dropping" I mean just happening to be in the slummy vicinity after making a trip expressly for that very purpose), making the irregular rounds of the theaters enough to be as up on the latest trends in smut as a racetrack tipster. Caution in my case being the better part of cowardice, I never had sex with a prostitute or ventured into the sicky-poo Krafft-Ebing side alleys of voyeurdom, priding myself on my vanilla tastes, pride being the better part of self-conceit. I intermittently haunted Times Square and it haunted me, the place exerting a pull even as it deadened the nerves, nerve deadening being part of the pull. Porn has all the attributes of junk, wrote Norman Mailer, and I interpreted his use of "junk" not simply as a synonym for trash but as a slang term for heroin and any other hook-sinking hijacker of body and soul. Porn was an addictive fix—masturbation as self-medication—and porn addiction doesn't carry the cautionary-tale romance of penthouse highs and gutter lows, just a sputtering stop-start series of catch-and-release buildups and let-gos that offered none of the humpbacked redemptive arcs of other addiction narratives. Porn hobbyists and rapid rejaculators with dark circles under their eyes and dull hair never reap the benefits of the dramatic gutter romance of alcohol or drug addiction, the binges and blackouts and bleary dawns in strange beds, the Christly withdrawal convulsions of the racked flesh and the beatific predawns that lead to the resurrection of recovery, reentry into society. For a porn addict, the blinds are always lowered and time inches sideways, other narcotics at least allowing one to forget oneself for a longer, self-losing spell, a deeper erasure. Kicking cocaine can be a conquering feat; kicking porn barely merits a back-pat and a discount coupon at Wendy's—the man with the flailing palm can't compete with the Man with the Golden Arm. I was once a guest at an AA meeting in which one of the regulars received a customary round of applause for saying how long he'd been sober, another round for how long he'd been nicotine-free, yet another for having given up caffeine, but when he topped it off by announcing it had been three months since he had masturbated to porn or images in his head, I was the only one who began to clap, stopping my hands in midair. Even for this receptive audience, he had pushed it a little too far, went for too many sympathy votes. Having run out of things to give up, he concluded his testimonial but looked tense the rest of the meeting.

Yet it wasn't necessarily all psychologically corrosive, the puppy stage of being a porn hound. It did have its vitamin side. It is standard operating procedure to decry the objectification of porn, its privileging of the Male Gaze (those mythical ray-beams that take colonial possession of the phantom of desire and pin it to the trophy wall), but there's something to be said for porn's de-subjectifying powers. At least there was back then, in the days when the printed word had a stronger muscle grip on our overstoked imaginations. For someone like myself, a bookworm with bulging lobes who drew most of his vainglorious ideas about sex, conquest, and the mercurial enigma of Woman from novels written by men who really knew how to grill up a hot paragraph, the actual act itself loomed like a parachute drop into existential night, where the chute might not open. The exalted glory of two bodies fusing into one and bursting into forked flame set the bar a little high for those of us fairly new to pole-vaulting. Each encounter seemed a test, a trial, pitting you against yourself and your grandiose expectations against whatever expectations she—She—brought to the encounter, your sexual pride and reputation riding on the line, at least in the amphitheater of your own mind. In his long story "The Time of Her Time," Mailer made the yeoman task of bringing a woman to orgasm into a symphonic clash of the titans, as if his stud alter ego were taking Omaha Beach against spirited resistance from one smart bohemian ball-busting recalcitrant, the aurora borealis of orgasm awaiting just over the shadowed ridge at the head of the bed. Mailer at least was super-vivid in his play-by-play description of this mattress prize-fight, as was Henry Miller whenever he got goaty under the slanted roof shingles of Paris. Half the time I didn't know what was going on in a D. H. Lawrence sex scene, only that man and woman had joined lava streams, which was of limited utility.

For us unfrocked English majors it was difficult navigating sex with this library of crescendos lodged upstairs—Lawrence coined the phrase "sex in the head," but who warehoused more sex in the attic than he did?—while having only the haziest idea of what we were doing and hoping word didn't get around. After several unsatis-factory off-Broadway tryouts in the sack with my first real girlfriend in New York, I horse-whispered to myself that I was Norman Mailer before the Ravel *Boléro* lovemaking soundtrack started, putting my hips into command mode and getting a pretty good locomotive head of steam going, indeed began feeling so devilish that I thought I might sprout a pair of warlock horns and a swishing tail, but then a strand of her hair got caught in my wristband and extricating it brought me back to reality, where I was at a distinct disadvantage. Also, I needed to rest a little more weight on my elbows, because (as she diplomatically put it) "I was kinda crushing her." Perhaps if I had read more sex-spiked novels by women, I would have gotten a better training manual to put into application, but the ones popular and prevalent then were of the bitter-blow-job roman à clef variety, in which the heroine would go down on a guy to get rid of him faster. I already knew plenty of girls who were quite happy to get rid of a guy without a lovely parting gift, so such fictions weren't much help, whatever their other merits as indictments of callous creeps by the women who debased themselves before them, practically throw-ing away their college educations.

Porn was all verbs and no adjectives. It got into your face mask. Despite liberal use of Vaseline on the lens for *Elvira Madigan* soft-focus lyricism, it couldn't keep up pretenses to pictorialism for long, innocent gambols requiring meadows and such. It developed its own bordello mise-en-scène. Old-school seventies porn is preferred by old-school porn enthusiasts because there were actual, if modest, production values, not simply a couch on which couples splayed, as has been the minimalist tack since digital turned every porn director into a human fly buzzing around the room. (Andy Warhol, a forerunner in so many fields, was the pioneer of couch porn with his 1964 black-and-white silent grinder, set entirely on the old Factory's well-ridden red couch.) And there were story lines too, however borrowed or imitative they may have been, with actual dialogue typed onto a page by human fingers, even though the actors mouthing them often sounded like hypnotic subjects dubbed into English. But what truly endowed old-school porn with a more relatable, mortal dimension were the bodies belonging to those actors on-screen, which exhibited the lumpy normalcy of our imperfect species rather than the later cloned master-race Las Vegas red-carpet ideal that would discard individual personality as if it were needless lipo. The bodies and behaviors belonged to flawed beings who had more moon than sun in their constitutions. Pre-Viagra, erections flew on a wing and a prayer. Once achieved, they didn't look like redwoods or swollen membranes, their veiny veins competing with the veins on the actor's forehead for aching intensity. And the women, especially the older women—there was something poignant about them, the veins in their hands, the ladylike manner in which they dressed and primped in the mirror and adjusted their lingerie just so (a single strand of pearls completing the routine), the way they tipped their chins slightly up in every dialogue exchange to make a point of their actressy dignity, this resigned determination to hold on to what they had left because in a few years it could all go. Kay Parker, Veronica Hart with her retroussé nose—they make the MILFs and cougars of today look like tramp-stamped dirigibles. One of the seventies hot mamas, Jennifer Welles, a favorite of Norman Mailer's, was like Gena Rowlands turned experienced call girl, a blond fantasy genie-rubbed from a jar of cold cream.

In the first few years after *Deep Throat* introduced a deathless new phrase into the American lexicon, porn carried a New York pallor, apart from firecrackers such as Vanessa del Rio. The entire industry hadn't wagon-trained to the West Coast to take advantage of the sunlight, advanced surgery, superior physiques, and Hollywood aura. Porn shot in New York featured aspiring actors whose peeled-apple complexions and concave torsos had the effect of making them seem smaller than life, until you saw them in the flesh and realized they were even smaller than the scale model in your head. Many of these Lee Strasberg school dropouts were furry specimens, and bushiness reigned likewise below with their female co-stars, the close-ups evoking *National Geographic* expeditions up the Amazon. One porn actor whom I used to see shopping at the local grocery, instantly identifiable by his caveman unibrow, was so spidery that he was usually cast as antic comedy relief, availing himself of a host of the unfunniest funny foreign accents heard to man that always sounded vaguely mad-scientist and paprika'd with Yiddish, as if he fancied himself X-rated cinema's Sid Caesar. (Only Caesar didn't hop from one foot to the other as if he always needed to pee.) I often wondered if that checkout-line porn actor pinched himself every night at the improbable wonder of somebody like him—a schnook—being paid to have sex with sexy younger women, or if he whined between takes about the room being too drafty, or his character's sketchy motivation.

If this neighborhood familiar was the Elisha Cook Jr. of porn actors, one of life's supporting players, others achieved a cult fame that didn't radiate into universal instant recognition but accrued into landmark status in the history of porn, most notably Jamie Gillis, whose curly black hair, sardonic eyes, and pent anger were tethered to a mind-gaming deck of cunning moves that reminded one of Philip Roth if Roth had been stripped of Kafka and radio voices: Roth in the predatory raw. At his shaggiest on-screen, Gillis looked like a more intense, unslouching Elliott Gould, but in most roles he was shark sleek. I saw Gillis now and again with the porn actress Serena, with whom he did nasty things on-screen, and strolling along drinking in the dirty air, they managed to suggest that they got up to even nastier things offscreen, all kinds of paraphernalia-intensive amateur theatricals that required ice packs afterward. Once I saw a fan approach to compliment them on their work. They thanked him with a gracious nod, like a couple of off-Broadway stars fresh out of the pages of *Playbill* acknowledging their public. Gillis became the boyfriend of the restaurant reviewer Gael Greene, who more than anyone turned food writing into gustatory porn, and a familiar at Elaine's, friends with the unlikely likes of the neurologist and best-selling author Oliver Sacks and James Watson, the discoverer of DNA. When the sex author Susie Bright, in a podcast interview with Gillis in 2008, noted that he had begun in the business in 1971, he replied, "[It] wasn't even a business. It was a dirty basement." A dirty basement that ate its way up into broad daylight and got bolder with every bite, just as a dirty bar on the Bowery became the manger for the squall heard round the world.

It was a logical segue for *Punk* magazine's former mascot and semi-lovable fumblebutt, Legs McNeil, to follow his oral history of New York punk, *Please Kill Me* (co-written with Gillian McCain), with an oral history of porn that made punk look like a romp in the pasture. Populated with an above-average percentage of sick twisties, both porn and punk were amateur uprisings from below deck, ragtag operations of low production values and high casualty tolls where fame was sought under an assumed identity. It was a short sharp hop from Linda Lovelace (porn captive) to Lydia Lunch (poet-punk dominatrix). Although porn performers occasionally tail-wagged into CBGB's—I once saw the porn actress C. J. Laing stroking a denimed bottom belonging to a stranger, judging by the exclamation mark on his face—and punk bands deployed porn motifs, the correspondences mostly remained on the mucky surface. Punk and porn both regarded the body as unconsecrated meat, a punching bag for blows inflicted and self-inflicted, pain being the price of admission into the sideshow. Punk, however, sought transcendence from a launchpad of sound, a release from bondage; porn operated under a lower ceiling, its repetitions feeding on themselves, a cycle of recurrence in which those who didn't become jaded simply became affectless, devoid, not much caring what was done to them, drugs and disassociation providing cloud protection. It wasn't too long before they looked on camera the way many punks looked offstage—slugged.

Punk was rooted in opposition to pretension, whereas porn adopted pretension as soon as it broke out of the basement and sought respectability, pursuing the fine cultural cachet of the art-house film where ennui hung heavy from the false eyelashes. A porn movie with a piano tinkle of sophistication such as *The Opening of Misty Beethoven* aimed to be a combination of *My Fair Lady* and *Modesty Blaise,* boasting location shooting, stylized sets (islands of white designer space), and an ingenue in the title role—the adroitly named Constance Money—who resembled a skittish foal, receiving instruction in the oral arts as taking her first clarinet lesson. (Jamie Gillis was the film's Professor Higgins, with a glop of gigolo.) It was one of the few hard-cores that marketed itself like an art-gallery preview and preened its cat whiskers and coat to a glossy finish. Its smug vanities were preferable to the bitter medicine that other directors spooned for our own good. After *Deep Throat,* its director, Gerard Damiano, got an acute case of auteuritis, his *The Devil in Miss Jones* a study in damnation that consigned its title character (a very moving, soul-bruised Georgina Spelvin) to an eternity of diddling without deliverance. The Mitchell brothers' moment-breaking *Behind the Green Door* was a satanic Black Mass where the white slave goddess—Marilyn Chambers, the all-American model on the cover of the Ivory soap box, a Warholian conceit that probably flipped the master's silver wig—was sacrificed to an African native in tribal war paint and necklace, a solemn traducing of taboo. *Fiona on Fire,* which took Otto Preminger's *Laura* and tarted it up, starred Amber Hunt, whose baby-cheeked appeal and scarves were visually echoed by Nancy Allen's in Brian De Palma's *Dressed to Kill* and *Blow Out.* (De

Palma knew his porn, wanting to cast the porn ice princess Annette Haven in *Body Double*.) One of the more interesting cross-mirrorings transpired between the more deluxe pornos and the sullen parables of Rainer Werner Fassbinder. Similarities: the oppressive furnishings that obstacle-coursed the bourgeois rooms like Douglas Sirk props, the wallpaper patterns and colors that looked like jaundice visiting for tea, the drag-queen soap-opera wigs and eyelashes that might have been daubed on with Magic Markers—and Fassbinder reciprocated the favor from Munich. "His strategies often indicate a study of porn movies, how to get an expanse of flesh across the screen with the bluntest impact and the least footage," wrote the critic Manny Farber in an essay from 1975, citing the scene in *The Merchant of Four Seasons* in which a "woman who had heretofore been all tightness is suddenly exposed in all her white length, being serviced from the rear by a stranger whose tiny smirk is hung on until its meaning is in your brain." The seventies were big on tiny smirks, which complemented the swinger mustaches.

If classic erotica from the Olympia Press and mortifications of the flesh such as *Story of O* gave off the ruby flicker of Catholicism gone bad, seventies porn had a more Jewish smack. Its profaneness was unfermented with metaphysical properties, allowing it to get much quicker to the beefy point. It wasn't simply the preponderance of Jewish performers in porn, especially on the protruding side (Gillis, Ron Jeremy, and mustachioed Harry Reems), that lent this impression, but the amplifying impact of cable-access TV in New York, where the two biggest porn hosts were Robin Byrd and Al Goldstein, the latter especially bloating up every Jewish stereotype into larger-than-life self-caricature that made the cartooniness of *Portnoy's Complaint* look like Victorian lithography. The editor of *Screw* magazine had no illusions about porn or its audience—they weren't ascoted gentlemen who read Aldous Huxley and appreciated a fine Chianti with their hand job, but losers who couldn't get laid unless they left money on the dressing table, or begged. Goldstein belittled and berated his readers with the zeal of an insult comic, not

wrapping his editorials in some larger *Playboy* philosophy of epicu-
rean wisdom (his weekly rag, *Screw,* looked like something to line
a sex offender's litter box), even though his commitment to free
speech and expression was as staunch as Hugh Hefner's and Larry
Flynt's. Like Flynt, the publisher of *Hustler,* Goldstein maintained an
unshakable conviction that First Amendment protections covered
filth as well as artistic merit and feints at redeeming social value;
censorship should have no part to play in quality control. The inadvertent comedy of Goldstein's interviews with porn actors and directors was that his questions could gross out even *these* veterans of the
trenches, so crudely were they formulated, so porcine his presence;
his interrogatory mode not even aerated with the aging-dirty-boy
glee that Howard Stern would bring to his radio interviews with
silicone starlets and their suitcase pimps. Where Stern still sends
the impression that two strippers spanking each other is a bar mitz-
vah special, porn for Goldstein was more of a wallow in the larger
mess hall of Manhattan, where connoisseurship consisted in being
able to spot and appreciate the better-quality slop. At one point
Goldstein tried to platform *Screw* into something more upscale and
slick, launching a spin-off magazine called *National Screw* (he was
never one for ornate package-labels), which mated porn and punk
on the masthead, using contributors from *Punk* magazine and running articles on Television, among others. The magazine came and
went without leaving a scent. As Goldstein's girth testified and his
words italicized, food was his true salivating lust, the vowels in his
enunciation of "pastrami" or "cream cheese" glistening more avidly
than any paean to some porn starlet's landing strip. He would end
up, over thirty years later, working as a greeter at a Second Avenue
deli for ten dollars an hour, a humbling comedown from his former
notoriety and yet fictionally apt, in an O. Henry story kind of way.

Watching *Midnight Blue* often made you feel dirty inside, dirty
outside too. Not the good kind of dirty that tingled of emblazoned
afternoons under the high-school bleachers, but the kind that put
you off your feed, like gazing upon buffet food that had been under

the heat lamp too long. But that the show was on TV at all and popular among New York's sophisticated lowlifes was proof that Lenny Bruce hadn't died in vain, though he might have wished his disciples had been more deserving primates. Seventies cable access would also be where reality porn made its first trudge out of the primordial bog in the semi-upright figure of "Ugly George" (real name: George Urban, so apropos), who trolled the streets of Manhattan in a bare-chested silver spacesuit outfit, bearing the bulk of a heavy backpack with a satellite dish attached that looked as if it belonged to a lunar land rover and a shoulder-mounted camera always ready for action. Ugly George, unlicensed provocateur, would approach attractive women on the street and try to coax them into taking off their clothes on camera with all of the sweet-talking charm he could muster, which wasn't much even by the meager standards of the day. Those who agreed to remove their tops for whatever occult reason he would usher into the nearest secluded alley or building hallway, where they'd peel off for the lens, as if it were a department-store changing room. Some would even accompany him to his basement apartment, which looked like a future crime scene in its seamy seclusion, a forensics field trip to collect a Jackson Pollock galaxy of DNA samples. Those who rebuffed Ugly George's come-ons had insults hurled at them for blowing their chance at stardom, a choice they evidently found more palatable than the prospect of blowing him. The situational suspense of each will-she-or-won't-she-show-the-goodies? episode is what gave the repulsive compulsion of *The Ugly George Hour of Truth, Sex, and Violence* (the violence was strictly verbal) its jagged teeth as a bottom-feeding enterprise.

Like *Midnight Blue, The Ugly George Hour* was a New York seventies phenomenon (the seventies: the mattress that exploded), must-see viewing for stay-at-home sickos and amateur sociologists; but like Al Goldstein, Ugly George himself was only capable of lateral movement in the slime field, limited by his lack of luster and immediate-gratification gluttony. Had he been a smoother operator and discovered Florida spring break instead of hulking and skulking the same old chewing-gummed sidewalks, he might have tumbled into the fountain of youth and beaten Joe Francis to the Girls Gone Wild franchise. Had he been able to talk a good art game and owned a more low-slung Dadaist imagination, he might have become the Harmony Korine of his time, Korine's 2009 movie, *Trash Humpers* (masked grotesques literally humping Dumpsters), availing itself of a VHS vomit-bag aesthetic that has Ugly George stamped all over it. But he went only where the snout of his camera lens led him, which wasn't high or far.

Not long ago I was on the M104 bus taking in the majestic sweep of upper Broadway—Gray's Papaya, Zabar's, the nail salons—when a man got on who reminded me of Shrek, if Shrek were the color of disgruntled instead of clay-green. It was, yes, Ugly George himself, still among us. Had his former notoriety not placed him for me, I would have taken him for just another Upper West Side scruffian, a category of unkempt malcontent in which many unmarried men in his age cohort seem to belong. He took a window seat, scanning the busy view for something to shoot. Video technology having advanced and sub-compacted in the intervening decades, the camera he was lugging wasn't the shoulder-strainer of his heyday. It drew no attention to its owner, and its owner drew no attention to himself, not like in the old days, when he was a clanking commotion. He aimed his camera lens through the window at any possible borderline-presentable woman in possession of youth who was passing by, even though she may have been passing by on the opposite side of Broadway; the bus was in motion, and he was shooting through the grimy glass of windows closed against the cold—no way could he have captured any savory images for his collection box, unless it was a motion-sickness documentary he was compiling. Ugly George had entered dirty-old-man stage in harness to a habitual mode he couldn't shed and now had no application even on the lowest digital rungs of postmodern porn. It was almost sad, a parable of sorts. *Mon semblable, mon frère,* that could have been me! No, not really, and yet I felt a shudder of remote kinship with this survivor from the Jurassic Park of porn, and relief when he left the bus, taking the flaking past with him.

It would be sentimental to romanticize the antiromanticism of Times Square in the seventies, mourning a lost vibrancy and Brueghelesque teem more authentic than the toy mall we have today, where few tourists will ever know the thrilling fear of having defecation thrown at them or being caught in the middle of a difference of opinion between two hookers ready to cut each other into unequal chunks. The human wastage of Times Square weighs too heavily against slumming nostalgia. Entire blocks looked as if they had a case of cirrhosis. Nearly every doorway had someone standing in it up to no good. The contempt for women that often wore a sneer in porn films on its liver lips was an everyday dragon-snort in Times Square, where women on their way to work often walked a gauntlet of crotch-grabbing solicitations and insulting commentary only to undergo a round-trip replay at the end of the office day, and then who knew what the subway ride would be like? Teenage hookers irregularly lined the far west avenues of midtown in miniskirts and rabbit fur jackets, their bare legs stalky-looking in the passing car lights as they teetered from one rolled-down car window to another. Every X-rated movie marquee, movie poster, video store display, was a semiotic form of aggravated assault, the live sex shows likewise no altar to Venus. I saw only one and that was enough for me, sis. It was in an Eighth Avenue emporium still standing today, then a bustling hive of peep-show booths, sex-novelty counters, and a small theater that may have been in the basement, but even if it wasn't, to enter it was to experience descent. The little playlet being performed was called "The Pimp and the Whore," a lightly scripted episode that dispensed with backstory and character development to present a compact lesson in what happens to a whore who disobeys her pimp: a cursing lecture, threats of bodily harm punctuated with a couple of stage slaps (the hands clapping as the face snaps sideways), followed by kneeling submission, simulated intercourse, a cry of pleasure-pain, and a few parting comments from mack daddy before the dimming of lights to the sound of the performers shuf-fling offstage without taking a bow, a round of applause being per-haps too macabre under the circumstances. What I remember more than anything that happened onstage was the booming distorted intercom voice of the porn theater announcer telling us over and over again, overriding the dialogue, the title of the vignette, "The *Pimppp* and the *Whorrrre* . . . the *Pimmmp* and the *Whorrre* . . . ," selling what we were seeing like a lascivious strip-club DJ. It was a better Brechtian alienation effect than anything I've ever seen in Brecht, the sense of dehumanization compounded by the knowledge that the performers of this sketch were repeating it four, five times a day, like the last damned dregs of vaudeville. Forget Sartre and *No Exit,* this is what hell must really be like: an endless reenact-ment performed by dummies for dummies, and you're one of the dummies.

After a disgruntled jazz musician and his girlfriend, about to be evicted, turned on the oven and stove burners and all the water taps before stealing out into the night, flooding my apartment and nearly turning the entire building into a minor replica of *The Towering Inferno,* I moved from my digs on the Upper West Side to a studio apartment on the farthest end of the West Village on Horatio Street. It was there that I was audience to a different sex show each week-end, with a quite distinct and varying cast. Moving into Horatio, I felt I had arrived: my first real New York apartment, the first empty space to call mine that didn't have someone else's history hanging around, the perfect snug fit for man and cat. Western light bathed the room with a warmer benediction than I had ever gotten in my old hideout (where the morning light seemed bloodshot), and my new place's one redbrick wall was a sign that I had finally landed my own parcel of the bohemian experience. It even had a fireplace, what could be better. I slept on a captain's bed, its three bottom drawers holding all sorts of bachelor necessities, and worked at a desk on a typewriter whose electric purr I would later associate with the sustaining hum of Transcendental Meditation.

It was a quite modern building, which meant that sound muffling seemed to have ranked low on the list of the Mafia's construction priorities. I could hear every sneeze and cough in the next studio as if the wall were a tent flap, and was able to follow the psychodrama of every loud telephone conversation as if it were an ongoing improvisation based on Jean Cocteau's *Human Voice,* a monologue once found in nearly every college drama department repertory. The young man in the adjacent apartment to me was having chronic boyfriend problems with Billy, whose name received extra *l*'s whenever my neighbor was distraught. "Billlllllly, why do you keep doing this to me?" Whatever it was that Billy was doing, he kept doing it, because the same desperate plea bargaining was played out over the phone again and again, as if the plaintiff were stuck to a script written on flypaper. Sometimes Billy would come over, and they would fight for a bit and then go out, or go out and then fight when they got back. I would pound on the wall, they would pound back, and really that's what being a New Yorker was about then. One of the regulars I would come to recognize in the hallway at 92 Horatio was a porn star named Marc "10½" Stevens, whom I had seen on-screen without considering myself "a fan of his work" and who sometimes appeared at parties painted silver, like a spaceship dashboard ornament. While in the army, stationed in Germany, Stevens found himself in the same bank of urinals as fellow soldier Elvis Presley. Legend was that the less endowed Elvis made a quick appraisal of the hose Stevens was holding and drawled, "Ya'll better take care of that thang." Words to live by, and Stevens's thang was later photographed by Robert Mapplethorpe, no mean judge of hangage himself. I would often see Stevens in the company of drag queens who partied down as if they had LaBelle's "Lady Marmalade" playing nonstop under their wigs. They sometimes popped poppers in the elevator on the way down to the first floor, wanting to hit the streets with an extra goosy bump.

Sunset aside, my studio hadn't much of a view. The windows overlooked a stretch of the underpass of the original High Line informally known as "The Trucks," named for the fleet of trucks parked there at night. My first summer on Horatio, I was standing at the window, wondering who the hell was honking the idiot car horn below (a perennial New York question), and noticed a man entering a gap between the trucks while another man exited from a different gap. Then another man emerged from that same gap, as if whatever business were being conducted with the first exiter had been completed. I wondered if drug dealing was being done, since it was being done most everywhere else. Perhaps it was, but that wasn't the main draw. It took a few surveillance moments to realize that my windows afforded the scenic view to a major cruising spot, this overpass shielding a Pac-Man shadow maze of pickup action. (Pac-Man hadn't been invented yet, but no other analogy quite dings the bell.) From the detached perspective of my overhead view, the intrigue had the abstract quality of a Jacques Tati comedy, a man on the hunt vanishing down one aisle and reappearing from another one soon afterward, as if he hadn't found what he was shopping for and was retreating into the shadows again while another man discharged himself from the lane between a different pair of trucks, he too having come up empty. One night I saw a man materialize between trucks in a pair of leather chaps over a pair of jeans that had been cut in the back to bare a heart-shaped bottom, his butt cheeks hosting a cucumber or a dildo shaped like a cucumber—in any case, something dark green was poking out. Had he inserted it himself, or did someone insert it for him and was he searching for the original owner? He paused on the sidewalk in a moment of Hamlet indecision, his "jewel pouch" carrying the seed of doubt, then turned back into the shadowed aisle between the trucks, his night not quite done and for all I knew may have been just getting started.

For those were marathon weekends many of the men in the West Village seemed to be putting in, stamina-testing contests, judging by their grizzled, battle-weary condition on Sunday mornings, some of them still bearing the darkness in their eyes like coal miners who had just come off a brutal shift. I, on my way to pick up the Sunday *Times,* would sometimes find myself downwind from a couple of sexual platooners who had pulled an all-nighter, a cloud of sweat, leather, alcohol, urine, semen, cologne, lubricant, and industrial might invisibly tentacling from them like a collection of short stories waiting to be written by Edmund White. The look of so many men on those mornings after the night before was the ink-drawn definition of "fucked out." Evidently, a lot more martial effort went into what they were doing than what their straight counterparts got up to on weekends, more ritual and regalia. Because gay life had been criminalized and stigmatized for so long, forced underground or into pocket enclaves, it had developed its own cryptology, but now the codes were more open, flashing in daylight. A yellow handkerchief in the back pocket signaled one thing, a black handkerchief signaled another, and left or right pocket designated whether one was a top or a bottom, although rueful word had it that there were a large proportion of men who claimed to be tops who were only fooling themselves and disappointing others. (Just as the ratio of masochists to sadists is so lopsided, putting a premium on the latter.) Post-Stonewall, the West Village was one of the prime vector sectors of seventies sex with the safety catch off. Monday mornings it was not uncommon to spot a businessman leaning back in the driver's seat of his parked car, receiving head from a drag queen before driving off to the office, one way to kick off the workweek. Horatio Street was a short throw from the meatpacking district, when it really was the meatpacking district and not a Marc Jacobs mini-mall, its brick streets, angled shadows, and abandoned atmosphere at night drenching the area with a Brassaï-photograph mystique or Jack the Ripper air, depending on the threat level in your head. The Anvil, which opened in 1974 and soon earned a niche as "a gay bar with a rough-trade rep" (in the words of the *Village Voice*), was on Tenth Avenue, its main action taking place downstairs. That's what a large part of the seventies was about, *venturing down-*

stairs, into the orphic melee, the gladiator pit of the members-only Mineshaft on Washington Street reputed to be even more of a docking station of battering-ram abandon.

A bystander in my own neighborhood, I only had the scratchiest outline of what was happening around me. It wasn't until Richard Goldstein's groundbreaking article in the *Village Voice,* headlined on the cover as S&M: FLIRTING WITH TERMINAL SEX and illustrated with a photo of a mannequin head encased in zippered leather mask (ideal for asphyxiation-training purposes), that the uninitiated got a field report on the complete panoply of specific practices grappling away in the groaning penumbra—the glory holes, the golden showers, the fisting. "People brag about how many fists they can contain, and there is even an organization, Fist Fuckers of America, whose insignia, a clenched fist, adorns the Anvil," Goldstein reported. Today, Fist Fuckers of America sounds like an apt name for whatever organization Newt Gingrich is fronting at the moment, but at the time it gave proof that pierced-cheek punks were clearly pikers compared with these pro leaguers at the punishing extremes of pain exploration—this leather guild of edgeplay. Although the S&M subcult that Goldstein depicted may have been padlocked off from everyday experience—its energy forces trapped and released behind its own containment walls, its violence consensual and ceremonialized—rough trade freelanced the night, and depending upon the kindness of strangers in the pickup scene could get you pulped. One heard unconfirmed stories of tricks roughed up by their johns, johns being stabbed and robbed by their tricks, bodies being found disposed along the piers. Sharpening the shadows were gay-bashing attacks carried out by gangs of youths, attacks not limited to the immediate radius of Christopher Street. (One horrific summer night, the gay cruising area in Central Park known as the Ramble was the site of a homosexual-hunting cull in which the serial victims were clubbed with bats. "Dialogue was sparse throughout the rampage," Arthur Bell reported in the *Voice.* "Each attack was guerrilla-like—swift, and without warning. Quick clubbings, then onward to the next target.") When the director William Friedkin started shooting *Cruising* in New York, a *noir policier* that took the first reverse-periscope look at the Crisco disco inferno, the *Voice* raised a ruckus and location sites were picketed, the extras who were trooping out of the bar scenes catcalled as "traitors" by waiting protesters. But for all of the finished film's howlers (including the spectacle of Al Pacino in Tom of Finland leather drag), it nevertheless captured the dark riptides of mortal danger and paranoia in the ambiguous prey-game. In 1978, a year before filming began, a twenty-three-year-old man—a disco dancer—was found dead one morning outside the Anvil, where he had been seen earlier that evening arguing inside with another man. He had been stabbed with a chef's knife.

The straight dating scene had its own homicidal overhang of "stranger danger." Pop historians recall the seventies as the decade of Erica Jong's 1973 novel, *Fear of Flying,* and the "zipless fuck," impromptu, liberated, guilt-free penis-hopping a bouncy pogo ride away. It was also the year that a teacher at a school for deaf children, a twenty-eight-year-old named Roseann Quinn, was found naked in her bed, fatally stabbed multiple times in the stomach and bludgeoned about the skull with a statue of her own likeness. The assailant was a stranger she had met on New Year's Eve in a bar across the street from her West Side apartment and taken back to her place for a one-night stand. The day after her brutalized body was discovered, the *Daily News* ran the headline story ONCE MORE, BACHELOR GIRLS ASK: WHO'S NEXT? Unlike so many tabloid horror stories, this one's shock waves didn't thin and recede with the next news cycle. They cut a neural pathway, put down tracks. Two years later, Quinn's "sex slay" was novelized by Judith Rossner into the sensational best-selling cautionary tale for girls about town called *Looking for Mr. Goodbar,* a catchphrase title that captured the prowling sweet-toothed hunger that vampired inside even nice girls. And two years after the novel arrived the movie version, starring Diane Keaton, taking Annie Hall out for a walk on the wild side, a creepy, defrosted William Atherton, and a jacked-up rabbit of Method-actor jism jive relatively new to the screen named Richard Gere (whose performance turned out to be the tryout run for the studly calisthenics of *American Gigolo*), and directed by Richard Brooks as if he were carrying a wooden cross and crying, *"Repent!"* A date movie for the damned, *Looking for Mr. Goodbar* looked as if it had been coated from floor to ceiling with contraceptive jelly, with a perv reading *Hustler* in the subway train in the very first scene, one slick barfly after another vying to worm into Theresa's panties, with Keaton's father, Richard Kiley, bellowing like a prototype Bill O'Reilly about kids today and their do-your-own-thing attitude: "I don't understand your crazy world—free to go to hell! Freedom! Tell me, girl, how do you get free of the terrible truth?" How do you get free from such terrible Arthur Miller–sounding dialogue? might have been the better question.

Looking for Mr. Goodbar was accorded the socially relevant deference that Miller's plays and Stanley Kramer's films (*Ship of Fools, Judgment at Nuremberg*) once received as Documents of Our Time until people sharpened up. *Looking for Mr. Goodbar* hammered like a judge's gavel, rendering a guilty verdict against the zipless fuck and everything it heedlessly promoted. It wasn't a lone psycho who killed this wayward wren, argued Molly Haskell in *New York* magazine; it was the Sexual Revolution and its miniskirt morals. "This is far and away Richard Brooks's best film. It is harrowing, powerful, appalling. It may even be an important film, particularly for the media gurus who propound the glories of swinging singlehood and sex-on-demand without ever setting foot in the bars, and who remain comfortably immune from the demons that the rhetoric of liberation has unleashed. Never has the gap between the rhetoric, the exhortations to 'control our bodies,' and the out-of-control reality been drawn more clearly." Pauline Kael, for whom the film had the "pulpy morbidity of Joyce Carol Oates," agreed that Theresa's cock-luring appointment with death ("Do it! Do it!" she orgasmically cries as the knife blade plunges into her) was intended to nail home "the consequence of living in a permissive society." But Pauline wasn't the impermissive type and rejected censorious brow-beating dealt from a stacked deck. "Terry has been maimed; her parents have neglected her and didn't notice that polio had affected her spine; as a result of her not having been loved enough, she is left with a scar on her back and a faint limp. It's as if a woman [who] wouldn't want sex unsanctified by tenderness . . . was crippled, psychologically flawed, self-hating." Such tragedies happen today, as witness the murder of the young designer in the hotel bathroom at Soho House, but they're treated in the press as individual collisions of intimate violence, not Indictments of the Times We Live In.

The threat of violence could thorn the atmosphere in New York almost anywhere you turned in the seventies, and yet I felt safer in the West Village than I did in almost any part of the city at the time. I didn't court danger, it didn't court me, no one had a monopoly on the night. While nipples were being thumbed under leather vests at macho-man bars, a cabaret known as Reno Sweeney (named after a character in the musical *Anything Goes*) was flourishing on West Thirteenth Street, a lyrical springboard for Karen Akers, Peter Allen, Marvin Hamlisch, Phoebe Legere, Andrea Marcovicci, Ellen Greene (later to excel in *Little Shop of Horrors*), and, for one engagement, the mummy-wrap style icon "Little Edie" Beale of *Grey Gardens* fame. It, along with similar showcases and piano bars, provided a melodic counterpoint to all the musclings going on, a Sally Bowles anthem call. I was living on Horatio during the summer blackout of 1977, the season that would go down in history as the Summer of Sam, on that humid night of July 13 that began as a collective inconvenience and erupted into what *Time* magazine would call an "orgy of loot-ing," with residents in minority neighborhoods streaming out in the streets to engage in five-finger shopping on an epic scale: "Roving bands of determined men, women and even little children wrenched steel shutters and grilles from storefronts with crowbars, shattered plate-glass windows, scooped up everything they could carry, and destroyed what they could not. First they went for clothing, TV sets,

jewelry, liquor; when that was cleaned out, they picked up food, furniture and drugs." Clothes were stripped from store-window mannequins and the mannequins knocked silly, their arms and legs strewn
like amputee spare parts. Car dealerships had their new inventories
commandeered, hot-wired, and taken for one-way test drives. What
freaked out New Yorkers and the rest of the country was not only
the hurricane strength and speed of the ransacking hordes hitting
the streets, as if on cue, but their merriment, the cries of "It's Christmastime! It's Christmastime!" as the orange glow in the city of fires
big and small suggested wartime London following a bombing raid.
Rickety-ribbed liberal platitudes about poverty and unequal opportunity would be wheelbarrowed out in the days and weeks ahead,
but they were no match for pictures of jolly teenagers considerately
helping their elders carry large appliances home during this special
one-time-only all-you-can-steal sale.

In the West Village, the atmosphere was charged with the radio-
static apprehension that was citywide, but windows went unshat-
tered and streets unmobbed, although there was word of a gay orgy
breaking out like a Broadway musical on one popular corner, a
rumor later confirmed in Jonathan Mahler's *Ladies and Gentlemen,
the Bronx Is Burning,* which placed the party on Weehawken Street.
While others robbed and raged, the West Village had its own way
of celebrating Christmas in July.

If this wasn't the last hurrah, however, there weren't too many
hurrahs left. No one could have known the magnitude of what was
heading down the tracks, the epidemic that by the late eighties
would give the West Village a haggard, ghost-ravaged air, a ground
zero of loss created not in a single morning but over the toll of years.
It amounted to a slow, unmerciful massacre that was both a human
tragedy and a cultural catastrophe, depriving the future of more
than can ever be measured and properly mourned, a mass grave of
unfulfilled promise. The creative ranks were skeletonized by what
was first labeled a "gay plague." Choreographers, designers, play-
wrights, artists, dancers, actors, photographers, and so many other

creatives whose names we knew made the obituary pages: Michael Bennett, the choreographer and deviser of *A Chorus Line,* the musical about aspiring dance gypsies going through the peeling exposure of the audition process that started downtown at Joe Papp's Public Theater and became such a public sensation that it was transplanted to Broadway, doing more to save Times Square from fatal rot than any other single production; the actor-playwright-director-impresario Charles Ludlam, whose Ridiculous Theatrical Company was the bedlam gingerbread cottage of camp; the fashion designer Halston, whose handsome rectangularity recalled Michael Rennie's distinguished interplanetary delegate in *The Day the Earth Stood Still;* the graffiti artist Keith Haring. Maybe I'm telling you what you already know, but I don't know what anyone knows anymore, those who came to the city after have no idea, they breathe a brighter air. As Fran Lebowitz points out in the documentary *Public Speaking* (it's the best monologue in the movie), it wasn't simply the talent lost to AIDS that was so calamitous; it was the devastation of an audience equally brilliant and alive. "An audience with a high level of connoisseurship is as important to the culture as artists," she said. "That audience died in five minutes." A discriminating, demanding, wit-appreciative audience for the performing arts that has never been regrown, replaced by a shipment of clapping seals for whom (in Lebowitz's words) "everything has to be broader, more blatant, more on the nose."

The audience whose loss Lebowitz mourned was still bumble-beeing when I made my first sortie into Lincoln Center, not realizing that I was about to embark on the longest romance of my life and the most incongruous. It began on a Sunday afternoon that might have otherwise lay fallow, with me lying fallow in it. I had bought a single ticket for a matinee performance of New York City Ballet, a seat in the fourth ring, the equivalent of the upper mezzanine at the old Yankee Stadium, absent the wind gusts and rustling hot-dog wrappers. I'm not sure what the source of the impulse was that tugged me there to Lincoln Center's State Theater that Sunday, but whatever was on the other end of the fishing line knew me better than I knew myself. Ballet was just a big fluffy cloud to me then, just as opera was a complicated bawl. I hadn't seen any ballet when I was growing up in Maryland, not even a childhood rite-of-passage *Nutcracker,* and my look-in on modern dance consisted solely in catching a touring performance of the Erick Hawkins Dance Company at Frostburg State, my primary takeaway being what a godlike torso Hawkins brandished, an Apollo shield form-fitted to his body and burnished in battle, even though he may have been in his sixties then. He made the rest of us look like cookie dough. Hawkins's history with Martha Graham, the mythopoeic roots of his choreographic philosophy and action-painting attack—of these I would have known nothing beyond what was in the program notes, assuming there were program notes. But that I went and that I remembered that I went meant it had dropped a dime in my imagination, made a deposit. Here I am, I thought, holding my program like a missal—my first ballet. If they could only see me now, I thought, "they" being nobody in particular. The arrival of the orchestra conductor, who it pleased me to think had just gotten off the phone to his bookie, was greeted with a flock of applause that sounded as if it were deriving from an adjacent banquet room, and as the musicians poised their instruments, the curtain rose with a wheely noise suggesting a crew hoisting sails.

It was probably *The Firebird* on the bill that tapped my interest when I was leafing through *The New Yorker*'s Goings On About Town listings, foraging for something cultural to do for my merit badge. *The Firebird* had a score by Igor Stravinsky, sets by Marc Chagall, and costumes by Karinska that from photographs really turned up the Cyd Charisse red. And choreography by George Balanchine, who even I understood in my heathen condition was regarded not simply as a creative genius but as God's junior partner, handing out one ballet classic after another like year-round holiday bonuses. *The*

Firebird would have made for just the sort of combo platter I was seeking in my continuing efforts at self-improvement, my knowledge of classical music, art, and theatrical costume needing some filling in, along with all the other cavities. I had an incomplete set of Time-Life books devoted to the great painters purchased second-hand at outdoor stalls in the Village—volumes on Matisse, Picasso, Cézanne, and Renoir—whose biographical content I would munch on before moving to the main course: studying the color-plate reproductions to educate my "eye." Mailer wrote about how the paintings of Cézanne and Picasso taught him to see in a new surface-destroying way, and my "eye" was still stuck on the boring flat-planed obvious. I also turned on the classical music stations (there was more than one then) whenever I felt it incumbent upon me to listen to classical music because I thought it was something I should be doing, but it usually wasn't long before my mind wandered out of the yard. Rock music had shattered my attention span into Flintstones vitamins, which may have been why I went to a mixed bill at NYCB rather than to a full-lengther such as *A Midsummer Night's Dream.*

The Firebird, my first ballet, didn't disappoint, but it didn't ring steeple bells either. I remember enjoying it, in a self-consciously "appreciative" manner, as if my eyes were set forward a fraction more than usual, the music holding me more than the dancing, which seemed subordinate to the costuming and a folk-legend storytelling that relied on a lot of portentous gestures prophesying terrible weather heading in our direction. The Firebird herself was performed by Karin von Aroldingen, whose tall, vanquishing presence lived up to her imposing name, but dancing-wise she didn't have that much to do under all that Vegas-red howdy-do. Afterward I felt a bit yawny, and no one ever truly yawns alone. History is made at night, as the movie title goes, and the afternoon dip of the audience's biorhythms and the energy-conservation mode of many of the dancers, who had perhaps danced the night before or were scheduled for that day's evening performance, made for a bit of a Valium drip. I didn't mind. I figured it was all part of the induction process, easing me into the wonder of it all with gentle massage. At intermission I went out to the viewing tier and looked down upon the promenade, where clumps of conversationalists and solitary figures were moving like Hitchcock miniatures in a high-angle shot or positioned like map pins, the rink book-ended by the Elie Nadelman marble statues that seemed smug in the rich plenty of their fertile hips. Also on the program that afternoon was *Afternoon of a Faun,* which had the tender intimacy and caressing delicacy of a recital piece, Debussy's piano notes strung like little drops of dew on your eyelashes. Nice, but nothing to write home from camp about.

My *Song of Bernadette* moment, my face bathed in miracle light, may have been Balanchine's *Serenade,* which I'm hesitant to admit since it has been the portal-opening ballet for so many converts, the dropped panel that divides Before and After, and I was so hoping to be different. It was the first ballet Balanchine did in New York, and from the opening tableau—the dancers in tulle skirts raising their palms in unison to salute the blue night—to the closing processional, the ballerina held aloft and carried off, her arms and back arched in rapt surrender, *Serenade* serves as an annunciation. Unlike the other early ballets I saw, it didn't have paraphrasable content, origin material; it seemed to have dreamed itself into existence, its seams and struts invisible. Proof that the pure products of modernism refuse to die! And it didn't depend upon a star dancer to send it through the uprights; everyone onstage seemed equally ensouled, answering the same votive call. Or could it have been *Symphony in C* that cinched the romance—its exhilarating marshaling of forces at the end, the small attack units of the corps, employed in slashing diagonals, uniting in a ranked surge, rallying to an excelsior finish? It may have been the stereoscopic power of both: the Rapture Vision and the Victory Romp.

After a couple of more incursions, I bought a matinee subscription to New York City Ballet, something affordable then even for a low-income, hardworking unpsychotic loner like me, and became a semi-semi-regular, seeing Balanchine's *Agon* and *Four Tempera-*

ments and other T-shirt ballets whose names I couldn't pronounce and still couldn't pronounce if you pop-quizzed me, such as *Cortège Hongrois* and *Divertimento from "Le Baiser de la Fée."* I saw Jerome Robbins's work for the company, including his insensibly maligned *Dybbuk* with beating music summoned from the bowels of the earth by Leonard Bernstein, which finally got its just due when it was revived in 2007. I began referring to dancers familiarly by their first names, as if we were the chummiest of acquaintances, hearing myself say things like, "I saw Patty last week in *Coppélia*"—Patty being Patricia McBride, one of my favorite principals at the company, the only ballerina who made *Coppélia* seem more like a candy factory. And Suzanne, referring to—well, there was only one Suzanne, as we shall see, make the sign of the cross when you hear her name. I should have known I was a goner once I started stopping after performances at the Ballet Shop on Broadway, which stocked, along with illustrated ballet storybooks, biographies, critical studies, and girlie souvenirs (ballerina figurines, baby toe shoes, music boxes), a cardboard box full of assorted back issues of *Ballet Review,* the magazine founded by Arlene Croce, who had since ascended to dance critic at *The New Yorker* and was virgin queen of all she surveyed. *Ballet Review* contained articles by her that were looser, swingier, and sparkier than many of her *New Yorker* columns, lacking the more raised-chalice tone of taut distinction that sounded like an abbess played by Maggie Smith with both nostrils. *BR's* contributors even graded new dances as Bob Christgau did with his Consumer Guide, a running scoreboard that gave the revival of Balanchine's *Donizetti Variations,* for example, a B at best, one critic docking it a D. A D—to Balanchine! *Sacre bleu!* Although *Ballet Review* didn't pie-face the reader with the messy, chop-shop layout of a punk zine, its curt *Dragnet* poker-faced diligence—every article in the issue looked as if it had been pounded out on the same old newsroom typewriter—registered its own resistance to the angel fluff and slatternly praise thrown about most places in print about dance. Its absence of photographic spreads picturing dewy dancers holding dewy poses—a text-driven emphasis perhaps from economic necessity or production limitations—gave *Ballet Review* a frank stare of intellectual rigor reminiscent of the literary quarterlies that built their reputations piling one plain block of text upon another in the forties and fifties, a brick wall of surety.

Hard to believe now, but ballet once had an intellectual constituency, an arty swank. The postwar exuberance of the mid-forties had carried all of the arts along on its dolphin crest, from painting to theater to music composing to fiction to poetry. "Even in ballet, previously hardly known, we were preeminent," observed Gore Vidal. (No stranger to the dance wings, Vidal had pseudonymously authored a murder mystery called *Death in the Fifth Position,* in which his sleuth "keeps one *entrechat* ahead of the police in their heavy-footed search for the killer.") Although Vidal brackets this golden age in the brief span from VJ Day in 1945 to the commencement of the Korean War, its glamorous legs stretched longer than that, long enough to bask in the glow of Camelot. Jacqueline Kennedy took ballet lessons at the old Metropolitan Opera House, hosted evenings at the White House where the invited guests included Stravinsky and Balanchine (indeed, Balanchine was the first guest invited to the Kennedy White House), and today has one of New York's leading ballet schools posthumously named in her honor. In his journal *The Sixties,* Edmund Wilson, the closest thing American literary criticism would ever have to Dr. Johnson in a Panama hat, records a gala evening in the mid-sixties:

Elena [Wilson's wife] and I went to New York May 19 and attended the first night, on the 20th, of [the composer Nicolas] Nabokov's *Don Quixote* ballet. Balanchine danced, or rather mimed, the title role, appearing for the first time in years and probably the last time in the night. It was not a very brilliant evening. Nicholas had told us beforehand that the score was made of "Ukrainian cafe music," but there were also invoked, on occasion, Rimsky-Korsakov and Stravinsky. The end of the first act consisted of one of those varied vaudevilles that occur in Tchaikovsky's ballets; but then the early part of the second act was a somewhat similar sequence. This broke up the dramatic line, which was not very effective anyway. Everybody was there. Nicholas had a section reserved for his friends in the middle of the first balcony: Kirstein and his brother and Mina Curtiss, Marianne Moore and John Carter were close to us. The New York Reviewers, Cartier-Bresson, and Marian Schlesinger [the then wife of the historian Arthur Schlesinger Jr.]; but the mob at the "reception" afterwards was so dense that it was impossible to talk to anybody.

"Everybody was there," a statement that affixes the royal seal of cachet, brilliant evening or no. The cachet hadn't diminished in the seventies, but it had acquired a brow of canonical sobriety, despite the raffish omnipresence of the artist Edward Gorey in his fur coat and tennis shoes, who was said to have attended every performance of New York City Ballet, racking up more *Nutcracker*s than mental health authorities should have allowed (he didn't even like *Nutcracker*!). The literary critic Richard Poirier, whose essay "Learning from the Beatles" was a landmark moment of highbrow recognition of the new Atlantis of pop culture, wrote about Balanchine and New York City Ballet for *Partisan Review,* Susan Sontag was a regular attendee, and even the easily chafed socialist thinker and literary critic Irving Howe had succumbed to the tulle, publishing an essay in *Harper's* in 1971 called "Ballet for the Man Who Enjoys Wallace Stevens" (a play on the title of the dance and music critic B. H. Haggin's primer for the harried mind, *Music for the Man Who Enjoys "Hamlet"*). In a 1972 entry in his journals, published posthumously under the title *The Grand Surprise,* the former *Vogue* and *Vanity Fair* editor Leo Lerman records the NYCB's principal dancer Edward Villella's effusion while standing on the pavement at 3:00 a.m., the hour of Fitzgerald's dark night of the soul, but not for Villella. "This is where it is right now. This is where I want to be—lucky to be.

Ballet's here with the New York City Ballet—the center—the living center—Balanchine's given us glory—the glorious opportunity."

To the faithful, New York City Ballet was the only true team in town, the diamond crown. I once asked a literary intellectual if he followed ballet, and his response was, with a distinct note of corrective, "I follow New York *City* Ballet," as if any other brand were simply too lower shelf. NYCB was the monarch Yankees and its closest rival for attention, American Ballet Theatre, the patchwork Mets, its bench strength and institutional heritage nowhere near as deep or storied. NYCB prided itself on not being fame-driven in its casting and promotional material (it didn't import internationally renowned dancers for B-12 ass-bumps of glamour) or yoked to lavish-scenery warhorse story ballets that made you wish the nineteenth century would go back where it came from. ABT, albeit performing works by Frederick Ashton and Antony Tudor, relied on a more MGM approach, refreshing yesterday's favorites with the stars of today. Hence there was more bravoing and brava'ing at its curtain calls, more flower-bouquet lobs from the balcony, accepted with courtly bows of humble gratitude from the gallant thigh-man in tights and Eve Harrington so-touched-by-your-generosity genuflections from the ballerinas, who would sniff from the presented rose as if its fragrance had been distilled from all the adoration of the cheering throng. Whereas the curtain applause for NYCB on the average night was more like a suitable tip left on the dining table while climbing into one's coat—rather Waspy.

The English professor and literary critic Robert Garis, in his one-of-a-kind critical memoir, *Following Balanchine* (imagine Frederick Exley of *A Fan's Notes* intoxicated by arabesques and never falling asleep on a stranger's sofa), chronicled two decades of the intellectual devotion and personal engagement with what he calls the Balanchine Enterprise. Each Balanchine ballerina was a vessel of devotional investment. "I remember an enjoyable argument at the 57th Street automat (that splendid large space was one of the places we went to for coffee and postmortems) with Haggin and Marvin

Mudrick, a friend of ours from the *Hudson Review,* after a performance: Haggin was supporting Verdy's style strongly against that of
[Allegra] Kent, Mudrick was supporting Kent against Verdy, whom
he identified as a 'soubrette.' Verdy was my special interest, and I
couldn't accept Mudrick's limiting category for her, but I really did
love Kent, too."

This would never happen today. It takes the spurious power of a
telepsychic to picture a pair of *New Yorker* arch druids such as James
Wood and Louis Menand—or any of the cybernetic brains from
newer literary journals such as *n+1,* or the policy wonkers seated
across from PBS's Charlie Rose debating the merits of Sara Mearns
versus Tiler Peck (two of the premier principal dancers in New
York City Ballet's current roster) under a rain-sheltering awning
on West Sixty-sixth, or co-analyzing the recombinant geometry
of Balanchine's choreography for the corps, its mandala designa-
tions. Longtime friends once fell out for good disagreeing over the
degrees of goddess stature of their favorite dancers, over a specific
ballet interpretation. The fraternal relationship between Garis and
the over-volted Haggin (a classic grievance collector who detected
hostility with every cilium of his being) irreparably ruptured over,
among other things, the super-supremacy of Balanchine's final,
greatest muse, Suzanne Farrell. "[Not] that he disliked Farrell, for
he admired her greatly, but . . . she did not seem to him as transcen-
dently special and new as she did to us." It was hell on the digestion,
breaking with a former comrade, as it must have been back in the
Trotsky era. Even after Farrell temporarily left the company, the
rift remained, the worry of being targeted by assassin eyes. "This is
the point at which my following the Balanchine Enterprise began
to drift . . . even the physical experience of going to the ballet had
become difficult since I had to be on guard not to run into Haggin."

Similar animosities rake the edges of the ballet scene today—
rival cliques retiring to opposing corners in the lobby, former buddies giving each other the leper treatment, veiled insults pressed
into print like thin cheese slices—but only among the shrinking

band of professional dance critics, its more partisan combatants and embittered shrunken heads. Literary critics with the pebbled subtlety and ardor of Garis and Mudrick interested in ballet or any performing art have become nearly extinct (literary critics of any word grain not exactly a going thing). Today's intellectual homeys are inserted so snugly into their visors of expertise that they patrol their particular beat like RoboCop, perhaps finding ballet too frilly for their brawny brains. Or they may have "issues" with the body ideals in ballet and gender representation, since everyone loves having issues as an excuse to stay home and darn their egos. Were a fledgling Irving Howe or Richard Poirier to flirt with an interest in ballet, there'd be no high lama for him to look up to for divine guidance, no Edwin Denby or Arlene Croce whose dance expertise serves as airfield beacon.

Croce's arrival at *The New Yorker* was a signature moment for the magazine and for dance criticism, another masterstroke by the editor William Shawn. In the seventies, *The New Yorker* was at the pinnacle of its cultural influence, and Croce's head-held-high prose and persona only extended the elevation. Reading Arlene, you never felt that her responses were saw-toothed by warring impulses, that ambivalences dug into her critical formulations and left tiny divots of doubt. In this she was unlike Pauline, for whom contrarieties were part of the jazzy rush of sorting out what you felt and thought. Witty, adventurous, mordant, occasionally slangy as Arlene could be ("In spite of its yuckiness, the *Sacre* remains in memory as the only tolerable [Pina] Bausch piece"), her *New Yorker* essay-reviews—like those of the art critic Harold Rosenberg or the literary critic George Steiner—radiated a fine chill of infallibility, which could have its own perfect-martini invigoration in the untucked seventies. She removed the valentine lace from dance writing that had gussied and gauded it up in the journalistic past with platitudes and sugarplum superlatives, covering dance as the demanding, exacting, grown-up art it was, not a rest-stop for tired minds wanting to look at legs. Her column seemed to have its own proscenium arch, a tremor of expectancy that heightened the stakes. She eagle-eyed why Suzanne Farrell was indeed worth warring over, what made her a figure of consequence, an altering force:

> Suzanne Farrell, one of the great dancers of the age, has rejoined the New York City Ballet. She returned without publicity or ceremony of any sort, entering the stage on Peter Martins' arm in the adagio movement of the Balanchine-Bizet "Symphony in C." The theatre was full but not packed. The lower rings were thronged with standees who did not have to push their way in. Sanity was in the air. As the long bourrée to the oboe solo began, the audience withheld its applause, as if wanting to be sure that this was indeed Suzanne Farrell. Then a thunderclap lasting perhaps fifteen seconds rolled around the theatre, ending as decisively as it had begun, and there fell the deeper and prolonged silence of total absorption. For the next eight minutes, nobody except the dancers moved a muscle. At the end of the adagio, Farrell took four calls, and at the end of the ballet an unprecedented solo bow to cheers and bravas . . .
>
> In that first moment of delighted recognition and then in the intense quiet that followed, the audience, I think, saw what I saw—that although this tall, incomparably regal creature could be nobody but Farrell, it was not the same Farrell.

I too was part of that audience that tremulous night and I sure didn't see what Croce saw and wouldn't have been able to articulate it if I had, even with a set of drawing pencils. What she saw was this:

> [Farrell] has lost a great deal of weight all over, and with it a certain plump quality in the texture of her movement. The plush is gone, and it was one of her glories. The impact of the long, full legs was different, too. If anything, they're more beautiful than ever, but no longer so impressively solid

in extension, so exaggerated in their sweep, or so effortlessly controlled in their slow push outward from the lower back. The largesse of the thighs is still there, but in legato their pulse seemed to emerge and diminish sooner than it used to, and diminish still further below the knee in the newly slim, tapering calf. Yet the slenderness in the lower leg gives the ankle and the long arch of the foot a delicacy they didn't have before. And it shaves to a virtual pinpoint the already minute base from which the swelling grandeur of her form takes its impetus.

Has any anatomy study ever swung that high? "Farrell and Farrellism" the essay was called, and its publication in *The New Yorker* had a sonic impact, exciting even among those who never went to the ballet and didn't know Farrell had left, much less returned, but knew something major was afoot. I know it made me sit up a little straighter when I went to the ballet from then on, working on my X-ray vision. After typing the quotation above into the text you're now reading, I flipped to the front of the original paperback of *Afterimages,* the collection that contains "Farrell and Farrellism," and saw, written in ink:

For Jim Wolcott,
In keenest admiration.
Arlene Croce 1980

I had forgotten that she had inscribed it for me. How could I have forgotten? Memory is a treacherous mistress, keeping so many past kindnesses from us.

What was it about ballet that won my allegiance? It was hardly the only thing hopping in tights. New York City—the entire country—was experiencing a dance boom in the seventies, a leotard liberation army breakout that was recognized while it was happening, as opposed to those golden eras known only in retrospect by their afterglow. The pioneer explorers who had made the Judson Memorial Church the Cabaret Voltaire of modern dance had matured, evolved, and dispersed: Kenneth King, Merce Cunningham, Yvonne Rainer, Meredith Monk, Lucinda Childs, Trisha Brown. Institutional largesse and arts funding kept companies solvent that had been formerly dangling by a shoestring. "Sexual liberation and gay liberation added momentum to the dance boom," the critic and cultural historian Holly Brubach told *City Journal* in 2011, "and you sometimes got the feeling that they were turning out because they were curious about bodies." Turning out and getting turned on. "Dance was the art in which the body woke up," recalls Elizabeth Kendall. "For us in our early twenties, the late 60's early 70's were about such dramatic waking up, that the awake body, the strongest metaphor for that, was front and center." From *The Exorcist* to Sam Peckinpah's *Straw Dogs* to *Looking for Mr. Goodbar,* the rudely awakened body was a war zone, the locus of sexual-social-political strife, the Supreme Court's *Roe v. Wade* decision in 1973 legalizing abortion setting a decades-long conflict between personal autonomy and government control. Alfred Kazin's walker in the city became the jogger in the park, trying to stay one frantic step ahead of the muggers and gnarly inquisitors. Where punk and New York–based movies such as *The French Connection, The Seven-Ups,* and Sidney Lumet's garbage-lid bangers shoved a street-level picture of clutter, graffiti, and the cracking vertebrae of the rotting infrastructure at the viewer, ballet—thanks to Balanchine and Robbins—proclaimed the water-towered rooftops and the silver-spired skyscraper skyline, the upward arrowing of energy and aspiration. Where nearly everything I enjoyed were provisional operations, making the most of make-do and snaring contingencies on the fly, ballet relied upon massive resources, exacting rehearsals, wealthy patrons, and a fine-boned sense of hierarchy, a bred-in appreciation of lineage, proportion, perpetuation, deference, decorum, unswerving devotion, acute sacrifice. It should have been out of joint with the jagged decade. Plus it had all that mime.

Elitist and reactionary to its detractors, it also lay on the wrong side of the class struggle, stroking its sable fur. In 1969, a professor of literature at MIT named Louis Kampf rabble-roused student radicals to cry havoc and unleash the dungs of war. Defile the cultural temples! Convert Lincoln Center into a field latrine! "Not a performance should go without disruption," declared Kampf. "The fountains should be dried with calcium chloride, the statuary pissed on, the walls smeared with shit." Kampf was more than just another fist-shaking, faculty-lounge, pocket-edition Lenin: he was then president of the Modern Language Association, so his preachings carried reverb. The revolutionary moment came and went without the New York Philharmonic or Metropolitan Opera coming under urinary attack from full-bladdered revolutionaries, and by the early seventies New York already reeked of enough shit and piss that manufacturing more of it to make a political statement would have seemed redundant. Further defilement was the last thing this rock pile needed, and what was solacing even to cynics about Lincoln Center was that it seemed to have earned a temporary restraining order against entropy; its blocky architectural sterility— more than one detractor referred to it as a cultural mausoleum—was a kind of comfort zone, a non-wild life refuge. True, the underpass that connected the uptown side of the IRT station at Sixty-sixth Street to Lincoln Center leaked from the ceiling and reeked from the puddled floor and back-splashed walls, such a dysentery stretch that even panhandlers shunned it, but once you sniffed prison freedom, it was as if the pause button had been hit on the fall of civilization. You could sit at the edge of the illuminated fountain, moisturized by the misty spray, and not fear for your life about a nearby drug deal gone bad or a psychotic breakdown in progress. You might see Balanchine himself strolling toward the State Theater, his head and neckerchief jauntily yachting across a choppy sea of mundane heads belonging to non-geniuses patronizing the sidewalk. It was an inspiriting sight, just knowing he was briskly alive, that Robbins was alive, Bernstein was alive, Martha

Graham was alive, Agnes de Mille was alive—they hadn't for-saken us.

And what I grew to learn about the ballet world was that, once inside, it was like every other subculture high and low in Man-hattan in the seventies. It looked like a members-only society only if you lacked the nerve and desire to enter; it wasn't warm and welcoming—what was?—but it offered its own gradations of grudg-ing acceptance, based not on money, breeding, boarding-school con-nections, Ivy League affiliation, the right address, or the ability to wield a salad fork like a neurosurgeon's scalpel but on the measure of knowledge, passion, and dogged curiosity for seeing what was out there to see because there was always something new to see even in things you had seen so many times before, a fresh interpretation that blew off the chalk dust. It made you come to it, rise to the challenging occasion. Piddlers need not apply. I went to modern dance performances, saw Cunningham's company, and attended a few events on the outskirts of the Village that seemed to belong to the Soviet bloc where the venues were inadequately ventilated (you left coughing coal dust) to give those avant-gardenias a try, but for me they didn't take root in the sky, seize the sun.

Perhaps ballet personified all of the nice things denied me up to then (by no one in particular, by the luck of the draw), things I thought I didn't feel I deserved, and in certain moods still don't. Without realizing it until the fug was washed off my windshield, I had grown up Beauty-deprived, a word I'm capitalizing to dif-ferentiate it from the beauty of a flower or the beauty of a sunset or the beauty of a smiling face or any of those other Kodak moments to paste in our memory books and tell ourselves are enough; and they're not. They're not genius-blessed. They're not Bach, they're not Balanchine, they're not Geoffrey Beene, they're not mind-woven enchantments of endlessly evolving, revolving fractals. No matter how Dewey decimalized your preferences and priorities may appear, you never know what you truly want in this pastiche world, because what you want is based on the tray of choices that were passed around during your upbringing, a limited selection that you believe is all that is available until a curtain parts, a light falls, and there something stands, in a state of expectancy, awaiting the cue. It would be leaning too hard on magnetic polarities to portray porn and ballet as the two opponents contending for my lapsed Catholic soul—a porn star perched on one shoulder, making lascivious mouth movements, Princess Aurora on the other, bourréeing to beat the band—but it would make a cool movie. Ballet was nearly everything I wasn't, and what I wasn't was what I must have wanted most. It also awakened the sensitive feminine side of me that had been lying dormant under all that Mailer and Peckinpah, an admission that I have usefully learned over the years can bring any conversation to a dead halt.

Classical ballet had its own rebel appeal. It stood perpendicular to the prevailing entertainment culture of the seventies, in a stance of stately opposition. Its conservatism, in retrospect, may have been the highest form of defiant resistance, a *Brideshead Revisited* breathing monument to faith, order, enduringness. Unlike Joffrey Ballet, which enjoyed a pop smash with its premiere of Twyla Tharp's *Deuce Coupe,* set to the songs of the Beach Boys (and the template for every Broadway jukebox musical ever since, from *Mamma Mia!* to *Jersey Boys*), New York City Ballet remained a pennant-bannered Monaco moated and aloof from the nagging needlings of the Zeitgeist to be relevant, socially concerned, hip, happening, and in harmony with the vibrating moment, its few veerings in this direction winced at as flights of fancy that turned into instant dodos, such as Balanchine's jet-age ode *PAMTGG,* pronounced "Pam-te-guh-guh." To those few who saw it, "guh-guh" was gaga. Its title taken from Pan Am's slogan jingle, "Pan Am Makes the Going Great," *PAMTGG* flurried out female dancers in icicle-spiked helmets and male dancers in customized Speed Racer helmets on a mod set that included a loose pyramid of transparent Plexiglas luggage, and such cavorting they appear to do. From the relatively scarce photographs of the production, it isn't commercial air travel being evoked at its most dashing chic, when stewardesses were the runway models of the plane aisle and the pilots in their uniforms looked like bronzed statues—it's way spacier. It looks like the first *Star Trek* ballet, a galactic greeting card from some planet a-go-go. I suspect that even more then (1971, when the ballet premiered) than now, the audience overlap between ballet fans and *Star Trek* buffs was a tiny crescent, ditto among the critics, who were similarly aghast. (The grades given it by *Ballet Review*'s bull-pen regulars ran the gamut of E to F—E meaning "Not Worth Keeping," F being "Insufferable.") *PAMTGG* was beamed up to oblivion, never to be seen again. After that, NYCB never strayed into pop, and even flirting with avant-garde experiment was greeted with frosty suspicion by the parishioners, as if somebody were trying to sneak something fancy through the vestibule.

Not a lot of hospitality was shown to a new Balanchine ballet I saw shortly after it premiered called *Variations pour une Porte et un Soupir* (Variations for a Door and a Sigh), an allegorical duet set to a musique-concrète atonality of squawks, squeaks, honks, clunks, amplified exhales of weary breath, and assorted thuds that suggested a futuristic netherworld in need of a lube job. Pierre Henry's score wasn't an alien contraption to anyone who had gotten temporary tinnitus from a John Cage piece or for that matter "Revolution 9" from the Beatles' *White Album,* and pictorially *Door/Sigh* was mystico-majestic, the male figure enveloped and devoured by a black billowing skirt large as night (the shadow image of the endless white veil streaming like the etherealized scarf from Cyd Charisse in the dream ballet in *Singin' in the Rain*), the victim of a she-serpent who conjures Louise Brooks's Lulu in *Pandora's Box* making a neat meal of her prey. Although the postgame wrap-ups in the lobby and later in print were undecided as to whether Balanchine was impishly showing he could beat the avant-gardists at their own racquetball game—see, here's how it's done, kids—or pulling an opaque Jovian prank, the reception was on the prickly side. This they weren't willing to lap from the milk bowl. One woman near me, who had been knitting socks during intermission, cupped her hands to her ears during the performance to block the dissonant din while others snickered and giggled, and at the fade-out came a smattering of hisses and boos, most unusual. I bet *Ballet Review* gave it lousy grades, too.

Unlike so much else dished up in that spread-eagle decade, classical ballet was sexy without being "sexy." It didn't fondle and flaunt itself, peacocking like John Travolta's Tony on the illuminated disco floor in *Saturday Night Fever* (authenticating Albert Goldman's insight in his coffee-table monograph *Disco* that "the real thrust of disco culture is not toward love of another person but toward love of self—the principal object of desire in this age of closed-circuit, masturbatory vibrator sex"), or steering its hands along its curves as if auctioning itself off, à la the chesty hopeful in *A Chorus Line*'s T&A number who sang, "Orchestra and balcony/What they want is what cha see." Both were Bob Fosse's department. With its stiletto stalkings and snazzy indentations (the bowler-hat cockings, the cool-cat dropped wrists, the pelvic thrusts and assy ripostes), Fosse's come-on choreography for the TV special *Liza with a Z,* the musicals *Cabaret* and *Chicago,* the revue *Dancin',* and the Felliniesque film *All That Jazz* became the defining theater-cinema dance style of the seventies, sexing everything up with its witch doctor "magic hands." When Fosse sexed up ballet itself, in a wet-dream fantasy set at the barre in the 1978 Broadway revue *Dancin'* between a shy bumpkin and a female classmate, releasing their inhibitions in a tumbling rhapsody of toes-pointed crotch-splits and scuba-diving cunnilingus, the only place I wanted to dive was under my seat. The worst lewd idea Fosse ever had (to be fair, he had loads of good lewd ideas too), it unwrapped like a *Penthouse* letter to the editor brought to purple fruition. It also reminded me of Gerard Damiano's psychosexual opus *The Story of Joanna,* which featured a balletic interlude performed by its eponymous heroine, played by the trained dancer Terri Hall (her rib cage resembling a birdcage), that dispensed with simulation for its shoulder-riding, face-mounting maneuver. Did the soft-core origami of Fosse's leotard lap dance have its origin in this hard-core divertissement? Perhaps not directly, but by that point porn had gone so viral that you could pick up its booty call in the prickling air just by walking around midtown without a hat.

All That Jazz (1979), starring Roy Scheider as Fosse's pill-popping, bed-hopping on-screen avatar, was shot in Times Square, and although it seldom spent time in the nasty streets, rotating from morning shower and first gulp of pills to rehearsal studio to editing room to home base day after day in a wheelhouse grind, the porniness of Eighth Avenue pitted the atmosphere of the film, the taste of cinders. One hotsy number, "Air Rotica," staged as a promo for the only airline to offer in-flight orgies, plunged Balanchine's *PAMTGG* into the polymorphously perverse, nose-diving into an orchestrated free-for-all bathed in a bathhouse fog presided over by a blond, bare-breasted Valkyrie named Sandahl Bergman, who, recumbent, lifted her left leg into a perfect forty-five-degree extension, her foot pointed at the ceiling like a pistol, making all men her slaves. It should have been a crowning image, the Christmas tree star, but the rest of the dance fell apart before your eyes, like a human pyramid sleepily buckling, tumbling into soft rubble. It was like the big bang with a boomerang effect. The inherent escalation in porn/erotica, the need to keep upping the kinky ante, had only so much room to multiply before the explosion of energy dispersed and diffused, leaving a dead core and a lot of mess for the maid to clean up afterward. Once you get to orgy, artistically there's no place left to go.

Ballet delivered a better bang, one that sunflowered and fanned out into the future. When Mikhail Baryshnikov defected from the Kirov Ballet in 1974 ("Glimpses of Genius" was the title of Croce's critical dispatch on Baryshnikov's pre-defection performances in Montreal, just as word of Bruce Springsteen's thundering thighs was traveling up from the Jersey shore) and made his U.S. debut with American Ballet Theatre in *Giselle,* it was not only a comet moment for ballet but one of the defining jolts to hit New York in the seventies. And this was a positive jolt, unlike the string of sucker punches that kept the city reeling from one *what-next?* crisis to another, stuck in a revolving turnstile of tabloid fright headlines, disap-

pointment being a portion of our daily bread during the protracted
death croak of the Nixon presidency. His thunderbolt arrival was a
Lindbergh-landing morale lifter from where I sat, which was in the
balcony of City Center on West Fifty-fifth, whose seats were a tight
squeeze even before the great expansion of American butts spread
across the vast prairie. It was there that I saw Baryshnikov's first
rabidly awaited performances and received a tutorial in star power as
paradigm shifter. "Ballet is Woman," goes the inevitable Balanchine
maxim, and, as Elizabeth Kendall writes in a bio-historical work
in progress about Balanchine, ballerinas were the drama initiators
and primary interpreters onstage, the searchers and choosers—that's
what made them heroines to many young feminists, eager to climb
out of their heads. But when it comes to the wider public, it is usually the herald infusion of male force, glamour, and elevation that
socks dance to a new level of matador excitement and supplies critical mass. Now, Baryshnikov was no Rudolf Nureyev, whose defec-
tion to the West in 1961 struck a Byronic chord that cape-whipped
through the decade, his dance partnership with Margot Fonteyn the
closest thing ballet ever had to an ongoing royal wedding. Baryshnikov wasn't dark, imperious, mercurial, and knightly; he didn't
possess a matinee idol profile, cruel amusement and passionate ardor
playing about his lips. (We didn't see the practiced-seducer panel of
his personality until the 1977 movie *The Turning Point,* where his
soulful dog eyes worked overtime.) He wasn't tall, and unlike some
other not-tall *danseurs nobles* he didn't project cloud-stature. The
altitude was in his jumps and whirlybird pirouettes, which seemed
to have not only more air around them than other spring-boarders
but a freeze-frame clarity even in fast motion; he achieved high-
definition before our analog eyes. The impact on the audience was
pandemonious, and when I left the theater, the night itself seemed
in an excellent mood. New York nights are like that, acquiring an
extra snap to remind you nowhere else will do. I made it a point to
see every Baryshnikov performance I affordably could, which back
then didn't require ransoming off a hostage or two, and when Gelsey

Kirkland joined ABT, he had a partner who transcended the rodeo tricks that some of the company's stars were prone to reeling off to crashing waterfalls of ovation and bouquets crapping from the rafters.

Gelsey. A name that falls in the mind's ear like a sprig of mint. I had fallen for her like a fool since I had first seen her at New York City Ballet, a dancer of Keatsian ethereality—such a cameo face—and yet utterly without coy affectation or approval-catering. Petite, precise, and imperishably young, she appeared enveloped in a personal quiet so profound that she seemed to dance under a glass bell, like an enchanted cricket. Not that she was crunchable. She was one tough little apparition, otherworldly and all there, her tiny little traveling steps in Balanchine's *La Sonnambula* while holding a candle a Gothic vision that escaped from the Brontë attic. Offstage, Kirkland was rumored to be a cactus handful, the sketchy rumors of her erraticism that one overheard at the line for the water fountain confirmed by her 1986 memoir, *Dancing on My Grave,* where she shocked the ballet world with her tales of coke-snorting, eating disorders, collagen treatment, and giving Balanchine back talk. The critic Wilfrid Sheed, reviewing a steaming plate of angry tell-it-like-it-is athletes' memoirs, once wrote, "The literature of nausea has come to professional football: the 'I Was a Vampire for the Chicago Bears' school for one crowd, and 'I Was a Rich Owner's Plaything' for another." *Dancing on My Grave* was the literature of nausea's first venture into tutus, but, onstage, in her prime, none of her personal demons poked through, at least to my un-clinical eye. She spun pure silk out of herself, so becalmed and mission-borne that she seemed to be erasing the connecting dots of the choreography in a continuous breath of movement, in thrall to a higher calling and a guidance system she had personally installed. Gelsey was more than poetry in motion; she could explode out of the bass drum with her own armory show of pyrotechnics, as in the can-you-top-this? trade-off solos in the *Don Quixote* pas de deux, where she tore off those pirouettes as if daring Baryshnikov to sass her back.

Technique and artistry animate ballet, as they do any performing art, but the mystery and alchemy of presence are what open the dome, making you realize there's more to this world than this world. Memory is such a patchy recording device of performance, and the fugitive clips of Baryshnikov and Kirkland together that surface on YouTube or other video portals preserve only tapestry pieces of their performances, a small, unrepresentative highlight sample that only traps the ghosts of those unrepeatable passing moments of live performance. But they also affirm that we weren't wrong then, they really were that graced, and nothing about them has dated, except Misha's Galahad mop of golden hair, more suitable for a Bee Gee. Baryshnikov made the cover of *Time* magazine in May 1975, the same month that *A Chorus Line* opened off-Broadway at the Public Theater before moving to Broadway; a month later, that ice bucket of dousing cynicism, *Chicago,* created by John Kander and Fred Ebb and choreographed by Fosse, debuted on Broadway. The astrological configuration for 1975's midyear must have been *awesome.* Gelsey herself went on to make the cover of *Time* in 1978, photographed snapping a fan in mid-jump as Kitri in *Don Quixote* above the head-line U.S. BALLET SOARS. The exuberance of the shot is a wistful reminder of Kirkland at the peak of her artistry and popularity, how broadly the dance boom had brightened into public consciousness, and how far the print media have culturally slid since then into the far side of moronica, the days long gone when any of the news-magazines would consider any of the performing arts cover-worthy, because none of their editors know anything apart from what they read online or what's memo'd on the inside walls of their bunker mentality.

When I think of what was waiting on the other side of the dance boom's soaring crest, the darker afterwash and long plateau, another matinee comes to mind, one quite different from my first at New York City Ballet, one separated by a decade. (By then, I had moved to a smaller mouse-hole in the East Village, just in time for the crack era.) This was the NYCB matinee when the principal dancer Darci Kistler was scheduled to perform after a long absence due to injury, a layoff that had seeded suspicion and resentment, rumors that Darci might be a perfectionistic head case like Gelsey. Her appearances had been sporadic even before this extended recoup, her name dropped from the cast abruptly like the scheduled 3:10 train from New Haven removed from the station board due to track failure. Darci was getting a George Jones reputation as a reliably unreliable no-show, though of course nobody imagined her knocking back Johnnie Walker Red in the back of a trailer. But her elusive butterfly dartings had become vexatious to those who loved her. So much had ridden on Darci's shoulders since she had first emerged from the stable that her absences were a deprivation, a denial of a great dancer in her prime. She had been the last of the Balanchine ballerinas, appearing first onstage at the age of sixteen in major roles and revealing a coltish, unself-conscious transparent cursiveness that had many reaching for the word "preternatural." She was the heiress of the Balanchine ideal and ballet's torchbearer for the future, a future that looked precarious after the death of Balanchine in 1983, whose last works were solos choreographed for Farrell, who would retire from the company in 1989. Without Balanchine as presiding, animating spirit, NYCB, ballet itself, was in danger of ossifying into a preservation society. Whatever doubts and irritation over the long gaps between performances, everyone wanted Darci's return to be triumphal, a faith-restorer, not so much a comeback (she was too young for that) as a coming home.

Everybody was there that sunny, light-spilling day. Arlene Croce and assorted other dance critics, forming clots. Susan Sontag and whatever scary person she was with. Regular faces whose names I didn't know, and a face whose name I did know who was a friend of both Arlene's and Pauline's, a literary critic who looked like Lytton Strachey when he held a cigarette aloft, the smoke chimneying upward as if leaving cares behind. He had a slight stammer too, as I recall, the fitful effort it took to insert a word into the loading chamber when he sensed his vocal mechanism about to jam, which also made me think of Bloomsbury, Oxbridge dons, the tapping of cigarette ashes. Though given that he had been born and raised in the Deep South, Tennessee Williams on the veranda would have been a closer invocation, but Williams didn't send off the scent of the library stacks; A. did. He was in a bad way, his uneven shoulders holding him up like a bent clothes hanger. He had lost noticeable weight, something had wrung out of him. It was difficult for him to stand, even more painful to sit, so much fleshy padding had been skimped from his bones. He said that he had come from his sickbed—adding, "Don't worry, I'm not contagious"—and knew that he shouldn't have, "but I couldn't miss this." This being Darci's return. He would die of an AIDS-related illness some years later, survived by his companion, a phrase more insufficient than most in the language of mourning.

After the performance, everyone was chatting madly away like song sparrows about Darci's return, how she moved and looked, the condition her condition was in. I can't remember whom I talked to, must have been someone. Here and there were coveys of young female dancers, all legs shooting upward and pony manes and wrist flicks, most of them students of the School of American Ballet dressed in their afternoon best, cliqued together going over Darci's performance with their own method of instant replay, imitating and mimicking her turns and combinations, how she extended her arms, positioned her pinkie fingers, came to a stop that was never a complete stop, the next step pouring out of it. Some of these ballet students would have flourished and entered the corps ranks of NYCB or some other company, they may have already come and gone in their dancing careers by now, had their shot and taken it. But on that afternoon they were loose bracelets of girls uninterrupted, still sprouting, graceful and ungainly, half-sophisticated, half-creaturely, chatting and laughing, their tiny pocketbooks slung over their shoulders, the bracelets breaking up as the bell-tones sounded the end of intermission. I go to the ballet now, I'm married to a dance critic, something that just had to be, and in the corridors and lobby and on the balcony overlooking the Lincoln Center square and geysering fountain, there are different girl dancers shadow-boxing now, marking what they've just seen, and yet they're the same girls, replenished. I love being able to look at them with unwanting eyes and careful not to look too long, looks being so easily mislaid.

PART V:

What Are You Doing Here?

For those of us who lived in New York in the seventies and felt as if this is where our real lives began despite wherever it was we were marking time before, the opening montage of Woody Allen's *Manhattan*—the city photographed by Gordon Willis in a black-and-white panorama of enshrining shadows and blinking signs; the elevated subway inching like a Lionel model train past Yankee Stadium, whose lights glow like birthday-cake candles; the mute mosaic of skyscrapers, silhouetted bridges, billowy steam clouds, snow-laden streets, thronged sidewalks, and traffic honks silenced as George Gershwin's *Rhapsody in Blue* builds to a fireworks climax— is more than a beautiful overture, a midnight valentine. It carries ambiguous undernotes, emotional motes that never quite settle. When the film came out in 1979, the montage appeared to soar with nostalgia for the present, the sense that (to quote the Carly Simon lyric) "these are the good old days." Even with the surefire laugh line in Allen's narrative voice-over about the city being "a metaphor for the decay of contemporary society," the Gershwin-Willis opening was a balm for every bruise that New York had taken in the seventies, a relieved sigh from the trenches signaling that perhaps the worst was over, somehow we had come through. To some, this relief had a tincture of wishful thinking. "In the most wry way, to anyone who knows the Manhattan of potholes and poverty and rudeness, the film is a fable—written by Woody Allen and Marshall Brickman—about a city of smooth rides and riches and thoughtfulness," wrote Penelope Gilliatt in *The New Yorker*. To others, it was an *ironic* fable, the grandeur of the cityscape, the vertical climb of the arrow-topped towers and Gershwin score, being so much grander a stage than its characters with their scratchy dilemmas and violin-tuned neuroses deserved.

Nineteen seventy-nine was also the year of the publication of John Leonard's *Private Lives in the Imperial City,* its title the perfect subhead for Allen's *Manhattan.* A collection of Leonard's columns from the *New York Times,* a weekly report from the bay window of Leonard's Zeitgeist receptor, *Private Lives in the Imperial City* was to the needily narcissistic seventies what Candace Bushnell's *Sex and the City* would be to the stiletto-clicking, dangling-price-tag nineties. It's difficult to overstate how omnipresent Leonard was as a baroque calligrapher of the bobbing cultural stream in the seventies, broadcasting on so many frequencies as critic and commentator, his sentences rolling across the page like a player piano programmed by the Irish absurdist Flann O'Brien on a liberal arts bender, tight yet loose compositions that yoked together cultural-literary-political-pop references in ragtime syncopation:

Since they stopped paying me to watch television, I don't do it much any more: *M.A.S.H.,* maybe, and *Lou Grant* on Monday nights; *The Rockford Files* on Fridays. (I would like to think James Garner is modern man. I used to like to think Dirk Bogarde was modern man. Modern man is probably Captain Kangaroo. On the other hand, why is everybody always kissing Yasir Arafat? ". . . and on a heath beneath winking stars a fox, red reek of rapine in his fur, with merciless bright eyes scraped in the earth, listened, scraped up the earth, listened, scraped and scraped," said James Joyce in *Ulysses.*) The Pope, of course, got me out of bed. But ordinarily I am upstairs listening to Joni Mitchell and reading Kierkegaard.

Idiosyncratic as Leonard's allusion-clustered prose was, his Private Lives column exemplified the *Times*'s thrust into lifestyle, service, and trend-spotting features under the managing editor, A. M. Rosenthal, who gleefully pirated Clay Felker's carbonated formula for *New York* magazine and brought out the Weekend Edition, which begat the Sports, Home, Science, and Living sections. Like Allen, Leonard in Private Lives had a specimen-pinning eye and a psychoanalyst's ear for the overthunk vanities of sophisticated brunchers tangling up their nerves on the soundstages of their overarching self-importance. Meanwhile, the spires of Manhattan stood by like obelisks, unmoved by such dramas, having witnessed millions of cast changes before.

But Woody's *Manhattan* was more than just a study of some private lives in the imperial city, a matte exhibition of love and confusion from the vantage point of Table 8 at Elaine's, his personal table. (It is at Elaine's where, against the Altmanesque rustle and bustle of egos, we first meet the Amazon nymphet Tracy, played by Mariel Hemingway, who, when asked the aboriginal New York question, "And what do you do?" answers with guileless aplomb: "I go to high school.") Visually, the movie joins the social and the spatial dimensions of the city together in tense embrace. For real estate was about to become everyone's demanding mistress. Compared with the tiny, rattletrap apartments of *Annie Hall,* the interiors of *Manhattan* look like shadow boxes, shipping containers for larger ambitions. By 1979, affluence has found room to stretch its bony arms, freeing more breathing space for the psychological fidgets and romantic quandaries of Woody's ensemble. The fading hippieboho spirit poured into the Modigliani string-bean figure of Shelley Duvall in *Annie Hall* (she was the *Rolling Stone* baby journalist who found a concert featuring a robed, garlanded guru "transplendent") is nowhere to be found in *Manhattan,* everyone being too busy beavering away at their careers. "In *Annie Hall,* Diane Keaton sings from time to time, at a place like Reno Sweeney's," wrote Joan Didion in a disdainful notice of *Manhattan* in the *New York Review of Books.* "In *Manhattan* she is a magazine writer, and we actually see her typing once, on a novelization, and talking on the telephone to

'Harvey,' who, given the counterfeit 'insider' shine to the dialogue, we are meant to understand is Harvey Shapiro, the editor of *The New York Times Book Review*." Actually, it's so inside it's pitch-dark, but let it go. The keenest perception Didion has concerns that famous list of things worth living for that Woody confides to his tape recorder, a roll call of redeeming greatness for the mediocre crapitude of existence that includes Groucho Marx, Willie Mays, Louis Armstrong's "Potato Head Blues," and Flaubert's novel *A Sentimental Education*. "This list of Woody Allen's is the ultimate consumer report," Didion writes, "and the extent to which it has been quoted approvingly suggests a new class in America, a subworld of people rigid with apprehension that they will die wearing the wrong sneaker, naming the wrong symphony, preferring *Madame Bovary*." That subworld was about to surface, conquer, and colonize. Consumerism in sneakers was where the culture was moseying before eventually sprinting in the eighties, our tastes on the lookout for any false step.

I, however, rode the rising surf in the wrong direction, managing somehow to move up professionally while knocking my quality of life down a notch. In the late seventies, my career had started to go slick. Still writing for the *Voice,* I would be hired as a columnist at *Esquire,* the Don Draper of sixties magazines, whose columnists at various times had included Norman Mailer, Dwight Macdonald, the English gadfly Malcolm Muggeridge (who, after his religious conversion, would enjoy a third-act career revival as "St. Mugg," the praise-singer of Mother Teresa), and Kingsley Amis, heroes all. *Esquire* had changed ownership in 1979, purchased by Chris Whittle and Phillip Moffitt, a team of Tennessee investors who were greeted with the askance condescension New York publishing kept on ice for anyone perceived as provincial and soft-padded, possible banjo-pickers. After the financially ruinous tenure of the previous editor, Clay Felker, who had converted *Esquire* from a monthly to a fort-nightly ("an ingenious scheme to lose money twice as fast," someone pointed out), the non-nudie men's title needed a savior, only the Tennessee Two didn't fit anyone's fantasy twin bill of the reincarna-

tion of *Esquire*'s founder Arnold Gingrich and Harold Hayes, the
editor who ran the ranch in its New Journalism renaissance. Who
could have? Their outside status may have immunized them to
the daunting weight of institutional lore that would have crushed
those who approached the magazine as a sacred trust. They took
proper care of the property. Unlike the entrepreneurs, arbitrageurs,
and turnaround kings who would vulture attack vulnerable busi-
nesses to strip assets, cut payrolls, and enrich shareholders, leaving
behind skeletal remains and a debauched brand, the Tennessee Two
weren't out for a quick kill. Where Felker had salvaged the *Village
Voice* by dragging it into the future with iron claws, Whittle and
Moffitt propped *Esquire* back on its feet with deerskin gloves, dust-
ing it off and making it respect itself again, no matter how much
the other kids laughed at it. Moffitt, who would become editor to
Whittle's publisher, conducted business in his office with a bluegrass
lilt to his voice that was as far away from Felker's seal bark as could
be imagined. It was like listening to a transcript of James Taylor's
greatest croons, and although *Esquire* revitalized itself by catering to
baby-boomer consumerism (yuppies in their puppy stage, discovering the talismanic powers of the perfect saucepan), it was little surprise decades later to discover that Moffitt had become a yoga guru,
preaching the dharma of nonattachment.

He was not the one who talent-scouted me. Contact was made by
Lee Eisenberg, who, knowing my devotion to a certain black feline,
had a bag of kitty litter delivered to my door. The editor to whom
I was assigned at *Esquire* was a young woman in her mid-twenties
named Dominique Browning, imaginative, scarily proficient, bound
for the higher rafters of magazine-dom, with transfixing crystal
blue eyes whose glance always seemed to catch you unawares even
if you had been looking forward to it the entire elevator ride up to
Esquire's floor. I had a crush on Dominique. Everyone had a crush on
Dominique. There was a secret society of Dominique infatuees who
stroked her name aloud as if it had dove wings. I probably fantasized
that *she* would be the editorial Suzanne Pleshette to my rippling

raw-talent James Franciscus in *Youngblood Hawke,* only Dominique wasn't droll and raven-dark like Pleshette posing in doorways and I couldn't quite get a Jungle Jim ripple going. It was certainly for the best, my opportunities for embarrassment more usefully deployed offstage, enabling me to maintain the facade of cool professionalism that existed whenever I practiced it in the men's room mirror.

In 1979, I also published my first piece for the *New York Review of Books,* a roundup of books about television, the subject mattering less than the fact that I was being initiated, if not fully inducted, into the intellectual Sky Club, where Gore Vidal, Susan Sontag, V. S. Pritchett, Elizabeth Hardwick, Isaiah Berlin, Mary McCarthy, and I. F. Stone were contributors. In my middling twenties then, I was probably the youngest of the paper's contributors, whose median age was somewhere around the half-century mark and would only climb to Methuselah heights. My first arrival at its offices on West Fifty-seventh underlined my unripened status. I was sitting in the outer office, waiting to go over my copy, when Barbara Epstein came out with an air of dispatch and handed me a manila envelope as if it contained codes that needed to be delivered to HQ, fast. "It's a doorman building," she said, "but make sure the doorman buzzes the apartment while you're there—" At which point the editor Robert Silvers rode to the rescue by popping out of his office and saying, "No, no, that's not a messenger—he's one of our contributors." That I was mistaken for a messenger might have been mortifying if I had owned much in the way of pride, but I prided myself on my lack of pride. (I was only sorry that I didn't get a chance to check out the address on the envelope, imagining myself "dropping something off" for Didion or Sontag.) Lack of undue pride, overprizing one's lack of pretense, has a self-punitive side, a penalty tax, I recognize now. If only such enlightenments arrived when they could do you some good. A healthier dash of self-worth and I might not have finished out the seventies where I did, pacing the ceiling.

Unable to pull enough together for a down payment on my apartment when the building on Horatio went co-op, I was in luck. I was offered an apartment on St. Marks Place that a former girlfriend was vacating, which I could sublet until the lease was up and have renewed in my name. Making the hazardous journey from West Village to East, I saw the apartment as a stopgap, a stepping-stone to the next chapter of my ruthless climb to the top of the middle, but I would stay there for ten years, as if serving out a sentence handed down from an unknown court. True, it was a rent-stabilized apartment, something so coveted in New York real estate that tenants would hold on to one until their toenails had turned yellow, their bodies had gone scarecrow, and they had become shut-in hoarders, until the inevitable day fell when neighbors would notice "a funny smell" wafting from the apartment, and out came the carcass, buried under a rotting pyramid of pet-food cans. I suppose there are worse ways to go. Incarceration wasn't too bad for, oh, the first six or seven years, but the longer I stayed, the harder it became to leave, despite the lack of amenities that less evolved societies took for granted. It was a studio like the one on Horatio, but smaller, darker, sulkier. Horatio had two windows into which sunsets could wash. St. Marks had one window that snatched a meager slice of morning light. No air-conditioning, no cable hookup, and a bathroom where I could hear every gurgle upstairs. I never had the walls painted, letting them fade to a festive laundry gray. Homeless alcoholics, holed up on the roof for informal meetings, deposited empty bottles in the rain gutters, sending water slopping over the sides during torrential storms and cascading down the back wall, often leaking through the tops of sills and giving the inside walls small-scale topographical maps of severe beach erosion. With my studio located on the floor conveniently above the garbage room, mice didn't have far to come to visit. I once dispatched a mouse with a broom after it dropped in around three o'clock at night, swinging at it like Dustin Hoffman in *Straw Dogs* while my cat, Gully, sedately sat by and monitored the situation, interested in seeing how this would turn out. Once the mouse was suitably flattened (not something I enjoyed doing, but glue traps seemed more sadistic and the snap of mousetraps too guillotine), I, sweat drenched on this summer night by the sudden exercise, gave Gully a silent look of reproach for falling down on the job as a mouser. I may have actually voiced something like this aloud, since a person who lives alone with a pet is prone to carrying on one-sided conversations. As I prepared to sweep the dead mouse into a dustpan, Gully trotted over to the radiator, reached behind it with her paw, and scooped out a decomposed mouse body that had been there so long it looked mummified, it too unable to give up a rent-stabilized apartment. Rather than tote the dead mouse in her mouth, she scooted it over with her paw and left it next to the fresh body, as if to say, Since you're disposing of that one, how 'bout getting rid of this one while you're at it? Cats really do have their nerve.

What I inhabited on St. Marks was a primitive, rough-draft "man-cave," a term that makes me shudder whenever I hear it on a real-estate show such as *House Hunters* or *Property Virgins,* a man-cave being something one needs to escape from, not a womb to revert to in middle age to revegetate. It was the only apartment I lived in in that high-crime era that was burglarized. I returned from a screening or some other outing one night and, reaching the top steps of the first-floor stairs, saw that my door was ajar. I heard nothing happening within. Whoever had been there had presumably left, unless they were waiting inside, as happened to someone I knew who had been face-punched as soon as he stepped in. I eased the door open, flipped on the light, and flinched as if expecting everything to leap to life, crying, "Boo!" What I saw was a shambles worse than the one that was the usual ordinary. Drawers open, their contents spilled on the floor, mattress askew, records and books strewn across the floor. But nothing major seemed to be missing. The TV and the VCR must have been too megalithic to lug in a jiffy down the stairs and through the narrow hall, and nothing else would have fetched much on the resale market. It wasn't as if I had a jewelry box where I stowed all my "nice things." It wasn't material things I was worried about, in any case. The fear in my throat was that vicious harm had come to my Gully, that she might be lying kicked-dead on her side, her life broken. Or that in a panic as the place was being tossed she might have darted out the door, and the rest of my night would be dedicated to going from floor to floor looking for her, hoping she hadn't somehow gotten out into the street. As worst-case scenarios were firing synaptically away in rapid overlapping succession, Gully poked her head out of the closet door, checking to see if the coast was clear, then stepped into the room, her meow sounding only marginally more cranky than usual. I filled her water bowl, which had been kicked aside by the intruder, and mopped up the spill as she sipped and enjoyed a late snack of dry crunchies. While she dined, I tidied up the debris in the living room, which was also the bedroom, which was also the workroom. Less than an hour later my girlfriend came over and we made love on the bed amid the disarray as if it were London after a blitz raid, then made love less romantically a second time, the encore having a lot more James M. Cain boiling on the stove. Next morning I phoned a professional, undergoing one of those meaningful and costly rites of passage for New Yorkers in that period, the Changing of the Locks. My saltine box of an apartment was now fortressed with the bolts and bars of a security cell at Rikers, but that was part of the package deal of living in the East Village, the trade-off for being at the nexus of everything it had to heave at you before it eventually turned into a simulation of itself, a watering hole for hipster doofuses on safari.

My apartment was in the rear (that's what made it man-cavey), a refuge from the street racket that gave weekend nights the festive melee spirit of Mardi Gras for the Mohawk-haired. St. Marks Place between Second and Third avenues in 1979 was still the Sunset Strip of bohemian striving and slumming, rinse-cycling at all hours with the creative detritus and chosen outcasts without whom any city becomes merely a business address for the embalmed. It was like the set for *Rent* out there on the block, without the piercing pathos that made *Rent* such an inspirational pain. On the southwest corner was Gem Spa, where the New York Dolls had been photographed in cocky dishabille for the back cover of their debut album. Farther west was Trash and Vaudeville, whose wares resembled a garage sale of the Dolls aesthetic with a healthy stock of punk fetishistica. Next door was the St. Marks Baths, where men in strategically wrapped towels adopting odalisque poses waited in cubicles for other men to drop by for a meet and greet (or, as one wag put it, "a meat and greet"). Across the street was the venerable St. Mark's Bookstore, before it migrated to the strip of Ninth Street where I had interviewed Patti Smith in her own saltine box. Nearby, on the same north side, was Manic Panic, the store founded by CBGB's Tish and Snooky, where fans of Kathy Acker's serrated fiction could get everything they needed to doll themselves up for the dawn of the dead. Farther east was a café where some of the hip, choppy-haired, beyond-caring waitresses could be as surly as the lesbian strippers in John Waters's *Pecker,* the customers too cowed to complain. The café had a courtyard dining area surrounded by apartment buildings on three sides where you could brunch amid potted plants and agnostically pray that an air conditioner wouldn't make a suicide leap. Farther east down on St. Marks was the apartment where W. H. Auden and Chester Kallman had lived for so many years, the poet punctuating conversations by taking a pee in the kitchen sink. "Everybody I know pees in the sink," he told a visitor. "It's a male's privilege." It was a male something, anyway. Across from the Auden preserve was Theatre 80 St. Marks, still operating, on June 20, 1979, presenting a Kay Francis double bill, *I Found Stella Parish* and *Confession,* which I was sure not to miss, being a Kay Francis fan long after it became unfashionable. Around the block from my studio was McSorley's Old Ale House on East Seventh, which I didn't visit the entire time I lived on St. Marks (too college-studenty), but found reassuring to simply know it was there if I wanted to pop in for a pint and a sneeze of sawdust. It's psychologically bracing having landmarks nearby, even if you avoid them. Most important, my new address positioned me equidistant between CBGB's and Max's Kansas City, within easy walking distance of both, the perfect triangle for bat flight.

Barricaded inside when nothing outside called, I made the most of the sensory deprivation, which did wonders for my productivity. So much work I got done there. It was like a sewing room for words. And though my memory may be mussed, writing didn't feel like drudgery at the time, a way to earn parole. It was as if I had the whole outfield to myself to run around in. In 1979, I did a review for the *Voice* of a Pete Hamill paperback thriller that was just too juicy for a joker like me to resist, though maybe I should have. Few remember Pete's thrillers today. He may only hazily recall them himself; for most prolific authors, books often recede from consciousness once they're pushed out the parachute door and sent praying. Hamill's career in fiction, though still riding backup to the pugilistic impact of his justifiably lauded newspaper journalism, is known largely from the late-flowering lyrical nostalgic word-daubing of *Snow in August,* from 1997, and the novels that followed. But in the late seventies, Pete cracked his knuckles and set out to do a series of smart urban action kiss-kiss-bang-bangs featuring a tough-guy-with-a-soft-cookie-center alter ego hero named Sam Briscoe, "who loves women, fast cars—and solving murders." Sort of like *Spenser: For Hire* with his own honorary bar stool at the Lion's Head (where Jessica Lange had waitressed in the mid-seventies before ending up in King Kong's paw) and a bust of Brendan Behan to bless the beer foam. The cover illustration of the paperback of *Dirty Laundry* featured Hamill's own handsome Hollywood head of hair with some icy dame in the background whose V-plunging cleavage was an open invitation for uptown snob and downtown knob to clash in the satin sack. For all of his ability to nail down a phrase and magnetize a regular-guy rapport with readers, Pete didn't possess the primitive guile and gusto of the phenomenal Mickey Spillane, the creator of Mike Hammer and such disreputable brute forcers as *I, the Jury* and *Kiss Me, Deadly,* whom I once had the opportunity to interview at a police equipment office, for reasons now forgotten. Mick was a swelluva guy, if I may be idiomatic. Spillane didn't believe in fancy setup fiction. Go in hard, get them hooked, and leave them happy, that was the literary praxis he lived by. "The first page of a novel sells that novel, the last page sells the next one" was his maxim, and it's a better one than most of the wrapped morsels of wisdom from those *Paris Review* "Writers at Work" interviews with various laureates who discuss their craft like medieval wood-carvers. Hamill tried to muster the door-busting pulp energy of a Mike Hammer-head ("I skulled him with the gun butt," growls his he-man avenger), but he was too much of a self-conscious poet of the common man to pull it off, which made his steamier passages worthy contenders for what would later in London earn their own Bad Sex Awards. Here is how my review of *Dirty Laundry* for the *Voice* ended:

> When Briscoe is naked and handcuffed, a Mexican whore unzips her jumpsuit and straddles the defenseless hero. As she rapes him, she keeps her boots on, the perfect porno touch. The funniest sentence in the book is when Hamill, after describing her up-and-down motions, writes: "She tossed her head, but the bun stayed in place." After her muffled orgasm, Briscoe grabs a gun and jams it in her gut. "Stop right there, sweetheart," he says. "Or you'll never come again."
>
> After 200-plus pages of pistol-whipping and kiss-my-boots kink, it's a bit disconcerting to flip to the front of the book and read the dedication:
>
> > *This book is for my Daughter*
> > *DEIRDRE.*
>
> Daddy, you shouldn't have!

Oh, I was such a scamp. Shortly after the review appeared, Pete did a column in the *Daily News* in which a buddy commiserated with him over my slam. Was it a real buddy or a ventriloquist's dummy? Newspaper columnists had a much freer hand with color-ful dialogue back then, in the heyday of Jimmy Cannon, Jimmy

Breslin, and similar heirs to Hemingway, John O'Hara, and salted peanuts. *He banged you up pretty good,* Pete's buddy said. *Yeah,* Pete conceded, like a weary sailor home from the sea, *but he's young, and someday he'll be on the receiving end, then he'll know what it's like.* Laugh while you can, buddy boy, but someday I'd be the one hurting, that was the word from the ring corner of the reigning champion. And of course Pete was right! Curse his perspicacity! I brought out a novel of my own years later, a novel Pauline Kael had tried to mother out of existence, and I got mine. Not universally, but the naysayers had a pecking party while I made like Tweety Bird with my little wing in a sling. (Showing his resilience, Pete revived Sam Briscoe in a 2011 crime solver called *Tabloid City,* and bully for him.) But, looking forward, looking back, what was the alternative? *Not* writing criticism, *not* trying fiction? The filthy secret about writing fiction is in the early ski runs, when no one's watching, it's *fun.* A reviewer's praise only means something to readers if it has a force of personality and conviction behind it that hasn't been compromised by too much cream filling in everything else you've written. Free-swinging writing was more expected in the seventies, and there was more room for it in print, but even in a rude decade it wasn't going to win you any popularity contests. One of the minor revelations I got after clocking a few years in journalism was how many writers *wanted* to be in the popularity pool, wanted to be invited for weekends at the Vineyard. Although I should have known better, being aware that one of the bedsores of Norman Mailer's resentment toward Norman Podhoretz was Podhoretz's inviting of Mailer's then-archrival William Styron to a party for Jacqueline Kennedy and not him, I couldn't understand how not being asked to certain parties or panel discussions or petition drives could plunge a can opener into a writer's pride and morale. I was naive enough to believe that such pouting ended once you graduated from high school, when it was replaced by a jolly new set of pouting opportunities and grudge breeders. It took me a while to learn that warm grievances fresh from the bakery do come along in life but they're simply piled atop the old, cold ones, a sedimentation akin to Philip Larkin's accounting of how Mum and Dad muck you up in "This Be the Verse" ("They fill you with the faults they had/And add some extra, just for you").

Going into writing for the social-climbing glory was never the goal, and not just because I didn't have any long-range goals, never picturing myself in the white mink palace of penthouse nooky and celebrities with all-cap names that gave the critic Seymour Krim such gnashed teeth. I was making my name almost solely as a critic, where restrictions apply. Being a critic isn't anyone's childhood dream, an occupation that schools set out a booth for on Career Day, a religious calling that glimmers in the goldenrod. It's impossible to imagine George Sanders's Addison DeWitt from *All About Eve* as anything other than a fully formed adult, issued from a printing press. To those literary cubs who fancied having a cigarette dangling from their mouths like Albert Camus or Jack Kerouac, or sharing a club table with Jay McInerney, Bret Easton Ellis, and Tama Janowitz to anteater a line of coke from here to the Vegas strip, or getting a Chinatown tattoo alongside Mary Gaitskill, or watching Jonathan Franzen adjust his eyewear (and who today would be happy just to get through breakfast without feeling as if everything's turned to gravel), to them, critics are the snipers in the trees that the director Sam Peckinpah heard whenever the palm leaves rustled. To creatives, the Critic is the undermining inner voice maliciously put on the intercom to tell the whole world (or at least the tiny portion of it that still cares), *You're no good, you were never any good; your mother and I tried to warn you this novel was a mistake, but, no, you wouldn't listen, Mister-Insists-He-Has-Something-to-Say.* Failed artists consider critics failed artists like themselves, but worse, because unlike them they took the easy way out by not even *trying* to succeed, critics not having the guts to climb into that Teddy Roosevelt arena that everyone likes to invoke as the crucible of character, or risk the snows of Kilimanjaro. Even prestige authors who flex their fingers at performing criticism as if filling in at the piano on Monday nights feign disdain of it as a secondary activity, siphoning off the creative juices necessary to keep genius fertile and gurgling. For some reason, the elegant retort "If doing criticism didn't cost Henry James, Virginia Woolf, D. H. Lawrence, and John Updike any candlepower, what makes you think you're too good for it, buster?" never seems to stick.

Journalistic critics such as myself were, are, and forever will be routinely disparaged as parasites, sore losers, serial slashers, Texas tower snipers, and eunuchs at the orgy (*what orgy?* where is this orgy we seem to have missed?), which would hurt our feelings, if we brutes had any. The journeyman critics who are both perceptive and funny—genuinely funny, not jokey, their wit flipping off their wrists like a sneaky curveball—can escape the accusations of jealousy hurled across the notions counter and earn the affection accorded durable entertainers. But there's a catch—there's always a catch, for everything. Like Woody Allen's comedians, such elegant wiseacres can often feel as if they've been denied a seat at the adults' table, unless it's the Algonquin Round Table that's their ideal, where they would have been right at home, passing the soup to Dorothy Parker. They can even start to talk about their reviewing as if it were a minor knack at which they got nimbly adept, like card tricks or shooting pool. But it was these Parcheesi champions with whom I felt the most kinship in the seventies and beyond, the ones unafraid to crack jokes that had a hickory snap to them, such as, yes, John Leonard. Though I didn't share his enthusiasm for that bevy of neurasthenic seismographs—among them, Elizabeth Hardwick, Joan Didion, and Renata Adler—he escorted round the cotillion whenever one of them had a new book out. He and I had a vaudeville moment in the seventies when I was entering the auditorium for the National Book Critics Circle Awards just as he was exiting and he halted, did a classic double take, and asked, "What are *you* doing here?" as if the purpose of the organization were to keep people like me out. Then he clapped a friendly hand on my shoulder as if to say, *It's okay, you can go in.*

Other serious comedians: the marauding balletomane and literary critic Marvin Mudrick (who, told by a young woman at the

Hudson Review, where he was a regular contributor, "You're the funniest writer I have ever read," beamed and said, "I could live the rest of my life on that compliment. I don't care whether it's true; I love it. That's what I *want* to be"); Alfred Chester, whose review of John Rechy's *City of Night* provided the template for every hatchet job Dale Peck would undertake decades later; and Wilfrid Sheed, a novelist of asperity (his *Max Jamison* of 1970 is the definitive poison-pen etching of a critic and the vale of vanities he inhabits—"He was in love with the way his mind worked, and he was sick of the way his mind worked. The first thing that struck you about it, wasn't it, was the blinding clarity, like a Spanish town at high noon. No shade anywhere. Yet not altogether lacking in subtlety"), primarily known as a critic who could spin dimes with every sentence. His defoliation of Norman Podhoretz's *Making It* was something to cherish, something I would sometimes lift from the milk-crate shelf and read in rainy moods like selections from Robert Browning:

This is the first impression of *Making It:* that of a burlesque queen solemnly striding up and down to the strains of "Temptation," and nothing coming off. Hour after pitiless hour . . .

. . . Ambiguity is totally alien to Podhoretz's book, which has but one gear and one track and rolls down it like a *Daily News* van . . .

. . . The names come tumbling out like clowns from a circus car. Mary and Dwight and Philip—but then he gets stuck. A gentleman doesn't rat on his friends. He simply uses them to pad his index . . .

. . . An anatomy of *Making It* should not bog down on the first navel it comes to. Why have we been brought here, anyway? Anyone who has paddled about in these literary wading pools knows at the very least that George Plimpton looks over your head and Podhoretz looks under your armpit and that

Macdonald looks you periodically right in the eye. (Our bad luck that the armpit man wrote the book.)

In the foreword to the expanded edition of *The Morning After,* where the *Making It* review was collected, Sheed recounts a party hosted by William F. Buckley Jr. where he was "accosted by a man I didn't recognize anymore who said, or rather sneered, 'I guess there's a statute of limitations, you son-of-a-bitch,' and turned on his heel." It was, of course, Armpit Man making the heel turn. Sheed: "Welcome to the world of Norman Podhoretz, where there obviously is no statute of limitations, even after thirty years, and where enemies are forever. In fact, Podhoretz had written a book around then called *Ex-Friends* in which ancient feuds still sound as fresh as this morning's razor cuts." Reviewing *Ex-Friends* for the *Nation,* John Leonard turned Podhoretz's travail into an unhappily ever after fairy tale: "It's an old story, and even my own, so let's be brief. Once upon a time you were a *Wunderkind,* and now, oh so suddenly, you're an old fart." A hard fact of life, which is why it's best not to linger on what awaits at the last depot and relish the memory of when we were young farts, and free.

I made enemies with my reviews but seldom ran into their gun-slit stares because my invitations to book parties were equally seldom, my one near altercation occurring when an innocent at a magazine fete asked someone whose book I had reviewed months earlier, "Do you know Jim Wolcott?" to which he snapped, "Yeah, I know the son of a bitch," and revved off, which in the brusque seventies barely even registered as bad manners. In his shoes, I wouldn't have wanted to say hi either, and if we ran into each other today, I'm sure we would amiably ignore each other, having amassed so many better enemies in the interim. I developed a reputation for being "a smart-ass" in print, but a smart-ass at least has some bounce to it, and my interest in literature was never liturgical. It was enthusiasm or forget it. Literature with a capital *L,* like a marble foot planted atop the reader's head, didn't interest me. I never accepted why there should be some invisible, wavy cutoff line separating Great Fiction from phosphorescent beauties and dollhouse miniatures, novels that contain a whole world in a snow globe. As Kael wrote in "Trash, Art, and the Movies," "I don't trust critics who say they care only for the highest and the best; it's an inhuman position, and I don't believe them." I did believe them, having seen how high they could raise the Communion wafer. Especially in lit-crit, there were those who could be believed when they professed undying fidelity to only the highest and the best, not only Sontag (for whom "seriousness" was the purring word she most liked to pet, telling an interviewer, "Sometimes I feel that, in the end, all I am really defending—but then I say all is everything—is the idea of seriousness, of true seriousness"), but *The New Yorker*'s supreme polymath and European curator George Steiner, and William H. Gass, who wrote in his essay "Even if, by All the Oxen in the World," "It is the principal function of popular culture—though hardly its avowed purpose—to keep men from understanding what is happening to them, for social unrest would surely follow, and who knows what outbursts of revenge and rage. War, work, poverty, disease, religion: these, in the past, have kept men's minds full, small, and careful." Which is one weird slant on the slaughterhouse of history (those small, careful minds that waged the Crusades, set Montezuma in motion, and so forth), as if literature has its own pacifying lies to tell, a finer class of platitudes.

I was once sitting with Pauline in the last row of a literary panel discussion downtown starring Cynthia Ozick and Joyce Carol Oates, who were trading honeydew compliments back and forth as if they expected Eudora Welty to show up with a wide-brimmed hat and a watering can. Ozick would compliment Oates on the dynamic fecundity of her bullet-train imagination and how it cowed her, confessing that she could only proceed to the next sentence in her own fiction after she had chipped and beveled the previous sentence to perfection, to which Oates would deftly respond, And that's what I so admire and envy about *your* writing, Cynthia, the exquisite crystalline luminosity of each beautifully chosen, carefully arranged

phrase and metaphor . . . Back and forth it fluttered, Ozick in her
girlish voice (so incongruous with her tank-turret head) and Oates
doing her shrinking-violet act, until Pauline side-whispered, "Can
you be*lieve* this shit?" We had a movie later to go to uptown, and
as Ozick and Oates appeared on the verge of singing a duet, I asked
what time our screening started. Pauline said, "It can't start soon
enough," and out we hastened, into the welcoming arms of liberty.
(Though when Ozick's "Shawl" appeared in *The New Yorker,* Pauline
was on the phone like a literary town crier to everyone she knew,
urging it on them, alerting them to its greatness.)

It was on such occasions that you felt literary fiction didn't need
any additional enemies, its own advocates and exemplars were doing
such a swell job draining its blood banks. Nevertheless, literary
quarterlies and critics with the long chins of undertakers found no
dearth of suspects responsible for the slow, desert-crawling Death of
the Novel, done in like an Agatha Christie victim by multiple assail-
ants, each taking a stab at the distinguished old crone, a mixture
of the usual suspects and new culprits: rock music with its invasive
rush of pure pop for now people; the summer movie blockbuster,
beginning with *Jaws* in 1975, its shark fin converting the American imagination into a drive-in screen; the academicization of literature by professors full of French cheese (a favorite theme of Gore
Vidal's, whose essay "American Plastic" joined Roland Barthes and
John Barth in unholy wedlock); the aversion of fiction writers to risk
bunions and discourtesy at their tender expense to do Dickensian-
Balzacian reporting of institutions, status-spheres, and the hidden
gear-works of class (an argument strung like Christmas tree lights
by Tom Wolfe in his introduction to the anthology *The New Journalism*); the inadequacy of fiction to keep up with the acceleration
and jump-cut transitions of our minds, the Godzilla rampages of
breakout of America's once-repressed derangements, something
Seymour Krim pegged back in 1967: "If living itself often seems
more and more like a nonstop LSD trip . . . what fertile new truths
can most fiction writers tell us about a reality that has far outraced

them at their own game? How can they compete with the absurd and startling authorship of each new hour?" This was the clamorous challenge that the narrator of Gilbert Sorrentino's 1971 novel *Imaginative Qualities of Actual Things* was mockingly determined to confront with a meat-hook in each hand: "My next book will be a novel, for you, tracing the fortunes of a typical American family, from the years of Depression up through the Swinging Sixties. It will be written in Abracadabra, have a number of brutally candid sex scenes, and the hero will be an alienated Jew who likes to Suck Off Christian movie stars and Fuck black girls in the Ass. Confronting Contemporary America in a Big Way. There will be no plot and I will exhaust everybody in sight by listing, at every opportunity, the contents of anyone's pockets and wallets and handbags."

Two years later, in 1973, a novel following Sorrentino's recipe for bathtub gin was published that truly confronted America in a big way, poking it in the face with a stubby penis, its very title a high-stakes provocation: *American Mischief*. Written by Alan Lelchuk, *American Mischief* was a campus novel turned reeducation camp whose inmates were well-known New York intellectuals: "'A.' has a 'boyish' unruly forelock and a propensity for going down on nubile seamen; 'E.' is a professor at Columbia, an Arnold and Forster specialist, who as a phase of his re-education is forced to watch fellatio being performed on Lelchuk's narrator (by a *girl,* thank God!)," Marvin Mudrick recapped in his review. A. was clearly meant to flag the multidisciplinary social thinker Paul Goodman, and E. could be none other than the patron saint of moral seriousness and T. S. Eliot tea-cozy decorum, Lionel Trilling, the author of full-length studies of Matthew Arnold and E. M. Forster. Norman Mailer appeared in *American Mischief* under his real name, assassinated with a bullet up his ass, perhaps intended as a bit of literary back atcha for the transgressive buggery of the German maid in Mailer's *American Dream.* But the real-life Mailer wasn't amused or appreciative of such a one-gun salute, vowing, "By the time this is over, Lelchuk, you ain't going to be nothin' but a hank of hair and some fillings."

(It was always a treat when Mailer talked Southern sheriff, as if he had been taking Broderick Crawford lessons on the sly.) This side-show stoked anticipation for the novel, like a scuffle at the prefight weigh-in before a major rumble. Excerpted in Theodore Solotaroff's *New American Review,* the most exciting literary publication of the late sixties and the seventies, its back issues as indispensable to comprehending the political and cultural storm systems of the time as any retrospective overview, *American Mischief* had the makings of a Big Mac of a succès de scandale, its picaresque effrontery something that the literary establishment was keen to embrace now that Roth's Portnoy had snapped the paper chains of propriety and everyone wanted to be with-it. It became a Book-of-the-Month Club selection, and indeed was a succès de scandale. I glanced at *American Mischief* years later, and it already seemed an overwrought period piece, overfueled by the same urgency that juiced even our most eagle-eyebrowed confabulators (Philip Roth in *Our Gang* and *The Great American Novel,* Robert Coover with *The Public Burning*) to overswing wildly for the fences and twist themselves into Twizzler sticks in their efforts to do vigilante justice to the grotesque, hyper-thyroid surrealism of the news in the age of Nixon.

I wasn't a size queen when it came to fiction, either as reader or as reviewer, though I wasn't as averse to heavy lifting as the devilishly suave Anatole Broyard, one of the *Times*'s daily reviewers, comically notorious among his critical brethren for his penchant for choosing the slimmest volume from the galley pile for his accomplished caresses and tango moves. *Aroused by Books* his 1974 collection was called, and as review collections go, it holds up much better than most precisely because its author doesn't apologize for prizing the pleasure principle over moral instruction, spiritual enlightenment, and intellectual muscle-building. Reviewing Alfred Kazin's *Bright Book of Life,* that cavalcade of American literature's Easter Island heads from Faulkner to Bellow and beyond, Broyard writes, "Mr. Kazin is what I would call an ideophile. He's in love with ideas, but though he generously shares that love with us, I know that I feel a certain lack . . . [I]t's all just a bit too platonic. Mr. Kazin seems to *think* about fiction more than he *feels* it." And Broyard was definitely more of a fingers-flexing feeler (which is to take nothing away from how keen, elegant, and mobile his spidery mind was), as was Alfred Chester, who wrote in a review of John Updike's *Pigeon Feathers,* "Despite the currency of the phrase, we really don't want writers to *say* anything because, as soon as they do, we get bored. What we do want is for them to *feel* something, and to make *us* feel something." Then Chester broke into peroration: "Teach us, O Artists, not to settle for guilts and anxieties, for twitches and embarrassments! Teach us, O Artists, to feel again! Because emotions are the only thing that artists have to say—and emotion can make us gigantic and tragic. (Ideas never can; they can only follow, like dogs. Ideas, however pertinent, however great, tend to remove us from reality; feelings always bring us back again. Ideas never explain experience; feelings *are* experience.)"

Whether or not a novel "holds up" over time means less to me than whether or not it *holds on*—if you can open any page and hear a voice coming through like a hypnosis countdown, initiating a one-on-one spell. When I think about the novels from the seventies, it isn't the big kahunas that project staying power in my crabby affections, bashing best sellers such as Thomas Pynchon's *Gravity's Rainbow,* whose prodigious set pieces were like the gargantuan meals in *La Grande Bouffe,* a grandiose glut with scatty arias of word-spew and a sprawling cast of characters with wacky, Dr. Strangelovian names (Lady Mnemosyne Gloobe, Lucifer Amp, Clayton "Bloody" Chiclitz); Saul Bellow's *Humboldt's Gift,* which constructs a too-unwieldy, top-heavy, and monument-minded edifice for the tragic unraveling of the poet of so much/too much promise undone by insanity, Bellow's friend Delmore Schwartz (who would become the subject of James Atlas's moving biography); E. L. Doctorow's *Ragtime,* a brilliant nickelodeon of a coup at the time, historical personages and fictional characters painted a bright enamel and set in pageant motion, but now something of a novelty item; William Styron's *Sophie's Choice,* a pretentiously sham Arthur Miller soap-opera exercise in moral breast-beating set in the Holocaust for maximum high-minded, grandstanding sensationalism; John Irving's *World According to Garp,* that Rube Goldberg Grand Guignol contraption of castration, self-mutilation, brain damage, and radical gender reassignment that the literary establishment found life-ratifyingly uproarious ("We not only laugh at the world according to Garp, but we also accept it and love it," wrote Christopher Lehmann-Haupt in the *New York Times);* even Norman Mailer's *Executioner's Song,* a half-great book that has the pared purity of a Japanese prose master such as Kawabata or Tanizaki in its mosaic account of the life of Gary Gilmore, but flabs up in the second half when it shifts to the media circus erected around Gilmore's execution and includes a heap of special pleading for Mailer's collaborator on the project, Lawrence Schiller.

No, the seventies novels that mean the most to me are the ones that expressed, distilled, and bottled a *mood,* mood being the most mysterious element in art, something beyond design and technique, the dark matter that permeates the grainy tilt of Robert Frank photographs, where roadside America seems viewed through skull sockets; the bleak winter of Robert Altman's *McCabe and Mrs. Miller* and the rancid sunlight of Sam Peckinpah's *Bring Me the Head of Alfredo Garcia;* the sonic dislocation and embracing estrangement of David Bowie's *Low;* the God-abandoned destitution of some of the best *Twilight Zone* episodes.

James Salter's *A Sport and a Pastime* has that for me, an erotic novel unsurpassed at recapturing that godly, awakening sense of two young bodies in bed being a new world unto itself, sealed behind shuttered windows that silence and hide the long white afternoons. "Now they are lovers. The first, wild courses are ended. They have founded their domain. A satanic happiness follows." Sorrentino's *Imaginative Qualities of Actual Things,* quoted above, crackles with caustic comedy steeped in a witches' brew of coffee grounds, shed hair on the sofa, and grease spots of mediocrity, with a fine selection of impotence on tap (sexual, literary, you name it) and at least one wisecrack on every other page that will unstitch your scalp and brighten your doomy day, bitter apostrophes about the life of a poet in all its avenues to disappointment: "The real poet was obsessed with his poems, his life, an egoist, selfish, boorish, rude, crazy. A great, romantic thing, into the breach, kill me tomorrow let me live tonight! and so on. Long hair and flowing lips, falling on the thorns of life, tortured to death in stifling university jobs, the Great Soul Writhing Underneath. Swift, intense, and destructive affairs with female undergraduates, too many vodka martinis, Fuck the Dean! Fuck the Chairman! . . . Anything. Everything." A frustration-driven novel, always glancing over its shoulder at the next nuisance to darken the doorway, with a mock lyricism that becomes the real impassioned thing by the end, as if it can't help itself. *Imaginative Qualities* is the only metafictional novel I can read without feeling as if I'm moving furniture up flights of stairs, the only one most animated by animal human vitality instead of marching through a cerebral encyclopedia. Why Sorrentino orphaned this snaggled line of attack in so many of his later naturalistic-mode novels (which dug their naturalistic knuckles into the brow until the reader cried, "Uncle") is one of those questions that, had it been posed to him, would have probably been met with a "gruff retort," like provoking Nabokov by asking about all the damned doppelgängers in his emerald fiction. Be grateful for what we're given, and don't muddle criticism with backseat driving.

Same with Don DeLillo. In recent years DeLillo must ask himself the cosmic question, "Why go on?," his later novels greeted with a fish-face without a trace of affection for everything he's done before, beating him up with his own achievements (*Libra, Underworld*) instead. His *Great Jones Street* of 1973 doesn't have the cybernetic density and conspiratorial mesh of his corporate-gnostic-algorithmic probes into power, chance, and paranoia, but its hungover mood evokes the exhaustion and pissed-away promises of the post-sixties, a psychological dehydration requiring a sequestering with none of the skin tingle of *A Sport and a Pastime*'s incognito air. I know, sounds like fun, and the novel's charcoal prose can read like a coroner's report: "I took a taxi past the cemeteries toward Manhattan, tides of ash-light breaking across the spires. New York seemed older than the cities of Europe, a sadistic gift of the sixteenth century, ever on the verge of plague." And yet its sense of time and place (I love that the novel is named for and set in an actual street with no mythic overtones until DeLillo endowed them) hooks me each time out: "I went to the room in Great Jones Street, a small crooked room, cold as a penny, looking out on warehouses, trucks and rubble. There was snow on the window ledge." How such passages recall rooms and views from my own past, as if my Horatio Street and St. Marks apartments had merged into one. I sometimes wonder if *Great Jones Street* might not be more highly esteemed if DeLillo hadn't dubbed his rock-star narrator Bucky Wunderlick, a Pynchonesque moniker that's hard to take seriously for a mystique-ridden Jim Morrison–like lizard king in self-exile. I can't see the name Bucky without thinking of Captain America's kid sidekick, one of the residua of having grown up religiously consuming Marvel Comics.

I sometimes wonder what would have happened had I found true fruition in book reviewing and taken up literary criticism as my sole vocation, setting aside childish things. I bet I'd be *real* bitter now. Staring out the screen door like Tommy Lee Jones in a bad mood, having long been farmed out by whatever magazine employed me and wishing I had drunk more so that I could write a sobriety memoir. Writing as deskbound craft, profession, and calling already comes pre-outfitted with so many diaphanous veils of solitariness that word-delight alone—the pleasure of all the billiard balls clicking and emptying into the pockets—doesn't compensate for an audience that doesn't answer no matter how nicely you call. I never felt this way writing about television for the *Voice,* even though television watching was considered then (less so now) a sedentary, light-bleached act of inanition that *The New Yorker*'s former TV critic Michael Arlen once compared to masturbation, which would presumably make writing about television like masturbating with both hands, no one's idea of heroism. There was always a sense of a larger audience out there, a fandom of fellow anchorites who watched *The Rockford Files* (James Garner as the perfect low-overhead, corner-cutting L.A. investigator for a recessionary time—a Lew Archer who can't step out of his trailer home without some cheap hood harassing his sideburns); *Kojak* (with the lollipop-sucking baldie detective who looked like a Ban Roll-on deodorant whose show even Lionel Trilling confessed to watching); Tom Snyder's late-night *Tomorrow* show, where the host's cigarette smoke ribboned the moody tension on the set, so different from the decompression chambers of studios today; the local Stanley Siegel talk show on WABC, where the Me Decade host bared his neuroses and had a regular segment on Friday mornings when he discussed the week in review with his actual psychotherapist (Siegel's national moment landing when a discombobulated Truman Capote appeared as guest and slurred, "We all know a fag is a homosexual gentleman who has just left the room," and a "Southern fag" is "meaner than the meanest rattler you ever met," as a prelude to venomizing Princess Lee Radziwill, with whom he had had a planet-fissuring falling-out); SCTV, the comedy ensemble whose satirical genius flickers intermittently today in the mockumentaries of Christopher Guest, absent the sketch revue; and Uncle Floyd, the New Jersey kiddie-show host with a puppet sidekick whose magicianship with minimalist stagecraft made him the Ernie Kovacs of the punk-decade mutant brigade (when the Ramones were guests on the program, they felt right at decrepit home). Writing about certain shows week after week (to the point where a few *Voice* editors got fed up with my recurring favorites) was like writing about your friends, the latest chapter of what they were up to. When I flick back at the book reviews I did in the seventies, I sometimes wince at the nasty incisions I inflicted on writers when I crossed the line between cutup and cutthroat (I won't quote examples—no need to re-inflict wounds). But what really retrospectively bugs me was when I got prescriptive, telling writers what they should have done, where their true gifts lie, the road they should take to get onto I-95 to reach Delaware by dawn. I recoil when I see reviewers doing it today, acting like talent management agents for some literary Almighty.

TV defied such dispensing morning-after pills to those involved. It was a collaborative push following its own set of tracks, and nothing a critic said was likely to lodge and peck inside its creators' brains for years after, building a nest. Even the sharpest dig didn't have the palpable impact of being spat at by a stranger in the street, to use one of Sheed's analogies for how a novelist feels having his latest work speared in print. In the seventies, before HBO, Showtime, AMC, and the networks built supertanker series with multichambered *Godfather* novelistic character bibles (*The Sopranos, Deadwood, Mad Men, The Wire, The X-Files, Buffy the Vampire Slayer*), television was more antihierarchical, prestige-resistant, and alien to putzy pretension. It didn't have any of the auteurist mystique and pantheon aura of film criticism, and to this day no collection of TV criticism swings the clout of Kael's *I Lost It at the Movies* and *Deeper into Movies*, James Agee's *Agee on Film*, Andrew Sarris's *American Cinema*, Manny Farber's *Negative Space*, or the roundups of Otis Ferguson's reviews for the *New Republic*. This was freeing for me, this acceptance of transience. It kept me balanced and responsive, not having a canon to lean on. I remember getting a report from a friend about a conversation he had with one of the *Voice*'s top theater critics who nosed up at the sound of my name as if it might trigger his hay fever. "Wolcott can be funny," he conceded, "but it's easy being funny about television. It's not a medium that makes many demands." "How *dare* he call me facile!" I fumed with the pretend ire I so enjoyed in P. G. Wodehouse's Bertie Wooster novels when this was related to me. I would have gotten more upset if it weren't for the fact that he had a point about TV requiring less deep-sea drilling and rock quarrying than theater-opera-dance reviewing. I couldn't pretend I was propping up any of the pillars of Western Civ when I descanted on *The Ropers,* the spin-off series from *Three's Company* that co-starred Audra

Lindley in a succession of misguided muumuus and Norman Fell, whose lips were caulked with a chalky white substance, no one quite knew why: a sitcom that I always mention when I feel my friend Elvis Mitchell could use a laugh. But being facile is harder than it looks, no one survives long as a chuckle bunny in print, and it wasn't all party tricks. I had to ladder up to a higher diving board to do justice to Paul Winfield's magnificent Martin Luther King in *King,* Dennis Potter's breakthrough lip-sync musical *Pennies from Heaven,* and the epochal miniseries *Holocaust,* because that was part of the job, being able to work at different altitudes.

My model was the Australian multi-talent Clive James (poet, novelist, literary critic, celebrity profiler, TV host), whose television column for the London *Observer* was as hilarious and high-wire an act as Kenneth Tynan's theater reviews had been in the sixties for the same paper. I stole from James as if copping his dance moves, mimicking his mimicry of anchormen and bogus dialogue, and later flew with him up to meet Pauline at her house in the Berkshires, an airsick excursion he described in "Postcard from New York" for the *Observer:* "We flew through a storm all the way. Lighting his cigarette one-handed, the pilot did a no-sweat Buzz Sawyer routine while his co-pilot made a great show of understanding the map. The aircraft behaved like a pair of underpants in a washing machine." As the plane came in for a landing, we looked out the window and saw the hills adjacent the strip full of summer-dressed people gawking upward. "What are they doing out there on the grass?" I asked, to which Clive replied, "Waiting to see us crash." Once we arrived at Pauline's, we chased away the jitters and relaxed before going out to dinner, Pauline and Clive standing and sipping wine while I sat on the couch, drinking cola. Somewhere between sips, Clive reflectively remarked, "I feel old enough to be his father." "I'm old enough to be his grandmother," answered Pauline. "Pa! Grandma!" I cried, throwing open my arms as if discovering my long-lost kin.

If it was the funnier columns that readers enjoyed and remembered, it may have been because, with identity politics coming more to the fore, many of my fellow *Voice*rs considered a light touch suspect, and some of the paper's political correctos—whose numbers would increase in the decade to come as the *Voice* in its new digs on lower Broadway would become an ideological honeycomb of minority caucuses competing for staff representation and column space—were grunting out copy as if handcuffed to a rowing machine.

Then again, as the irritable tone of the theater critic implies, maybe I was just getting on everybody's nerves. I can see now why others might have found me abrasive, overfull of myself, acting as if expecting a star on my dressing room door any day soon. The TV column was increasingly popular at the *Voice,* and popularity translated into higher visibility, and higher visibility translated into the *Esquire* column, the call from the *New York Review,* feature assignments from *The New Yorker* that were never published or completed (including one where I spent a sunstroke week in New Mexico on the set of Sam Peckinpah's delay-plagued *Convoy,* where he called me a pussy in front of the crew, which I was told not to take personally, I was but the latest in an infinite line), and similar offers that no one at the paper was being treated to, with the exception of Ellen Willis, who by the late seventies had phased out of *The New Yorker* and *New York Review,* and the Press Clips columnist, Alexander Cockburn. The *Voice*'s brightest journalistic star, Cockburn could get away with it better in the office because along with his stylistic brilliance he was English and sexy, whooshing in and out of the building on a jet stream of daredevilish charisma. I didn't have that going for me then, and it isn't something you pick up later along the highway of life. I probably came across as bumptious, though I didn't conduct a survey. If I no longer hunched my shoulders like Norman Mailer ready to plow through the defensive line to tackle the bitch goddess of success, I was dropping Pauline Kael's name and her latest asides with mad abandon, and not just to annoy the Andrew Sarris faction in the office whose bat ears picked up everything and transmitted it uptown to His Tetchiness himself. That's how things were done in the days before tweeting and texting sped up the hamster wheels of competitive tattle.

The irony was that I was seeing less of Pauline for most of that particular year. Nineteen seventy-nine was when she took an unprecedented leave of absence from *The New Yorker* to make the trans-coastal hop from film critic to film producer at the behest of Warren Beatty, seducer of all he surveyed. She would be given an office at Paramount as a producer on Beatty's next project, *Love & Money*, based on a script by James Toback. It has been argued in at least one stewpot biography of Beatty (Peter Biskind's *Star*) that luring Pauline out to the coast was a Machiavellian ploy by the ageless superboy to teach her a humility lesson, let her know what it was truly like in the major leagues, and cut her down to size, render her inoperative. This is motivational conjecture raised to the plane of advanced calculus. A true Machiavellian knows what he wants and plots the angles in advance to achieve his aims, and Beatty was too indecisive to be a true Machiavellian, his ideas and choices subject to constant, worrying revision and his conversation (as interviews reveal) a golden cloud of coy, cagey, hazy, noncommittal indirection. And one would have to assume that Beatty simply enjoyed buying a new toy to break to explain the personal hostility needed to set such a trap into motion. It was Pauline who championed *Bonnie and Clyde* and was the first critic to treat Beatty seriously as an artist, who hailed the Beverly Hills sex farce *Shampoo* as a Mozartean bed-hopper ("The central performance that makes it all work is Beatty's. [The hairdresser], who wears his hair blower like a Colt .45, isn't an easy role; I don't know anyone else who could have played it"), and if she thought that the remake of *Heaven Can Wait* emasculated Beatty's talents (he "moves through it looking fleecy and dazed"), well, she was hardly alone. And she would be working on *Love & Money* with friends, not just Beatty and Toback, but Dick Albarino, who pitched in with Pauline on the polishing of Toback's script. I saw various versions of the script, which became progressively sharper, funnier, and structurally firmer, and what happened to that screenplay I do not know. I do know that at some point Beatty evanesced out of the project and with his withdrawal went the money interest. What was conceived as a big-budget jeweled elephant starring Beatty, Laurence Olivier as his father (or was it grandfather?), Laura Antonelli as the love interest (Isabelle Adjani was also discussed), and a lavish backdrop ended up a much runtier film that looked as if it were shot just off the turnpike with Ray Sharkey pipsqueaking as the hero, the aged director King Vidor in the Olivier role (who died months after the film's release), and, in the role of the imported white chocolate, the gorgeous Ornella Muti, whom Pauline and I so appreciated in her slinky catsuit as the vixen in *Flash Gordon,* which we caught in a theater in Times Square where the rodents outnumbered the customers. *Love & Money* played a brief engagement when it was released after some delay in 1982, already something everybody involved wanted to put behind them. Friendships were severed over this film, certainly Pauline's and Albarino's was. She successfully lobbied at Paramount for David Lynch to direct *The Elephant Man,* but that seems to have been small consolation for what others have since told me were indeed miserable months out there for Pauline, a mortifying letdown. Though I don't believe the rumor, repeated in Biskind's book, "that she would go over to director Richard Brooks's office, complain that she had been put out to pasture, and weep." The weeping sounds so unlike her, and Brooks was not a director with whom she would have been on confiding terms, and vice versa, not after her panning of *Looking for Mr. Goodbar.* Like so many of the anti-Pauline anecdotes in *Star* from studs now in their sinking suns, this strikes me as sexist payback.

Pauline never spoke to me of her unhappiness at Paramount, not then, not later, not even alludingly. When she phoned from the coast in the summer of 1979, it was to hear what movies I had seen, what I was up to, if there was any talk about some recent story or review in *The New Yorker,* her amusement over an item in Liz Smith's syndicated gossip column that she had "gone Hollywood" and was taking driving lessons—"me, at my age," she scoffed. "As if I'd even be able to see over the steering wheel! Who *feeds* her this stuff, garden gnomes?" Were there clues in our long-distance conversations to the emotional wringer she was going through that I was too tone-deaf to detect over the phone? I don't know. I'd like to think I wouldn't have been that obtuse, but subtext wasn't something Pauline trafficked in. I had a closer view of the buffetings that were to come, the shaky underpinnings in her voice this time unmistakable. The decade was about to dim.

Coda

Here's how I remember it, the moment for me when the door-knob turned and the seventies were truly over.

It was after an evening showing at the now-gone Loew's Tower East of *The Competition,* starring Richard Dreyfuss and Amy Irving as rival concert pianists whose inconvenient romance prickles every passive-aggressive nerve in Dreyfuss's acting quiver, his character's male ego in danger of developing a bald spot from too much rubbing. He wants her so bad, but can't accept that she might out-Rachmaninoff him! For some reason, Pauline Kael hadn't caught the film when it was screened for critics, and so her review would run late, weeks after its December release. After her sojourn in Hollywood, Pauline had returned to active duty at *The New Yorker* in June 1980 with a long take on Stanley Kubrick's *The Shining* that seemed to mimic Kubrick's Steadicam tracking through the remote snow, followed by a state-of-the-art polemic called "Why Are Movies So Bad? or, The Numbers," in which she took what she had learned at Paramount, shaped it into a plasticine bomb, and set it off. Colonized by conglomerates that knew and cared nothing about movies themselves, studios were now run by executives who hedged their bets by green-lighting package-deal projects whose premise could be boiled down to a sound bite: "The higher the executive, the more cruelly short his attention span." Beneath the bureaucratic inertia and servile bowing to the balance sheets, chaos. "Nobody really controls a production now; the director is on his own, even if he's insecure, careless, or nuts." If her sabbatical had been a sour education, worse was on the way now that Pauline was back home. In August, Renata Adler, she of the bell-ringer braid, a longtime *New Yorker* contributor who had been one of the relievers rotated out of the bullpen to review movies in Pauline's absence (along with Roger Angell, Veronica Geng, and Donald Barthelme), fastidiously shoved a steel safe off the roof of the *New York Review of Books*, an eight-thousand-word flattener titled "The Perils of Pauline." Judgment had fallen. It read like an autopsy report filed by the archangel of death whose pen was her scalpel.

Occasioned by the publication of Kael's latest collection, *When the Lights Go Down,* the scale of the vivisection combined with its methodical thoroughness indicated months of preparation intended to deliver a coup de grâce. Once upon a time, when unicorns gamboled, Adler had entertained fancies that Kael might be a critic to marry the distinguished mind of Robert Warshow with the frequency of the political columnist Walter Lippmann (how'd *he* get in here?). But the cucumber slices had fallen from her eyes. "Now, *When the Lights Go Down,* a collection of her reviews over the past five years, is out; and it is, to my surprise and without Kael- or [John] Simon-like exaggeration, not simply, jarringly, piece by piece, line by line, and without interruption, worthless. It turns out to embody something appalling and widespread in the culture." It was as hyperbolic an exaggeration as Mary McCarthy's assertion that every word of Lillian Hellman's was a lie, including "and" and "the," and Adler was just getting started. The publication of "The Perils of Pauline" hit Pauline hard. Not so much the meat and particulars of the essay, though these damaged and vexed. "She's trying to take away my language," Pauline told me, "to make me so self-conscious that every time I ask a rhetorical question or do something jazzy I'll catch myself and worry, 'Is this something everyone will jump on?'" And she found Adler's elevation of "the intermittent critic" over those who covered a critical beat absurdly snobbish and patrician, as if anyone who had to meet deadlines for a living were some kind of bum. More unnerving was the gloating jubilation it ignited in the press, including a feature article in *New York* magazine by Philip Nobile that called it a "crucifixion," and Andrew Sarris climbing like a rooster atop the henhouse to proclaim that Pauline was now "naked to thine enemies." Gary Indiana, a former colleague of mine at the *Voice,* would later muse in *Artforum,* "I have a fond memory of devouring that essay with Susan Sontag, peering over each other's shoulder, in the donut shop that used to occupy the corner of Third Avenue and Fourteenth Street, both of us nearly gagging with laughter at the sly, inexorable trajectory of every sentence, the devastating conclusion of every paragraph, the utterly damning thoroughness with which Ms. Kael's grotesquely inflated, even sacrosanct reputation had been laid out like a corpse for burial." Sontag gagging with laughter is not a picture to linger over. It was more than simple Schadenfreude at work; it was more visceral and hooting, a vulture party, reminding me in its circling glee of the footage of Frenchwomen having their heads shaved in public after the liberation. Which is not to argue that Pauline was an innocent, defenseless victim, or that Adler's article was unanimously endorsed. I did a jokey riff on the controversy for the *Voice* and for my jesting found myself vaguely threatened with a lawsuit, a prospect that seemed to excite our resident civil liberties advocate, Nat Hentoff, who always enjoyed having a First Amendment case to warm his hands over.

What made this harder for Pauline to weather than the high-powered hits she had taken before (such as Mailer's bull run at her over *Last Tango in Paris*) was that Adler's attack had the acid residue of an inside job, a takedown encouraged with a nod and a wink by those at *The New Yorker* who thought the Minotaur mama's vulgarity and bullying had gone too long unchecked. A few claimed they did more than nod and wink, directly assisting in the mechanics of the piece. The high-altitude novelist Harold Brodkey, whom we met earlier, boasted that he had helped Adler with the essay, suggesting solecisms and signature mannerisms to toss in the evidence bag. Of course, Brodkey had an extravagant sense of his own diaphanous influence, placing himself as the lightning rod of every literary creation that had happened since he attained consciousness, claiming that he was the unattributed model for Bellow's *Henderson the Rain King,* the Devil in Updike's *The Witches of Eastwick,* and Leander Dworkin in Adler's novel *Pitch Dark.* A fun guy, he resented the fact that the New York Mets ace Dwight Gooden made more money on the pitching mound than he did at his desk as a writer, to me a distinct sign of a madman. So his testimony always had to be filed under "Dubious" or "Iffy." But Brodkey was also a notoriously sly malice-spreader who liked to keep busy, so it's quite possible he did put his Iago insinuations into play here. In any case, Brodkey *wanted* partial credit, even if no credit was due, and he made sure Pauline was aware his fingerprints were on it. Other *New Yorker* colleagues let slide smiles of royal court approval over Adler's onslaught, and it was conjectured that William Shawn himself tacitly condoned the piece, distressed over the coarse improprieties Pauline kept traipsing across the stage like a burlesque queen's tatty boa. "Some *New Yorker* watchers feel that the genteel editor is in secret sympathy with Adler's analysis and wishes that Kael, whom Brendan Gill characterizes as 'foul mouthed' in *Here at The New Yorker,* would clean up her column," Nobile wrote in *New York,* citing those unnamed sources whom no journalist can be without. Granting an interview to Nobile, Shawn denied that this was so, but that the elf wizard himself felt compelled to speak on the record indicated how roiling this was intestinally for the magazine. The last paragraph of Nobile's piece read, "Adler observed in [her nonfiction collection] *Toward a Radical Middle* that 'no essay form becomes as quickly obsolete as an unfavorable review.' She is mistaken. 'The Perils of Pauline' will most likely haunt Kael for the rest of her career." It didn't haunt the rest of her career, but it cast a blight over the rest of the year, which wasn't done.

A few months later, Woody Allen's latest film, *Stardust Memories,* was screened, an evening high with anticipation. Seated in the row in front of us, Dick Cavett, crickety with excitement, turned to Pauline and said: "Pauline, let me ask you something. Do you think it would be worthwhile learning German to understand a pun John Simon recently told me?"

Without missing a beat, Pauline shot back, "Why are you talking to John Simon?"

That was not the response he expected, and, innocently unaware that fraternization with John Simon carried the risk of Senate censure, Cavett expressed his fondness for puns by way of explanation, then turned around and faced front as the lights dimmed. How well I recall the film that followed. The abrasive whining about fame and the parasites it attracted. The Felliniesque scattered remains of a carnival that's left town. The conflation of private angst and historical atrocity. The Grosz-like close-ups of the Jewish characters as they swooped into frame, exhibited like gargoyles. ("Here comes another nose," Pauline muttered unhappily at one point during the screening.) If Pauline was dubious about much of *Manhattan* and *Interiors,* now *Stardust Memories* had bared Woody's sour desire to blend into the tasteful WASP wallpaper (or sink between a pair of shiksa thighs) and be free from clawing Jewish cling. "The Jewish self-hatred that spills out in this movie could be a great subject, but all it does is spill out," she wrote in *The New Yorker.* "He may be ready to become a Catholic convert." The review was so blistering—*"Stardust Memories* doesn't seem like a movie, or even like a filmed essay; it's nothing"—that it drove a stake into her and Woody's friendship for good. How close that friendship was, I didn't know, but it had been at one of Woody's New Year's parties that Norman Mailer, still stung over Pauline's slam of his Marilyn Monroe biographical photo album, gun-slingered up to her with his elbows extended and proposed that they butt heads to square things. She declined the invitation, like a sane person. In a portrait of Pauline published years later in the *Atlantic,* her friend and Massachusetts neighbor Roy Blount Jr. recounted how during a car drive a fellow passenger expressed what a shame it was that Woody had taken the review so personally, and Pauline replied, "Oh, no. It was vicious." She accepted that casualties were part of the price of practicing criticism, one of its lousier sacrifices, which didn't make it less painful. Walking into rooms to meet waves of resentment loses its novelty appeal after a while, and losing friends only makes each entrance more exposed.

We got through *The Competition*, Pauline murmurously pleased whenever Sam Wanamaker appeared as the snowcapped Leonard Bernstein maestro who wore his sweater tied around his neck like a cape, and scoffing at Lee Remick's stiff-postured projectile launch of such unsayable lines as "It will turn your tits a lovely shade of puce." We gathered ourselves together and ventured out into the December night to signal a taxi to take us downtown. The mood in the taxi was strange, wrong somehow, a bubble of trapped air of heavier density than that outside. The sound from the car radio was turned down low, but not for long. Pauline gave the driver the destination, and he said, as the taxi found the lane it wanted, "Guess you haven't heard the news—John Lennon got shot tonight. Outside the Dakota. They're saying it was carried out like an assassination." The driver turned the radio up to one of the all-news channels that had reporters on the scene relaying the latest bulletins. "God," Pauline said, "anyone with a gun can have his day." The faces on the street through the passenger windows looked stunned, everyone moving at three-quarters speed, or maybe that's memory slowing down the videotape. We said the usual hopeless things one said about the sadness and awful senselessness of it all as the soft machinery of shock and mourning took shape elsewhere in the city, the candlelight vigils to come, the chorusing of "Imagine" and "Give Peace a Chance."

The Christmas lights in midtown looked incongruous, an irony we could have done without. The driver had lowered the radio volume again, as if respecting our quiet, or sensing we had heard enough, and beside me Pauline said, "I wish the movie had been better. It had so much going for it." "I guess this just wasn't our night," I said. "It wasn't anyone's night," Pauline said, and it got quiet again as the Christmas lights continued to go by.

ACKNOWLEDGMENTS

First and foremost to my editor, Gerald Howard, the sort of editor everybody insists doesn't exist anymore, but how wrong they are, as I and this book can attest. He initiated the idea for *Lucking Out* and kept the project alive with encouragement and enthusiasm during its choppy passages at sea after I had swallowed the compass. Thanks too to editorial assistant Hannah Wood at Doubleday and to copy editor Ingrid Sterner, who tweezed the text with nimble precision. My agent, Elyse Cheney, is the dynamo every writer dreams of having in his corner. And the last two decades of my life as a writer would be unimaginable if it weren't for the creative support and spirited generosity of Aimee Bell, my editor at *Vanity Fair,* and of the magazine's editor, the phenomenal Graydon Carter.

Grateful acknowledgment is made to the following for permission to reprint previously published and unpublished material:

Alfred Music Publishing Co. Inc., and Hal Leonard Corporation: Excerpt from "Loudmouth" words and music by Johnny Ramone, Dee Dee Ramone, Tommy Ramone, and Joey Ramone, copyright © 1977 by Mutated Music (ASCAP), Bleu Disque Music (ASCAP), and Taco Tunes (ASCAP), copyright renewed. All rights for Bleu Disque Music and Taco Tunes administered by WB Music Corp. All rights for Mutated Music administered by BMG Chrysalis. International copyright secured. All rights reserved. Reprinted by permission of Alfred Music Publishing Co. Inc., and Hal Leonard Corporation.

Rhoda Wolf: Excerpt from letter from Dan Wolf to James Wolcott. Reprinted by permission of Rhoda Wolf.

The Wylie Agency LLC: January 1972 letter from Norman Mailer to Dan Wolf, copyright © 2011 by the Norman Mailer Estate. Reprinted by permission of The Wylie Agency LLC.